REINVENTING
KNOWLEDGE

REINVENTING KNOWLEDGE

From Alexandria to the Internet

IAN F. McNEELY

WITH LISA WOLVERTON

W. W. NORTON & COMPANY
New York   London

Frontispiece: Western and non-Western knowledge systems in contact. Charles D'Oyly, "A European Gentleman with His Moonshee, or Native Professor of Languages." From Thomas Williamson, *The European in India* (1813), courtesy of the Special Collections Library, University of Michigan.

For information about permission to reproduce selections from this book, write to Permissions, W. W. Norton & Company, Inc., 500 Fifth Avenue, New York, NY 10110

For information about special discounts for bulk purchases, please contact W. W. Norton Special Sales at specialsales@wwnorton.com or 800-233-4830

Manufacturing by Courier Westford
Book design by Dana Sloan
Production manager: Anna Oler

Library of Congress Cataloging-in-Publication Data

McNeely, Ian F.
Reinventing knowledge : from Alexandria to the Internet /
Ian F. McNeely, Lisa Wolverton. — 1st ed.
    p. cm.
  Includes bibliographical references and index.
  ISBN 978-0-393-06506-0 (hardcover)
1. Intellectual life—History. 2. Learning and scholarship—History.
3. Civilization, Western—History. 4. Civilization, Modern—History.
I. Wolverton, Lisa, II. Title.
  CB358.M37 2008
  909—dc22   200801900

ISBN 978-0-393-33771-6 pbk.

W. W. Norton & Company, Inc.
500 Fifth Avenue, New York, N.Y. 10110
www.wwnorton.com

W. W. Norton & Company Ltd.
Castle House, 75/76 Wells Street, London W1T 3QT

1 2 3 4 5 6 7 8 9 0

To Jing and Margot

Contents

Introduction

IMAGINE PUTTING the entirety of knowledge on the World Wide Web. Every book and every article from every branch of study, every manuscript and every artifact from every ancient culture, every painting and every musical recording, every DNA base-pair sequence and microchip blueprint: everything we call knowledge would be faithfully digitized, universally accessible, completely indexed, and easily searchable. This is no longer just a science fiction fantasy but potentially a reality for Internet behemoths like Google, which is already busy scanning the contents of some of the world's largest libraries.

Now consider an alternative project, one dreamed up by a different group of cyberspace visionaries: a 10,000-Year Library, whose aim is to preserve knowledge for the distant future rather than make it instantaneously available in the present.[1] This project would allow us to send mail to the future and (when we get there) receive it from the past, to store time capsules and remind us when to open them, and to stockpile handbooks for reconstructing civilization in the event of global catastrophe. The 10,000-Year Library is not a projection of technological confidence but a recognition of an Achilles heel. Its aim is to make us mindful of time in a way that our fast-paced society has forgotten. As some see it, the current "information age" threatens to make knowledge as ephemeral as an electronic pulse flitting through a fiber-optic cable.

We are living through one of the recurring periods in world history when far-reaching changes in economics, culture, and technology raise basic questions about the production, preservation, and transmission of knowledge. How do we adapt to vastly new circumstances to ensure that we can reproduce ourselves as a culture? What new institutions will we need to organize and transmit the totality of our knowledge? Are conventional libraries obsolete? How must the traditional university change? Can we continue to expect that scientific advances will improve our lives? What will digital media do to the production and distribution of knowledge in words and images?

In this book, we ask what light history can shed on these questions. But instead of worrying about where knowledge is headed in the future, we want to recall the drama and dynamism surrounding the pursuit of knowledge in the past. Instead of chronicling the growth of an educational system about which many are all too complacent, we want to convey how different and exciting and even dangerous the life of the mind could be for those confronting similar upheavals hundreds, even thousands of years ago. Before the age of multibillion-dollar university endowments, high-profile government labs, digital media, and wireless broadband, scholars were pioneers and renegades, and knowledge was a hard-won treasure. Everything new they learned was in danger of being lost and forgotten, whether through the hostility of those who feared new ideas or, more insidiously, through the simple neglect of those unwilling to organize and preserve a collective civilizational memory. Today, as we again face the daunting task of organizing all our knowledge, we would do well to study the example of those who showed an equal boldness to do so under far more adverse conditions.

This story includes a rich array of events and characters, from the medieval Christian monks who devised schemes to preserve knowledge as the Roman Empire crumbled around them to the scholars who set up an international "Republic of Letters" to unify early modern Europe as it was being torn apart by Protestants and Catholics at war. It includes Peter Abelard, the arrogant medieval logician who tangled with his masters, seduced his star pupil, Heloise, and wound up watching his books burn and suffering castration at the hands of his lover's uncle. And it includes the public and private struggles of Marie Curie, one of the first women scientists, who literally poisoned herself to death with radiation to explore the structure of the atom.

One of the unlikeliest results of the efforts of these men and women, and many others, is a body of knowledge common to all who live, work, and study in the so-called Western world, and increasingly elsewhere as well. Medieval theologians like Abelard and atomic physicists like Curie had very different reasons for pursuing knowledge—to know God, to unveil the secrets of nature—and yet both contributed to what is often deemed the "Western intellectual tradition" and thus to the story we have to tell in this book. We would argue that "the West" itself is better defined by its institutions for organizing knowledge than as a set of cultural values or a region of the globe. Imagine a group that includes ancient Greek shepherds, French aristocrats, Soviet apparatchiks, Californian commuters, and perhaps even students at the University of Malaya in Kuala Lumpur. These "westerners" differ radically in language, ethnicity, and lifestyle. Historically they have been concentrated in Europe, but they have since spread to its colonies and beyond, all over the world. Most now subscribe to the so-called Western values of democracy, secularism, science, and individualism—but others have endorsed the exact opposites. What they chiefly share is a common intellectual heritage. But how can that heritage be defined? And where is it heading? If we can understand where it came from, perhaps we can make educated guesses about where it is going.

This book attempts precisely that. It traces the production, preservation, and transmission of everything deemed worth knowing in what has become the "Western" tradition. Such knowledge comprises all the subjects debated in Plato's Academy, from law and politics to love and poetry, as well as everything that has since been added to—and subtracted from—this list. This book is not a history of philosophy, though it engages with the philosophical ideas that animate our educational practices. Nor is it a history of education, though it argues that the way knowledge is conveyed from generation to generation is inseparable from the content of that knowledge. Most obviously, it hardly touches on informal knowledge, the type of knowledge we get from reading a newspaper, fixing a motorcycle, parenting a child, or creating a work of art. Formal knowledge, the kind organized by institutions for the wider public world, is our province. Our approach is necessarily selective, even as it aspires to encyclopedic breadth. We take examples from Christian theology and nuclear physics, Homeric Greek and corporate law, the mapping of continents and the study of the mind.

This book is about the West, but it generates an understanding of this term by drawing comparisons with the world's other great literate cultures. For the sake of this book, we can reduce these to three: China, Islam, and India. China had the world's longest-lived alternative tradition to the West, a parallel universe of scholarship and civilization that came to an end only in the twentieth century. Islam shared with the West both an origin in Near Eastern monotheism and the absorption of Greek knowledge and philosophy. India, a region with one of the world's oldest homegrown knowledge systems, founded on Sanskrit, has been enmeshed in complex webs of influence involving the rest. In all four traditions, academic institutions grew up to solve problems universal to literate societies, problems for which

Western scholars simply found particular, enduring solutions. These include how to produce knowledge, by converting oral philosophical traditions into written scholarship; how to preserve it, by copying manuscripts, establishing a canon of scriptures, and ensuring that the meaning and sense of their language is maintained; and how to transmit it, by animating the dead letter in face-to-face discussion and debate or surmounting the impossibilities of face-to-face contact by resorting to letters. Periodic glances at the solutions of other cultures to these problems highlight not the intrinsic superiority but rather the historical specificity of European, and later American, variants.

This book is thus a history of institutions of knowledge. It chronicles the six institutions that have dominated Western intellectual life since ancient times: the library, the monastery, the university, the Republic of Letters, the disciplines, and the laboratory. Together these institutions have safeguarded knowledge through the ages by acting as interfaces between scholars and the rest of society. Each was formed, amazingly enough, to organize the totality of knowledge. Each coalesced in reaction to sweeping historical changes that discredited its predecessor or exposed its limitations. And each parlayed dissatisfaction and disillusionment with existing ways of knowing into an all-encompassing new ideology legitimating its mission for the outside world. In times of stability, these institutions carried the torch of learning. In times of upheaval, individuals and small communities reinvented knowledge in founding new institutions. These moments of transition and innovation provide our exclusive focus in this book, for once a template is established, later incarnations of an institution carry on the same basic mission—until knowledge is again reinvented.

A focus on institutions directs attention beyond individual personalities, ideas, schools of thought, and even disciplines and toward the ways in which seekers of knowledge have practiced their craft. Readers will recognize many of the names (Curie or Saint Augustine) and ideas (heliocentrism or Taylorism) found in these pages. Yet many of the "giants"—Newton, Darwin, and Einstein, for instance—appear fleetingly, if at all: their contributions, however momentous, fit comfortably within existing institutions. We in fact aim to avoid the usual "great men and big ideas" approach to intellectual history. Instead we examine shifts occurring, often without conscious direction, among entire communities of scholars pivotally situated in history. Thus Galileo and Descartes make cameo appearances in the chapter on the Republic of Letters, but more for their epistolary style than for their scientific doctrines. Other, lesser-known figures, such as Demetrius of Phaleron, Wilhelm von Humboldt, and Vannevar Bush, contributed more to the organization of institutions than to the progress of ideas, always at transitional moments in history. Architects behind the scenes, they deserve the limelight for their far-reaching institutional innovations.

Ideas, great or small, can communicate their effect only through the institutions that organize them. Some of the most powerful ideas are those with the capacity to reorganize the ways in which people pursue knowledge: who pursues it, where and how they do so, and how they judge themselves to have attained it. Before seekers of knowledge in any age can even begin their quest, certain fundamental questions need to be settled. Do they debate their colleagues in verbal confrontations or write books in solitude for faraway readers? Do they scrutinize nature as they find it or trick it into doing the unexpected? Do they engage with their contemporaries or labor on behalf of scholars past and future? Do they close ranks to preserve embattled truths or spread learning for the benefit of all? These are but a few of the issues affecting how the life of the mind has been constructed and reconstructed over centuries. Intellectuals build very different houses for the pursuit of knowledge, but they share their raw materials with institution-builders in other walks of life. Among these are speech and writing, images and objects, and provisions to overcome the limitations of space and the ravages of time. Also important are decisions about privacy and publicity, whom to exclude and whom to include. We highlight these by examining women's varying access to the world of knowledge and the gender-saturated ideologies governing both men's and women's contributions to it.

The most novel experiments, the most fundamental discoveries, the most stupendous feats of academic genius exert their influence over us because their creators said, wrote, and did things that reorganized the activity of other, lesser minds. Institutions give meaning to those who live by their rules, and even to those who rebel against them. Upheavals in the organization of knowledge, in turn, follow from institutional innovations that anyone with a vocation for learning can appreciate. For example, it would be impossible to survey, even cursorily, the accomplishments of each individual discipline from anthropology to zoology. But it is not hard to grasp that when a mass market for education first arose after 1800, a new specialization of intellectual labor creating these fields was the natural result. Such insights unlock the whole of intellectual history, for all its arcana, to the layperson's understanding. None of this is to suggest that the majesty of ideas can be reduced to the crude, material circumstances of their production. Between the medieval cathedral and the contemporary skyscraper, architectural practices were radically transformed by the shift from stone to steel. And while this observation hardly suffices to explain the achievements of architects Gothic or modern, it can nonetheless serve to illuminate their respective forms of genius. In a similar way, this book aims to demystify knowledge and to construct a skeleton narrative of its development. It seeks to catalog the raw materials from which knowledge is fashioned, and examines the institutions that transform these raw materials into powerful political, social, and cultural forces.

From the moment, about 2,300 years ago, that knowledge first expanded beyond the compass of one person's mind—or the minds of a single community of scholars engaged in face-to-face debate, like Socrates and his followers—organizing knowledge became as important as knowledge itself. It is not enough to pile up all the great books in a room and assume that they will inspire the thirst for knowledge. As the founders of the first library, at Alexandria, well knew, one had somehow to categorize learning, or there would be no way to grasp its meaning and relationship to other bodies of knowledge. As the founders of the first universities knew, one still had to present it in lively lectures and debates, or it would become stale, lifeless, and increasingly irrelevant to the lived world. And as the founders of the nineteenth-century scientific laboratory knew, one had to put it to practical work improving the human condition, or there would cease to be any rationale for its continued support among a multitude of pressing social needs.

The ways in which we organize intellectual activity remain crucial to how we create new knowledge and draw on it for moral and practical guidance in daily life. We have recently witnessed the emergence of a new technology, the Internet, with great potential to reshape the way we produce, preserve, and transmit knowledge around the globe. But innovation in technology does little in itself to guarantee the progress of knowledge as a whole. We risk committing a serious error by thinking that cheap information made universally available through electronic media fulfills the requirements of a democratic society for organized knowledge. Past generations had to win knowledge by using their wits, and never took what they knew for granted. Recalling their labor and travail is, if anything, more important than ever if we are to distinguish what is truly novel about the "information age" from what is transient hype.

Certainly the contemporary university, however all-encompassing its claims to knowledge, is not the culmination or pinnacle of everything that has gone before it. The history of knowledge is a discontinuous one, full of paths not taken, and the current system may not be the best of all possible worlds. The following pages are filled with stories of people pursuing knowledge in surprising—and perhaps superior—ways. Students in Europe and India once gravitated to verbal disputation, not passive listening to a lecture, as the heart of learning. Gentlemen in Europe and China once carved leisure time out of busy lives full of social obligations in order to carry on academic traditions. Scientists in Europe and Islam once saw the mastery and manipulation of nature as complementary, not antagonistic, to religious and humanistic understanding. Many alternative ways of knowing, of learning, and of teaching have been lost or submerged beneath the layers of history that underlie the present organization of knowledge. If the life of the mind is indeed undergoing a structural transformation, it is all the more important to recall what history has seemingly discarded, to turn a potentially destabilizing situation into one that will revitalize the pursuit of knowledge in the future.

Most important, we must strain to unearth the core rationales for knowledge embedded—often unnoticed—in the histories of institutions we have inherited from the past. Each chapter of this book therefore tells the story of a familiar institution from an unfamiliar perspective, emphasizing what made each one novel at its inception. At every unpredictable juncture, changes in the wider world, not the activities of specific geniuses or intellectuals generally, have driven the reinvention of knowledge. But whenever a new institution of knowledge crystallizes, it exerts a remarkably pervasive influence. So comprehensively has each one refashioned the life of the mind that even the most enduring and entrenched practices of knowing submit to reform and renovation under its aegis. As we will see, even today's "knowledge society," for all of its apparent novelties and radical departures, is but the continuation of this millennia-old pattern.

REINVENTING
KNOWLEDGE

1

The Library

300 BCE–500 CE

BY TRANSFORMING A LARGELY ORAL SCHOLARLY
CULTURE INTO A LARGELY WRITTEN ONE, THE LIBRARY
MADE THE GREEK INTELLECTUAL TRADITION BOTH
PORTABLE AND HERITABLE.

THE MAN who founded the most famous library in the Western world wore makeup, dyed his hair blond, carried on affairs with married women and adolescent boys, and led a life checkered by political intrigue. Demetrius of Phaleron (ca. 360–280 BCE), who initiated the construction of the library at Alexandria, ranks among the least known but most pivotal figures in the Western intellectual tradition. Demetrius began his career in Athens, where he was a student at the famous open-air school founded by Aristotle, the Lyceum. By 317 BCE he had become tyrant of Athens, courtesy, if only indirectly, of another student of Aristotle, Alexander the Great. Alexander and his father had put Greece under Macedonian control, with formerly democratic Athens now subject to their overlordship. In part puppet dictator, in part philosopher-king, Demetrius ruled Athens with a high-handedness arguably typical of intellectuals in power. Somewhat hypocritically, given his own flamboyant habits—he was notorious for his orgies and lavish banquets—he initiated a series of crackdowns on excess and luxury in dress and entertainment. By 307 BCE he had made so many enemies that he sought exile in Thebes.[1]

By this time, Alexander the Great was long dead and his generals were busy carving up his legacy in Asia. The general in charge of Egypt, the future Ptolemy I, invited Demetrius to emigrate to Alexandria after the leader of the Lyceum declined a similar offer. Demetrius jumped at the chance and became in effect Ptolemy's court philosopher. Before he managed to disgrace himself again (by alienating Ptolemy *II* in a succession controversy), he first initiated and then supervised the construction of Alexandria's library and its equally famous Museum.

There are at least three ways to tell the story of the library, each from a different perspective but all overlapping. The first approach is institutional: the tale of how libraries were founded and funded; how books were produced, collected, copied, categorized, and stored; and how scholars made use of them. Such a story might begin with the libraries of ancient Mesopotamia. It would reach its apex in the Ptolemies' unprecedented decision to collect all the world's knowledge at Alexandria. And it would conclude with the glories of Islamic scholarship, which transmitted and expanded the knowledge of antiquity across the greater Mediterranean and beyond.

The second approach is intellectual, and begins with the philosophical rationale for collecting books in the first place. Organizing and managing a library is, after all, a monumentally tedious task, in need of a deep-seated prior commitment to justify its utility. In particular, libraries rest on the conviction that writing is the best way of organizing knowledge. Yet as recently as 1800, Enlightenment encyclopedists and Romantic university lecturers still disagreed over whether writing or speech is preferable. Given that such philosophical greats as Socrates and Plato preferred to debate rather than scribble, the decision taken by their immediate successors to found the first Greek libraries is a surprising development in need of special explanation. Greek society, like most archaic societies, revolved around oral tradition, the memorization and recitation of the Homeric epics. If hearing the *Iliad* and the *Odyssey* gave you cultural literacy, if epic poems achieved their highest expressiveness in theatrical performance, why write them down? Here a direct line connects Demetrius to Aristotle: their common decision to support writing as comprehensively as speech, to write everything down, store it in libraries, and base scholarship on the analysis and synthesis of texts rather than on verbal argument.

Mention of Aristotle, who served as Alexander's boyhood tutor, brings us back to the Macedonian world conquests and to a third approach, which might be called political. Alexander's successors, in particular the rulers of Egypt and Asia Minor, brought Greek culture out of its confinement in the city-states, or poleis, which give us our word for politics. The libraries they founded enabled knowledge to flourish for the first time in the radically different social environment of the Hellenistic empire. Since then, libraries have been supported by an astonishing variety of political systems down to the present day. Any institution that has lasted well over two millennia has to have appealed not just to scholars and academics but to society at large. It must have fulfilled some of the deepest aspirations of ancient people, reflected the wishes of those commanding influence and resources, and meshed with the structures of social and political power. Understanding why the Ptolemies—and others of Alexander's successors—saw fit to establish libraries, of all things, gives us insight into why large-scale political powers so often make patronage of learning a key part of their competition with rivals.

With politics as our guide, then, but with institutional developments and intellectual rationales in mind, let us sketch the origins of the Hellenistic library. Academic knowledge first emerged in the society of the Greek polis at Athens. But only the eclipse of this world, and with it classical Greece itself, made possible the rise of the library and its characteristic forms of scholarship. Sumptuous institutions conceived on a grand scale, libraries reflected the wealth and ambition of Hellenistic empire-builders newly emboldened to assert the hegemony of Greek learning over the known world. Nothing in the ancient world compared with their achievement—except in China, whose epoch of unification also inspired a great library to organize knowledge. There too cultural standardization went hand in hand with the end of classical philosophy and its replacement by imperial patronage of scholarship. Equally true, the profound differences between Chinese and Hellenistic libraries reveal what was historically specific about the scholarly culture that emerged in the West. Alexandria, not Athens, was its first center. Alexandria's library became a model for three other imperial civilizations of Mediterranean antiquity, Rome, Christendom, and Islam, all founded on the Greek legacy.

SPEECH AND WRITING IN THE CLASSICAL POLIS

Among the most disquieting features of the ancient Greeks, a people we often regard as the fount of Western civilization, is their profound devaluation of private and family life, the sphere of women, children, and slaves. Public life—the only life that really mattered—was the domain of men. Celebrations of the phallus, graphically depicted on numerous vases and sculptures, announce a culture of frank and aggressive masculinity.[2] Equally troubling to modern sensibilities, the Greeks showed a distinct preference for pederastic relationships between adult men and postpubescent boys. Misogyny and homoerotic swagger under-lie the vibrancy and brilliance of Greek philosophy, even while raising the puzzle of why it ever took written form.

The male-male love for which ancient Greece is famous had its origins in military comradeship. Adult men and teenagers—fifteen- to nineteen-year-olds, not children—tried to prove themselves to each other, the older ones taking younger comrades under their wing. Sometimes such relationships did take the form of explicit carnal contact, though this was generally looked down upon; homosexual intercourse was viewed more as adultery is today than as pedophilia, as an all-too-human weakness of the flesh rather than a perversion of nature. The norm was instead a kind of passionate friendship. Greek education was designed to transform the male erotic bond into a bond between mentor and protégé, to make pederasty into pedagogy.[3] (An analogous blend of sexual and educational fellowship flourished among women on the island of Lesbos.) Physical education was as important as, if not more so than, mental training; gymnastics derives from the word *gymnos* ("naked"), indicating the Greek mode of male exercise. Over time, however, mastering effective speech came to outweigh prowess in the martial arts.

Speech was central to the functioning of small-scale, personal politics like that practiced at Athens. For a long time the Greek poleis had been ruled by tyrants or aristocrats, but political conflict in the sixth and fifth centuries BCE gradually led to the establishment of democracies. The shift from tyranny to democracy intensified the need for pedagogy in effective public speaking. We tend so much to the reflexive praise of Greek democracy that it is easy to overlook its inherent weaknesses: take a group of people trained in combat, chronically at war, poor by modern standards, and confined to a small space, and, emancipated from traditional authority, they would likely proceed to clobber one another even more vigorously. In such a climate, spoken competition, in political debate at the town square, provided the means to channel violent conflict into nonviolent conflict.

These aspects of Greek education, society, and politics came together in the epic poems attributed to Homer, the *Iliad* and the *Odyssey*. Both center on masculine identity, the *Iliad* on the comradeship of war (one launched by a fight over a woman), the *Odyssey* on the lone individualist, the man who for ten years

8

prefers exploration and adventure to the company of his long-suffering wife, Penelope. The two epics also focus on Greek political cohesion: in narrating the Greek city-states' war against the Trojans of Asia Minor, they establish a group identity that held Greece together amid its tendency to degenerate into civil war. Passed down through the generations, they constituted a repository of what it meant to be Greek. Both epics were transmitted orally, memorized by professional bards or poets who roved from town to town.

For competitive speech, though, one needed not bards but coaches: the Sophists, a rival group of wordsmiths who came from all over Greece, converging in democratic Athens in the later fifth century BCE. The Sophists gathered in public spaces already frequented by men engaged in self-betterment, specifically the gymnasiums. Professionals for hire, they explained epic and archaic poetry, Homer in particular, and taught their clients to speak well. The ability to win any argument—the skill the Sophists purveyed—paved the road to influence and power in the polis. Literary knowledge was more important than scientific knowledge in this world, as it was throughout the premodern period. Effective speech conferred mastery over people, which in an age before advanced technology counted for far more than the mastery over nature that science offers.

Sophists addressed the challenges of democracy by systematizing the art of persuasion and the pedagogy of speaking well. In so doing they became the first true practitioners of textual scholarship.[4] The careful, methodical study of Homer meant getting the words exactly right, which entailed an emphasis on grammar, rhetoric, and roughly the field we now label linguistics or philology. For this the Sophists relied heavily on the written word, and in particular on books. They became infamous for the refinement of their linguistic distinctions and made lawyerly arguments drawing their evidence and citations from poetic precedents. Books, as references, were indispensable handmaidens to the sophistic style of argument.

But the Sophists were not only nitpickers, they were hucksters and cynical profiteers: this was the damning view of Socrates, foremost among the circle of elitist philosophers suspicious of democracy's tendency to put knowledge up for sale. Socrates believed that the Sophists' exaggerated faith in the written word weakened physical memory. A conservative, he hearkened back to the living, erotic, verbal bonds among men. The Socratic method, a robust question-and-answer, is the expression of an oral pedagogy founded on the productive friction between masters and students. It also reflects the Socratic belief that speech leads to truth: to judge the veracity of an utterance, one may also consult the reputation of its speaker, a central habit of mind in the face-to-face polis. The written word, by contrast, is untrustworthy and corrupting because it is detached from the actions, honor, and character of whoever uttered it.

What we know of Socrates, given his principled disdain for writing, comes inevitably from his pupils, mainly Plato, who for his own part acted to tip the balance back away from speech. Plato's dialogues took written form and by their very nature accommodated difference and disagreement among rivals (including Socrates himself), working through their arguments logically. Equally important, they acted as a conduit for the Socratics' most innovative departures from the scholarship of the Sophists. For painstaking analysis of verb tenses in the Homeric epics, Plato and his circle substituted a style of metaphysical speculation associated with the eclectic philosophies of the pre-Socratics, who argued over such questions as whether atoms, numbers, or elements (earth, air, fire, water) were the ultimate constituents of reality. In essence, they fused the pre-Socratics' penchant for abstract contemplation with the Sophists' emphasis on practical scholarship.[5] This brought a newly systematic viewpoint to perennial practical questions on the best ways to live, to form character, to constitute society, and to design institutions. Dialogues made this feat look natural. Not so much literal transcriptions as textual recreations of spoken debates, they paraded hard-won insights as the apparent products of extemporaneous philosophizing. This clever illusion confronted the Sophists on their own turf and created a lasting tension in academic culture between true wisdom and mere rhetoric. "Philosophy," the ideology of ancient learning, emerged as a calculated bid counterposing a public-minded love of wisdom to sophistic opportunism and private profit.

Institutionally, what Plato, his followers, and their dialogues together created, and what later imitators copied, was the philosophical school. Plato proved his devotion to wisdom by inviting rivals to join him, and his Academy—a brotherhood of scholars constituted in an Athenian grove—ranged freely over the entirety of what has come to be known as academic knowledge. When Plato's student and rival Aristotle failed to succeed him as leader of the Academy, Aristotle's followers in turn created their own school, the Lyceum. Both institutions had close ties to the gymnasia for which they were named and as such conformed to the classic ideals of Greek pedagogy, establishing new oral traditions in acts of ritual love and public conflict among men. As an institution for organizing knowledge, the school engenders passionate commitments among individuals united, despite their own rivalry, around a charismatic founder. Its institutional continuity is by the same token threatened by the death or defection of leaders and prominent members. Aristotle confronted exactly this problem, finding in Athens and elsewhere a plethora of schools besides his own vying for intellectual position.

Aristotle was able to coopt his rivals by grounding his scholarship decisively in writing. He determined to synthesize positions represented by contending schools, his method being to group discrete doctrines and treat their differences and similarities with an aim to unraveling their apparent contradictions.[6] Many find Aristotle's books insufferably bland for this reason. His kitchen-sink philosophy teems with sober categorizations—his typology of causes as material, formal, efficient, and final, for example—and lacks the spark of dissent that enlivens Plato. Others find Aristotle inspiringly capacious, able to incorporate all the encyclopedic detail, on everything from flora and fauna to political constitutions, that Plato lacked. Such a style is eminently suited, in any case, to the shift from speech to writing. Speech thrives on one-sided positions, so argument can go on indefinitely around the same questions; writing makes an inclusive, ecumenical approach both possible and desirable.

So too the library embodied on a large scale what Aristotle's books embodied in miniature, which makes Aristotle not just the personal but also the intellectual link to the Hellenistic world that emerged through his student Alexander. Every library comfortably contains writings and juxtaposes ideas that, if they were represented by their proponents in the flesh, might contrast violently with one another. Yet there they sit, on shelves, awaiting such scholars as may chance upon them to confront their latent contradictions. Libraries reduce complexity not by proposing a new simplicity—a bold philosophy advancing air, not water, as the ultimate constituent of matter, for example—but by constructing a well-made intellectual edifice where every doctrine has its proper place. Where schools fade or fragment, libraries persist; where schools sustain fixed arguments and preserve intellectual lineages, libraries absorb new knowledge and accommodate newcomers to learning. This made Greek learning, incubated by oral competition, newly portable to non-Greek landscapes. Abroad, for the first time, writing enabled the accumulation not just of philosophical perspectives but of knowledge of the world more generally.

ALEXANDRIA: GREECE ABROAD

Ancient books had been in circulation on the open market long before the first Hellenistic libraries, but their collection was a private affair, not a public one. Books, or rather papyrus scrolls, were produced by trained copyists operating out of commercial bookshops or working as household slaves for wealthy patrons. The physical act of writing carried the opprobrium of all manual labor and was disdained by cultivated men; scholars who "wrote" books in fact dictated them to their scribes. Together with the emphasis on speech in politics and philosophy, this limited the extent to which books could be—or could be seen as—the authoritative storehouses of knowledge in classical Athens. Only with the shift from polis to empire and the founding of libraries at Alexandria, Pergamum, and elsewhere did the collection of books become a public affair.

In 323 BCE, Alexander the Great died (one year before Aristotle), and this unleashed a struggle among his several successors. Poleis and city life continued, but larger-scale political organization became the rule. Empires now competed where cities had before, generally under the patronage of a wealthy ruler or family rather than a body of democratic citizens. Superseding the polis, these new states elevated cultural competition from the level of individuals to the level of dynasties without in any way undermining the centrality of Greek language or culture. Such dynasties simply commanded, for the first time, the resources to establish institutions outlasting their founders and tied to the longer-term fortunes of the states that sponsored them. The wealthiest and most powerful of these was in Egypt, where the Ptolemies lorded it over the Nile Valley from their capital at Alexandria, a military-administrative outpost located where the river delta met the sea. Vying with other empire-builders in Antioch, Pergamum, and back in Macedonia and Greece, the Ptolemies made their city a magnet for ambitious emigrating Greeks. Alexandria grew under their tutelage to become the multicultural city of antiquity par excellence.

The Ptolemies were uncommonly cultured rulers and established as a paradise for scholars a lavishly endowed temple to the Muses, the Museum. Imperial patronage marked a critical shift away from the self-sacrificing public-spiritedness of Athenian philosophers toward a newfound concern for scholars' private lives, and in particular their incomes. Certainly the emphasis once given to character formation in the classical polis receded when politics began to center less on competitive speech than on palace intrigue. Pampered, coddled, secluded in a royal compound set apart from the hustle and bustle of a busy, polyglot port city, Museum members enjoyed hefty tax breaks and free use of residence halls, dining facilities, personal servants, teaching rooms, colonnades and open spaces, and, most important, the famous library. Resentful outsiders called it a "birdcage" for politically emasculated bookworms. But the Museum was part and parcel of a very shrewd policy to lure talent from all over the Greek world by providing all the creature comforts and cultural amenities of Greek life. The same thing happened on a smaller scale with the numerous gymnasia, baths, festivals, and theaters also established in Alexandria to weld the Greek diaspora into a ruling class.

The Ptolemies were anxious to attract the best Greek scholars to their capital and paid them handsomely. Among those who flourished under their patronage were Euclid, the great synthesizer of ancient geometry; Eratosthenes, whose measurements established with impressive accuracy the circumference of the earth (which, incidentally, he knew to be round); and Archimedes, the polymath best known today for his study of hydrostatics. Later, under the Romans, Alexandria hosted Galen, the giant of ancient medicine, and Claudius Ptolemaeus (or simply Ptolemy—no relation to the Ptolemaic dynasty), architect of the geocentric solar system ultimately overturned by Copernicus.

But it was Demetrius of Phaleron who became the pivotal figure. No one better embodies the link from Aristotle to the library and the shift from polis to empire. Through his initiative, the Ptolemies set about acquiring as many books as possible. They paid huge sums, utterly indiscriminately, for whatever was available on the Mediterranean market. They even ordered incoming ships at port to yield up their scrolls for confiscation and copying; the copies, not the originals, were later returned to their owners. Books were an even better investment than scholars. Scholars come and go in a competitive world, but books can only accumulate. Ancient (albeit unverifiable) reports number the holdings of Alexandria's library during its heyday at over half a million. Though most books took up several scrolls, meaning that the quantity of discrete texts was perhaps a third as many, the Alexandrian library was still by far the most comprehensive library of antiquity.

Hellenistic scholarship

Greek knowledge pursued under the aegis of empire took on a more depoliticized character. Not only did charged speech at last yield to scholarly writing, but the all-encompassing pursuit of "philosophy" dissipated among the various fields of learning for which Alexandria became famous: literature, philology, poetry, geography, ethnography, medicine, mathematics, and experimental science. Philosophy itself failed—almost uniquely among learned pursuits—to thrive there, at least early on. Not only does philosophy feed on oral interaction, but it arguably profits from a dearth of texts: without the seductions of a research library, scholars are thrown back on their own intellectual resources. Amid Alexandria's embarrassment of riches, by contrast, public intellectualism was easily sacrificed to private curiosity, and philosophy was transmuted into something more recognizably academic.

Collation, translation, and synthesis: these were the particular forms of scholarship first established at Alexandria. Far more than a place merely to amass scrolls, the library became a place to collate them: to edit and recopy manuscripts, to recombine their contents and add commentary and analysis. In an age before print technology, even the most faithfully hand-copied texts were irremediably inaccurate. The great classics especially circulated in hopelessly many versions around the Mediterranean. Establishing a reliable edition of Homer's epics thus became Alexandria's particular point of pride. Disdaining other scholars—at Pergamum, for example—who contented themselves with establishing Homer's overall allegorical meaning, Alexandrians set particular store on getting every paragraph, every sentence, every word right.[7] Quite often this led them to make inferences that did more harm than good to the texts concerned. A line from the *Iliad* in which Aphrodite carries a seat for Helen offended the critics' belief that a goddess would not stoop to serving a mere mortal.[8] But the decision to elevate precision and rigor over substantive moral message illustrates better than anything else the extinction of classical Athenian speech in Ptolemaic Egypt and its replacement by a text-centered academic culture.

Even more consequential than editing Homer, a Greek poet for Greek speakers, was the translation effort that began to establish the hegemony of Greek learning among non-Greek cultures. Alexandria was a multicultural crossroads with a large (albeit oppressed) native Egyptian population and a wealthy and influential Jewish minority; it was also quite close to the great civilizations of Persia and Mesopotamia. In this unique environment, the Ptolemies undertook to make the most important books of the various Mediterranean peoples—the known world, to them—available in Greek. Included were Roman law, Egyptian history, Babylonian astronomy, and, first and foremost for its impact on later history, the Hebrew Bible. Demetrius himself may have initiated the production of the Septuagint, so named after the seventy-two Jewish scholars, six for each of the Twelve Tribes, reportedly brought from Palestine to Alexandria to translate the Hebrew Bible into Greek. Although each one was sequestered from the rest, all seventy-two allegedly produced exactly the same text. This proved both the accuracy of the translation and its divine sanction.

Eventually the Septuagint became the patrimony of Alexandria's ever-growing Jewish community, which had already begun to adopt Greek, displacing Aramaic and Hebrew, as its primary language. But its initial production reflected distinctly Ptolemaic interests. Hellenistic rulers combined genuine intellectual curiosity about "alien wisdom" with the politically shrewd insight that governing subject peoples required knowledge of their laws and customs.[9] As explained in the Letter of Aristeas, one of our few sources on the library's early activities, Ptolemy wanted to gain the allegiance of Jews who had been forcibly relocated from Jerusalem to Egypt by the Persians, as well as a large number of Jews forced to serve in the Ptolemies' own armies: "Now since I am anxious to show my gratitude to these men and to the Jews throughout the world and to the generations yet to come, I have determined that your law shall be translated from the Hebrew tongue which is in use amongst you into the Greek language, that these books may be added to the other royal books in my library."[10] In later centuries, some of Alexandria's most famous philosophers, including the Jew Philo and the Christians Origen and Clement, drew on the Septuagint to reconcile Greek philosophy with divine revelation and forge true theology out of Hebrew monotheism. Few efforts better encapsulate the way in which Hellenistic learning had become enmeshed in the politics of multiethnic empire.

Synthesis was the final accomplishment of Alexandrian scholarship. This simply reflected the influence of Aristotle's encyclopedic approach. The luxury of roaming along endless bookshelves inspired scholars to cherry-pick those choice bits of knowledge that their predecessors had ransacked the world to discover. The truest practitioner of this art was Callimachus (ca. 305–ca. 240 BCE), famous both for his erudite poetry and as the compiler of Alexandria's first library catalog, the *Pinakes*. These "tables" were a vast improvement over first-letter alphabetization, itself invented by Alexandria's first librarian. They enabled Callimachus to search library scrolls for lists of rivers, cities, myths, fish, rituals, gods, unusual words, and strange customs from peoples all around the world. Natural and human wonders, like "salt water which tastes sweet" and "precious metals that grow like plants," became staples of what is called "paradoxography," a genre he invented.[11] All this information he kept at hand as a store of references, learned allusions, and fascinating facts with which to pepper his verse. His thematic groupings and cross-references made his collections available to other library scholars—to the detriment of their poetry, in the eyes of their critics. "Soldiers of Callimachus," wrote one vitriolic detractor, "you hunters of grim verbal combinations, who like '*min*' and '*sphin*' [archaic pronouns], and to research whether the Cyclops had dogs, may you be worn away for eternity."[12]

The categorization of knowledge, whether in tables, trees, or Dewey decimals, has exerted a fascination among modern-day scholars far disproportionate to its actual importance. Classification schemes are arbitrary conveniences. What matters is not whether history is grouped with poetry or with politics and what that says about the ancient mind, but simply whether such schemes make books readily and rapidly accessible to roaming encyclopedic intellects. To judge by the quality of substantive synthetic scholarship emanating from Ptolemaic Alexandria, this is exactly what Callimachus's *Pinakes* and similar works accomplished. Some of the ancient world's best cartography and ethnography was done by scholars who never ventured outside the city walls, or perhaps even the Museum grounds, to gather data but instead simply drew together the best and most reliable maps and travel reports from library holdings. Euclid's geometry falls into the same category: more a synthesis than an original work, it nonetheless ranks as history's most influential mathematical textbook.

Critical reading became "a source for further writing" at Alexandria, spawning new genres like the commentary, the glossary, and the index.[13] Erudition, eclecticism, and a penchant for system-building, still the vices and virtues of the scholarly mind, were the manifestations of the new scholarly style. This was far from the style of the philosophers, for good or ill, but it is unlikely in any case that true philosophy could have survived outside hothouses like fifth-century Athens. The patronage of rulers made all this knowledge available—in modified form—to others, including ourselves.

Cultural patronage

We may well wonder why great rulers, from the Ptolemies of Egypt to the Medicis of Italy to the sultans, mughals, and emperors of Asia, have so often patronized academic scholarship. It cannot be simple chance, the mere goodwill of powerful figures who happen to take an interest in the life of the mind, that higher learning has prospered under such extensive financial and political support.

One explanation is straightforwardly, even cynically political. It holds that rulers invest in cultural capital to burnish their reputations and paint their rivals as base warlords by comparison. Especially in a culturally unified but politically fragmented world such as the Hellenistic one (or for that matter Renaissance Italy or "Warring States" China), centers of higher learning tipped the balance in an otherwise equal contest among a limited number of rivals. Other means, however, such as the patronage of religion or the construction of monumental architecture, accomplish this goal more directly, by conveying the impression of kingly magnanimity to much larger groups of people. The Ptolemies' predecessors, the pharaohs, had done exactly this with massive pyramids and temple complexes. Royal patronage of this sort was a millennium-old tradition throughout southwest Asia, and this the Ptolemies well knew.

Somewhat more satisfying is the argument that scholars play a special role in the establishment of languages of power and commerce. After Alexander, Greek had not yet supplanted Aramaic (the language of Jesus Christ) as the lingua franca of the eastern Mediterranean, but it bid fair to become one if the various administrators, sailors, traders, soldiers, and craftsmen hailing from the Greek city-states could be induced to offer their talents to the service of empire. For them, the Museum/library complex, embedded as it was in an ethnically alien host population, acted as a beacon as surely as the gigantic lighthouse the Ptolemies erected in Alexandria's harbor. Then again, it is doubtful that scholars in a birdcage were truly consoling presences to a thin stratum of conquerors acclimatizing themselves to foreign peoples and foreign languages.

Neither of these explanations, in any case, can account for why specifically writing—written scholarship, the mania for collecting books, the penchant for precision, and all that the library represented—offered the Ptolemies the most efficient means of achieving their objectives. For answers to this we must look to antiquity's most writing-centered civilization, the Chinese, and to a situation quite the opposite of the Hellenistic one, in which cultural uniformity already existed but political competition had recently ended.

GREEK VS. CHINESE

A first glance at ancient China seems to confirm, if not the magnanimity of the Ptolemies, then at least the advantages of Greek competitiveness over the monolithic repression of oriental despots. China's "Warring States" epoch had been philosophically brilliant, a lot like classical Greece: this was the era of Confucius, Plato's rough contemporary, and of a host of dynamic rival schools—Legalist, Daoist, Mohist, and many others. But in 221 BCE, the Qin ("Chin") emperor, from whose dynasty China gets its name, put an end to this. First he brought the warring states to heel and created China's first unified empire. Then his chief minister, Li Si,* himself an accomplished Legalist scholar, clamped down on all rivals to the Qin state philosophy, Confucianism especially. The philosopher-potentate proceeded to mandate a general burning of the books. In a notorious memorial to the emperor, Li Si explained that having access to private learning meant that scholars trusted their own teachings instead of the emperor's orders. A direct correlation could be drawn between the multiplicity of philosophical teachings and the fragmentation of China. Only one recourse remained: "Your servant suggests that all books in the bureau of history, save the records of Qin, be burned; that all persons in the empire, save those who hold a function under the control of the official scholars, daring to store the classical literature and the discussions of the various philosophers, should go to the administrative and military governors so that these books may be indiscriminately burned." The punishment for noncompliance would also be severe: "Those who dare to discuss the classical literature among themselves should be executed and their bodies exposed on the marketplace. Those who use the past to criticize the present should be put to death together with their relatives."[14] Diversity and dissent perished in this holocaust, or so goes the argument, and

*Pronounced "Lee Suh," and also spelled Li Ssu.

political unity was bought at the steep price of cultural conformity. Thank goodness none of the Ptolemies or their ministers were ever in a position to enact such a scheme.

However great the temptation to demonize Li Si as the anti-Demetrius, his book-burning policy is inseparably connected with another, more positive cultural policy: the standardization of written Chinese. China's beautiful, complex script has long signaled a greater fascination with writing than the somewhat utilitarian alphabets of the Mediterranean. Whereas Greek writing developed from the commercial scrawl of Phoenician merchants, China's nonalphabetic characters were objects of timeless aesthetic and religious veneration. Dynasties of remote antiquity, starting with the Shang, made inscriptions on stone, jade, and especially bronze to communicate with ancestors and gods as well as with future generations. Calligraphy, an elegant art intended for learned cultivation, carried a prestige unimaginable to a Greek scholar dictating to a slave. But Chinese characters came in many historical, functional, and even regional variants. Li Si and his associates eliminated these variants, made characters simpler to write, and established a trend, which culminated several generations later, replacing the curvaceous ancient "seal" script with the recognizably angular characters Chinese has today.[15] As with the book-burning, he intended to clear the cobwebs of history and establish Qin as the zero hour in China's subsequent development.

It is little exaggeration to say that in doing so, Li Si saved Chinese civilization, which depends on the uniformity of its writing system. Chinese was and is an exclusively written language in that its script bears an arbitrary relation to the sounds people speak. It lacks not only an alphabet but a syllabary: seeing a written character offers no reliable help in how to pronounce it, and conversely, each spoken syllable corresponds to multiple written characters. Alphabets, by contrast, whether Greek, Hebrew, Roman, or other, provide at least rough guides to pronunciation and as such are tied to the everyday tongues spoken by common people as well as scholars. The Chinese cultural region, which includes Japan, Korea, Manchuria, Mongolia, and Vietnam, is as linguistically, topographically, climatically, and ethnically diverse as the ancient Mediterranean and the Near East combined. Yet the latter never counted as a coherent unit, certainly not under the Greeks, whereas China (or at least China proper) did—and does. This is because Chinese scholars speaking different dialects, precisely because they could not understand each other face to face, had to communicate in the purely imaginary realm of writing. This gave them a cohesiveness and common bond they most certainly did not have with the uneducated hordes with whom they daily rubbed shoulders. China was an empire of scholars. Its unity reposed in its textual tradition. Dynasties came and went, but the Chinese classics, and the script that unlocked them to understanding, kept the dream of a unified Chinese civilization alive during epochs of upheaval.

Among such upheavals, the Qin book-burning was no exception but rather the best illustration of the rule. Despite aiming to eradicate past wisdom, it had the unintended effect of preserving it. Not only did it spare writings on medicine, pharmacy, divination, and agriculture, but it exempted state scholars by aiming its fire only at "private teaching" and suffered from limited and ineffective enforcement, so that many, many books survived. The whole episode functioned less to damage China's literary heritage than to awaken in subsequent dynasties a sustained determination to recover the knowledge believed lost.

China's first imperial libraries date to the Han dynasty, which supplanted the Qin and aimed to recover all it had destroyed, especially the Confucian classics. Han scholars charged with this task confronted problems of textual editing and collation even worse than those of their Alexandrian counterparts. China's standard writing materials, bamboo and silk, were far more perishable than the papyrus and parchment used by Greeks. Chinese books were also more prone to physical collapse and discombobulation than their Mediterranean counterparts. Characters were often inscribed vertically on bamboo strips which were then tied together; when strings broke, texts fell to pieces and coherence was lost. Loss of sequence was much less of a problem with the smaller number of ten-foot-long scrolls that composed even the longest Greek book. Some scholars have even argued that the Han restoration, which involved piecing together lost texts, rearranging their contents, and sometimes fabricating missing elements, all on the basis of dubious inferences and subjective editorial decisions, did more harm to the authenticity of ancient literary works than the Qin book-burning itself.[16]

But the Han imperial library followed a political logic that easily overrode the sort of philological scrupulousness found at Alexandria. It was paramount not only to save China's literary heritage, but to reconstitute it in full as a perfect mirror of a lost Golden Age. This imaginary double for the present would act as its guide during periods of turmoil and stability alike.[17] The drive for permanence and canonization accounts for the Han dynasty's most impressive act of scholarly patronage, one certainly comparable in scope and vision to the Alexandrian library. Han scholars, having laboriously reconstructed the corpus of Confucian classics, then erected them on massive stone tablets. Begun in 175 CE and lasting eight years, the effort required between forty and fifty refrigerator-sized slabs to record the 200,000-plus characters comprising the six Confucian classics.[18] These were arranged just outside the National Academy in Luoyang. Scholars from all over China flocked there by the thousands to make rubbings of the inscriptions and thereby acquire indisputably reliable copies of these canonical texts. Only a unified empire could command the resources—the manpower, the materials, the commitment and organization—to stage such a feat. Only a unified empire could enforce a decision to canonize a particular set of works by fiat. Only a unified empire could then set out in later centuries to produce a far-flung elite of loyal scholar-officials by indoctrinating and testing them in a single corpus of literary texts—the basis of the Confucian examination system, which provided government officials until 1905.

The use of permanent materials, not to mention the mechanical reproduction it made possible, was unknown in the Hellenistic academic world. The Chinese carved characters on stone, bronze, and jade; the Mesopotamians wrote cuneiform on clay tablets; the Egyptians under the pharaohs etched hieroglyphics on obelisks and temples; the Greeks themselves made numerous epigraphic inscriptions. But durable writing was never a part of either the Greek or the Hellenistic *scholarly* tradition. The multiplicity and indeed practical infinitude of scholarly writings simply made permanent public inscription a moot prospect.

Scholars at Alexandria would doubtless have turned down any opportunity to inscribe their achievements in stone even if they had had the chance to do so. And here we come to the point of this comparison: whereas Chinese libraries were founded to stem the decay of a vanishing and partly destroyed intellectual tradition in their own homeland, Hellenistic libraries developed to render an existing body of knowledge reliably reproducible and physically portable. The Greeks, both by inclination and by circumstance, lived in the present. Newcomers to the world stage, peripheral to the great Asian empires, they lacked the sense of deep time and rootedness in place that oriented Chinese scholarly culture so decisively toward reconstructing the historical past.

This made the Greeks forward-looking, innovative, explorative. It also made them historically shallow and sometimes startlingly naive. The two most famous historians of classical

Athens were Thucydides, who wrote only about events in his own lifetime, and Herodotus, who wrote about foreign peoples with notorious credulousness. Nothing in the Greeks' cherished epics, set in a familiar Aegean world ringed with monsters and marvels, prepared them to rule and understand foreign peoples. And yet in Egypt they confronted a civilization they recognized as vastly more ancient than their own. Ruling the land of the pyramids, the Ptolemies styled themselves after the pharaohs and may even have built the Museum after the plan of Ramses' temple at Thebes.[19] Above all, Greeks abroad acquired a new self-consciousness about their own history.[20] The Alexandrians were the first to canonize the Greek achievement, to view their own scholarship, however creative, as derivative from it, and to establish a precedent whereby the spark of Hellenic wisdom might migrate from one place and political system to another and yet be seen as part of an organic tradition—what we now call "the West."

TALES OF DESTRUCTION AND LOSS

Regarding the destruction of Alexandria's library we know precious little; indeed, there are several rival accounts, none of them factually satisfying. One holds Julius Caesar responsible. The great Roman general, having pursued his enemy Pompey into Egypt, soon took up with Cleopatra, the last of the Ptolemies, and supported her rise to power around 47 BCE. In the ensuing warfare, Caesar found himself trapped in the royal palace complex and had to burn his way back to his ships. Since the palace complex included the Museum and the Museum contained the library, a large number of books reportedly went up in smoke. Some scholars doubt the accuracy of this story, arguing on the basis of literary detective work that the great conflagration must have been confined to some waterfront storehouses far away from the palace complex.[21] Others, accepting the basic fact of Caesar's destructiveness, repeat a well-worn and probably apocryphal anecdote whereby Mark Antony, when *he* was courting Cleopatra a decade or so later, stole 200,000 books from the rival library at Pergamum and gave them to Alexandria as compensation for its past losses. If this is true, it helped the library to go on after Rome finally conquered Ptolemaic Egypt in 30 BCE.

These variants hint at the essential truth, yet none captures it: that Greek knowledge, and libraries in particular, benefited enormously from Roman conquest. The Roman general Sulla loved Greek books so much that after he conquered Athens, he carted off its entire library to Italy, complete with the original texts of Aristotle's works. Later Roman emperors continued appointing library directors at Alexandria for several centuries, helping the city retain its reputation as a center of scholarship. More important, they caused other libraries to be built all over the Mediterranean and especially at Rome itself. Sometimes as stand-alone temples, sometimes as adjuncts to public baths, they had spacious reading rooms and wings for both Greek and Latin and stood open to men and probably women as well. Julius Caesar became a great patron of libraries, and his adoptive son and dictatorial successor, Augustus, an even greater one. The Byzantine Empire, as the eastern Roman Empire became known after its split, tended Greek texts for fully a thousand years, long enough to transmit them to Renaissance Italy before its own capital was sacked by the Ottoman Turks in 1453. Whatever the ultimate reason the Ptolemies had for building libraries, then, their conquest by the Romans did nothing to end the precedent they set for imperial patronage of scholarship.

The same holds true for another tale of military destruction, this time coming from the East at the hands of the Arabs. Some say that in 640 CE, an Arab Muslim general, in the course of evicting the Byzantines from Alexandria, came across the library and sent a message to his superior, the caliph Omar, asking what to do with the books. Omar, known more for his military zeal than for his tolerance or intellectual subtlety, apparently replied with an inescapable syllogism: if the books at Alexandria conflicted with the Quran, they were heretical and should be burned; if they did not, they were superfluous and should likewise be burned. Again, there is reason to doubt, if not the facts of this story, then certainly the message it conveys about Muslim bigotry. Omar's dictum was not the final word on Islamic policy toward Greek "philosophy." Dubbing it *falsafa*, Muslim scholars soon appropriated Greek learning wholesale, first from Syriac translations and then from the Greek originals.[22] They also did more than the Romans to spread libraries and scholarship geographically, founding learned centers from Baghdad's House of Wisdom in the east to the libraries of medieval Spain in the extreme west; from Samarkand, on the Eurasian silk road, to Timbuktu, south of the Sahara Desert.

Islam, like Byzantium, is often viewed as a passive caretaker of Greek learning until it could be transmitted to the more dynamic societies of Western Europe. But the Muslims were no more passive or derivative than the Romans, who likewise pursued knowledge on a firm Hellenic foundation. Islamic scholarly institutions were in fact for centuries a good deal more vibrant and original than Western Roman ones, but to appreciate this we have to wait for Europe to catch up.

The final story of destruction and loss at the Alexandrian Museum concerns one of its last attested members, Theon, and his daughter, Hypatia. Theon was a respected mathematician, astronomer, and poet. He was also a devotee of alchemy, astrology, and divination, three "Hermetic" arts that reflected a kind of synthesis between Greek science and Egyptian folk magic.[23] Hypatia, who presided over a school of Neoplatonic philosophy, was even more accomplished than her father. Comfortable among men of power, she owed her reputation to her virtue and wisdom, not to her femininity, and reportedly once repulsed an infatuated male admirer by producing her sanitary napkin. But in 415 CE, five years after Rome was sacked, Hypatia was brutally dismembered by a bloodthirsty paramilitary force set upon her by Alexandria's Christian bishop, Cyril. Cyril had spent his early days in office launching a pogrom against Alexandria's Jews, a campaign Hypatia actively opposed. He then turned against Hypatia for resisting this anti-Semitic power play. Accusing her of black magic, Cyril's followers stoked popular rumors surrounding her father's interests in the occult. In reality, Hypatia was immune to the otherworldly mysticism that marked the waning Roman Empire.[24] What really infuriated the rabble-rousing Cyril was that Hypatia was the last of the pure Hellenists, a true, albeit elitist, follower of Plato dedicated to virtue, dialogue, and spiritual ecumenism.

The point of this story is no more to castigate the Christians than the point of the previous one was to exonerate the Muslims. Late antique Alexandria was rife with religious tension and communal violence on all sides, pagan, Jewish, and Christian. Political authorities were simply losing their power to hold this mix of cultures together, and Greek learning had lost its role as intellectual arbiter among them. Knowledge was now the contested patrimony of a fractious multicultural metropolis. Jews and Christians used it, as we saw in the case of the Septuagint, to refine their religious doctrines. Hermetics used it to lend prestige and give depth to Egyptian folk magic. Hypatia's colleagues threw around their philosophical weight—unsuccessfully—to defend the pagan Serapeum temple (home to the Museum's daughter library) against Christian onslaught. But philosophical pagans no longer had anything like a lock on Greek thought or the power it had in the past.

For centuries, under the Ptolemies and then the Romans, *paideia*—Greek learning—had given men of widely different ethnic and geographic origins the chance to compete on a level playing field, as elite possessors of what for many of them was not in fact their native language and culture. The power of persuasion, first incubated in Athenian democracy, welded together these elites even under authoritarian rule, as the empire-wide currency of political influence.[25] But between the caesars and the caliphs, Greek learning, borne aloft by spiritual ferment, had leapt the Museum walls. Nothing better illustrates this than the fact that its last devotee was a woman. Learning was now tied to the fortunes of the city as a whole. It would prosper as long as political authority—Ptolemaic, Roman, Byzantine, or Muslim—provided at least the semblance of order. This is precisely what the empire west of Rome now lacked. Even the maintenance of order back in Alexandria was not enough to save the library itself. Put simply, the famous scholarly complex now had no one left to tend and preserve it. Its collection ebbed away rather than burning up, and decayed as the result of neglect rather than destruction.

2

The Monastery

100–1100

MONASTERIES NOT ONLY PRESERVED LEARNING
THROUGH CENTURIES OF CIVILIZATIONAL COLLAPSE BUT
FORGED NEW LINKS FROM THE STUDY OF WRITTEN TEXTS
TO THE MARKING AND MEASUREMENT OF TIME.

IN 529 CE, the Academy at Athens founded by Plato, a relic of pagan philosophy in a now thoroughly Christian world, was shuttered by imperial edict. That same year a monastery was established at Montecassino, eighty miles south of Rome, which flourishes to this day. Located on a mountain "whose top seemed to touch the very heavens," it lay near the epicenter of the western Roman empire. But in sixth-century Italy, the civilization of classical antiquity was in a state of advanced collapse: "Towns are depopulated, fortified places destroyed, churches burnt, monasteries and nunneries destroyed. Fields are deserted by men, and the earth forsaken by the ploughman gapes desolate. No farmer dwells here now; wild beasts have taken the place of throngs of men. What goes on in other parts of the world, I do not know; but here, in the land in which we live, the world no longer announces its coming end, but shows it forth."[1]

These are the apocalyptic sentiments of Gregory the Great (ca. 540–604), who at the nadir of Rome's secular power witnessed— and contributed to—the birth of a new civilization, Latin Chris-

tendom. The first monk to become pope, Gregory also popularized the holy life and deeds of Montecassino's founder, Benedict
of Nursia, whose Rule has provided a written guide for centuries
of Western monks and nuns.[2]

Montecassino has suffered much since Gregory's day, repeat-
edly losing precious texts to fire, war, and natural disaster. In
577 it was sacked by Germanic invaders from the north, in 883
by Arabs from the south. Several times its monks had to flee,
once carting Benedict's bones off with them. Not until the
eleventh century would Montecassino's scriptorium—the room
where, in a familiar image, copyists hunched over parchment in
hushed silence—begin systematically to acquire and reproduce
manuscripts from Cicero and Ovid, Byzantium and the Arab
world. Then an earthquake in 1349, following hard upon the
plague of the year before, hastened another reversal of fortune.
Six hundred years further on, in 1944, an Allied bombing raid
against Fascist Italy reduced the place to rubble. Through all
these vicissitudes, the monks at Montecassino reconstituted
their spiritual traditions while adapting to changing times. The
1,500-year-old cloister has recently established its own website
(www.officine.it/montecassino/main_e.htm).

The library at Alexandria, as we have seen, succumbed to the
withering of urban amenities and the withdrawal of political
patronage attending the collapse of ancient empires. Indeed,
none of the schools or libraries of antiquity escaped extinction.
But unlike them, Christian monasteries were formed in conscious retreat from urban civilization, well before that civiliza-

tion collapsed. They were therefore remarkably well adapted to the preservation of learning in times of decay and devastation. They rank among the longest-lived continuously existing institutions of any kind in the Western world. Longevity is integral to the monastery, part of its institutional DNA.

A profound attentiveness to time is programmed into the monastery and its practices of preserving and deepening knowledge. The monastery's guiding ideology, Christianity, structures its sense of time around the life and death of Jesus Christ, whose eagerly anticipated return gives history direction and meaning. It offers, in the interim, a body of scripture and other literature to guide individuals in their personal and collective decisions about life, death, and salvation. Emphasis on the written word of God provided a religious rationale for the preservation of written knowledge after the infrastructure of civilization collapsed in the West. As the most devoted Christians, monks and nuns relied especially on texts, both sacred and profane, to mark out every hour, week, and year of their lives together in monastic communities. It was also monks who developed the system of enumerating time "in the year of Our Lord's Incarnation," *anno Domini incarnationis*, A.D., today ascendant in all parts of the world, Christian and non-Christian alike.*

Contrary to the popular image, the monastery was more than an institution devoted to tending lifeless manuscripts

---

*Recent historians have replaced A.D. with CE (Common Era) and B.C. with BCE in recognition of this commonality, albeit with only a surface change of nomenclature.

through centuries of darkness, bridging two periods of light, classical antiquity and the European Renaissance. Instead, its dual devotion to texts and to time constituted a reinvention of knowledge all the more impressive for the humility, diligence, and unbelievable patience with which it was undertaken.

CHRISTIANITY AND THE WRITTEN WORD

For all the importance of the Hellenistic library, the ancient world never ceased to honor the skills of the orator and the rhetorician above those of the writer and reader. Romans in particular consistently prized speech and made it central to public life and public values. Schools taught young men the trivium, the three arts of proper Latin grammar and diction, persuasive rhetoric, and dialectic (that is, how to mount a logical argument). Oral education offered more than vocational preparation for the law courts or imperial administration. Personal morality itself was anchored in an individual's public reputation, won through verbal exchange with other elite men of leisure. Nearly four centuries after Christ, Augustine of Hippo (354–430) could still observe in disgust that aspirating the "h" in the word "human" counted for more among the educated than exhibiting true Christian humanity. This remark came in the *Confessions*, the earliest autobiography in the Western tradition; in it, Augustine crafts a life story around his conversion from pagan morality to Christian faith. A philosophical work brimming with biblical citations, it marshals chapter and verse to bolster his case against "the man with a reputation for eloquence" who "attacks his opponent with ferocious animosity."[3]

Thanks in no small part to Augustine's works, Christian scripture finally began to displace Roman rhetoric in the formation of personal character and values. Reversing the balance between writing and speech, Christianity spawned an incredible wealth of texts to guide everyday believers, to shape their conscience, and to mold their behavior. Such writings offered to the humblest individual—and to philosophers—the opportunity to engage with the word of God, to craft one's life on earth to fit it, and thereby to pave a road to salvation in the hereafter.

Christianity began as a sectarian cult within Judaism, which, uniquely in the ancient Mediterranean, held a well-defined body of written texts, the Torah, at the heart of its religious practice. Even as the followers of Jesus began to distinguish themselves from Jews, they took for granted Jewish notions about the written word of God. Discussions of the Hebrew Bible figured prominently in early Christian groupings, where it was recited from the Greek Septuagint translation and reinterpreted in light of Jesus' messianic life and redemptive death.[4] But the Christians' own holy book, called the New Testament to contrast with the Jews' old one, took a surprisingly long time to coalesce. Stories of Jesus's life and teachings circulated orally for decades before being committed to writing. We thus have four separate, discrepant versions of his time on earth, the Gospels of Matthew, Mark, Luke, and John. Other, "gnostic" gospels, steeped in currents of esoteric mysticism, competed with these four canonical ones through the third century but were later judged heretical.

The Gospel of Judas, rediscovered in the 1970s and published only in 2006, depicts the disciple who betrayed Christ to the Romans as in fact acting on his behalf, as an instrument in Jesus' secret master plan.[5]

The oldest extant Christian writings, Paul's Epistles, were the work of a man who clearly expected Jesus' imminent return, heralding the end of time. In the first century, Paul relied on the Roman Empire's famed road network and thriving postal system to found and support fledgling communities across the Mediterranean. His letters to the Corinthians, Thessalonians, Romans, and others answered urgent questions arising in small and disparate gatherings groping for a common Christian life. (His remarks to the Corinthians on love are quoted at countless wedding ceremonies today.) Passed from town to town, they also helped form a larger community of shared belief.[6] Circulating outside any kind of formal academic and educational institution, Christian texts were from the beginning adapted for the immediate practical use of believers. By no means especially literate as a group, early Christians relied on those with rudimentary education, both men and women, to read aloud to others and to copy by hand the books they needed. Worshipping in the homes of wealthy believers or in the open air, Christians would gather to read before a communal meal. According to Justin Martyr (100–165), once "the reader ceases, the president speaks, admonishing and exhorting us to imitate these excellent examples." Prayer followed, then bread, wine, and water. Regular use in settings like this, scholars believe, eventually established some texts as more doctrinally authoritative or "canonical" than others.[7]

For centuries, fundamental issues of doctrine, large and small, were actively discussed, asserted, challenged, and supported, much of this in written letters and treatises for swift distribution across the empire. There was neither a clearly defined orthodoxy nor any means to impose it. Debate even infected the manuscript copies of scriptures themselves. Unlike the slaves or paid professionals who acted as copyists in the Greco-Roman tradition, Christian scribes held a personal investment in the texts they disseminated. A reference to Joseph as Jesus' father, for example, might be altered to reinforce Jesus' crucial status as the Son of God in all subsequent copies of a text—a process known as orthodox corruption, in this case directed against Arian heretics who denied the divinity of Christ.[8] A rough-and-ready democracy prevailed, in which an individual's decision to transcribe and possibly change a text constituted a vote for its continued use in future generations. Women as well as men could be found among these copyists, testimony to the penetration of textuality into a private sphere far removed from the all-male world of Roman public discourse.[9]

Uncoordinated by any central authority and driven by immediate needs for spiritual guidance and instruction, Christian writing practice long militated against the formation of a canon or Holy Book. Texts adapted for practical use even differed in appearance from the Jewish Torah scrolls, treated as ritual objects in synagogue. Christians instead were among the first to adopt a new physical format for the book, the very one we use today: the codex. Recall that the vast majority of ancient writing, including the books stored at the library of Alexandria, took the form of papyrus or parchment rolls. But by the first century, Christians were tying loose-leaf sheets of papyrus or parchment together in tablets that opened down the middle. These codices were compact enough to be carried around in a satchel and produced at prayer meetings. The codex had two other advantages over the roll: with writing on both sides of the surface, it was more capacious; and whereas rolls had to be read sequentially, codices enabled readers to turn to individual pages at separate points in the book—rather like the difference between a videotape and a DVD. Outside Christian contexts, the codex was nothing more than a handy notepad, chiefly reserved for administrative note-taking. Only the Christians favored these utilitarian notebooks for convenient, on-the-spot access to the contents of their guiding texts.[10]

Translations of the New Testament, written originally in Greek, soon appeared not only in Latin but also in regional vernaculars like Syriac, Coptic (Egyptian), and eventually Arabic. No divine authority attached to these translations as it did to the miraculous Septuagint, rendered identically from Hebrew into Greek by seventy-two separate scholars. It was more important to get the word of God out. Nor did Christians possess anything like Judaism's rabbinic tradition to give holy sanction to the tending and transmission of scriptures. Jews developed schools to teach both the written Torah and a separate oral Torah (the

Talmud), notionally derived from Moses himself, to complement and explain the written scriptures. Christians were forced to rely on Greco-Roman educational institutions for the basic learning required to understand their sacred writings. The rapid spread and success of Christianity in a pagan empire meant that devotion to written texts came to rest on prior training in the classical trivium of grammar, rhetoric, and dialectic.

Christian thinkers agonized over their reliance on the fruits of pagan learning. Tertullian (ca. 155–230) threw down the gauntlet early, asking what Athens (philosophy) had to do with Jerusalem (religion). The great translator Jerome (ca. 347–420), before he determined to render the entire Bible from Greek and Hebrew into Latin, was beset by nightmares in which a divine judge accused him of loving Cicero more than Christ. Augustine, for his part, deployed in his *Confessions* the full arsenal of Latin rhetorical devices to justify his repudiation of Roman mores and his espousal of a Christian life. Indeed, a rhetorical question crystallized his critique of the love story at the heart of Virgil's *Aeneid:* "What is more pitiable than a wretch without pity for himself who weeps over the death of Dido dying for love of Aeneas, but not weeping over himself dying for his lack of love for you, my God?"[11]

Augustine's soul-searching vindicated the application of scholarly acumen, derived from classical learning, to the Christian practice of self-scrutiny through texts. He perfected a tradition, begun by Clement and Origen of Alexandria, of eliciting philosophical profundities from popular Christian texts. Later generations venerated Augustine for saving ancient philosophy, Platonism in particular, by assuring it a central, if subordinate, place in the world of scripture. But in his insistence on word and text, Augustine departed even from the philosophers of his time, who still crafted their moral lives in Roman fashion around face-to-face encounters. Stoics, Cynics, and particularly Neo-platonists always formed a counterculture within the Roman elite, adopting lives of voluntary austerity in tight-knit circles of disciples—cults of personality, in effect. The reputation for holiness they enjoyed had to be won and defended orally against flesh-and-blood rivals, Christian ascetics and Jewish rabbis in particular.[12] Recall Hypatia, Augustine's contemporary, who lost her life when she entered the fray of Alexandrian ethnoreligious conflict.

Viewed from this perspective, Christianity's contribution to knowledge consisted of more than festooning the writings of an upstart cult with philosophical notions. The religion provided a way for learning to survive even in the absence of the living oral competition that truly defined the ancient world. By Augustine's day, Rome's power in the West was beginning to disintegrate. The uneasy cohabitation of pagan schools with Christian scripture in late antiquity would come to an end with the disappearance of the urban communities that sustained them. But Christianity had long since established itself as a religion that could exist outside the matrix of civilization and its institutions. As long as its texts survived, so too would its teachings.

BOOKS IN THE WILDERNESS

In 410, the Visigoths sacked the city of Rome, an event comparable to the World Trade Center disaster in 2001 in its shocking effect on contemporaries. In the *City of God*, his greatest philosophical treatise, Augustine tried to defend Christians against claims that their otherworldly religion had left the empire weak, corrupt, and vulnerable to attack. But as he lay dying in 430, his own North African city, Hippo, was already encircled by the Vandals, another among the Germanic peoples labeled "barbarians" by the Romans, who soon overwhelmed the political apparatus of the western empire. The slow collapse of Roman civic culture would continue for more than two centuries. The society to emerge from it would be nearly its opposite: illiterate and oral; rural, underpopulated, with a subsistence economy; dominated by warriors constantly in conflict with each other; and yet—profound testimony to the universal appeal of Jesus' message—homogeneously Christian. The task of learned men two centuries after Augustine was not so heady as the reconciliation of Plato and Christ. In an exclusively rural environment, it had devolved into the preservation of written culture per se. The knowledge needed to derive meaning from scripture would have to come from another source—a key function taken over, in the West, by the monastery.

The monastery was not by any means new in the sixth century, nor an institution whose origins lay in Rome's collapse. In part its inception reflected Christianity's success. Emperor Constantine's battlefield conversion in 312 gave official sanction to a religion that had by that time made deep inroads across the empire. Prior to this, the persecution and martyrdom of Christians had ensured that they all shared in Christ-like suffering. As the faith gained legitimacy and majority status in Mediterranean cities, however, those disaffected with the laxity of what had become a mass religion sought hardship and isolation as a conscious choice. A steady stream of believers took themselves to the deserts of Egypt and Syria in search of a purer life closer to God. Simeon Stylites (ca. 390–459), admittedly an extreme case, lived for thirty-seven years perched atop a pillar in Syria. The word "monk" comes from the Greek *monachos*, meaning "solitary one," as in our prefix "mono." And yet as many as five thousand of them swarmed the deserts of Lower Egypt alone by the end of the fourth century.[13] There they lived both as hermits and in communities. News of such men spread the ideal of individual ascetic purity to those living outside desert settlements. Accounts of lonely ascetics inspired other Christians to reform themselves in life. Augustine himself decided to convert on the very day he heard of Antony (ca. 250–356), the archetypical monk who abandoned Alexandria for a desert abode.

Antony's withdrawal from the Mediterranean capital of knowledge aptly illustrates early ascetics' committed rejection not only of the cultured world of Roman cities but specifically of its traditions of learning. Augustine was profoundly ashamed to learn that while Antony was illiterate, he knew his scripture by heart and truly embodied its precepts. The rejection of learning, especially of the sophistry of philosophers, stood at the heart of a monk's vocation as Antony exemplified it. But soon a communal alternative to the desert hermitage emerged, also in Egypt, and these first monastic groups inevitably came to rely on texts. Reciting scripture at weekly meetings gave lonely novitiates a needed sense of fellowship. Meditating on a well-chosen verse, a monk might learn to ward off the demons of boredom, despair, and temptation, as Antony did. Repeating a particular psalm over and over again steadied and calmed the mind. Focusing on words of love and power drawn from the Bible helped to drive out words of anger and dissipation uttered against fellow monks. Asking an elder to "speak me a word" was a means of apprenticing oneself to him. None of these practices involved what Roman Christians would call scholarship. Instead, desert ascetics, like cloistered monks later, built their lives around a different attitude toward words and texts: *lectio divina*, meditative reading, akin to prayer, devoted to God.[14]

The monastery was the first institution of knowledge specifically adapted to the absence of civilization, to the wilderness. And by the sixth century, all of Western Europe, whether non-Roman or post-Roman, was indeed such a wilderness. Though temperate and fertile instead of hot and barren, Europe had already proven receptive to the desert model. Pilgrims like John Cassian (ca. 360–433), who emigrated from the Holy Land to found two monasteries near Marseille, helped plant the seeds. But it was written texts—Cassian's *Institutes* and *Conferences*, and later the Benedictine Rule—that truly broadcast the ideals of monastic life and offered detailed regimens for its realization.

Western European monks molded their lives around written texts, just as previous desert hermits had done and indeed all Christians did. But lacking the luxury of steady traffic between desert and city—always a feature of the eastern Mediterranean—they had to bring an entire culture of learning with them. In establishing a new model for European monastic scriptoria, Cassiodorus (ca. 490–580s) drew the next logical conclusion: that monasteries must be deliberately designed to preserve ancient manuscripts.

Flavius Magnus Aurelius Cassiodorus was a Roman senator from a well-to-do, if arriviste, family who served the Ostrogothic kings who usurped Italy from the Roman emperors. His initial plan was to found a Christian school at Rome, but "raging wars and upheaval in the Italian kingdom" made this impossible. Eventually he returned to his family villa at Squillace, in Italy's toe, where he took up his books and writing, a common reaction for disillusioned aristocrats since Cicero's time. Soon, however, Cassiodorus transformed Squillace into a monastic community he called Vivarium, meaning "fish pond," after a notable feature of the well-appointed rural retreat. There he embarked on a bold new course, systematically collecting the great works of antiquity and training his monks to copy and correct them. Drawing on and modifying Cassian's writings, Cassiodorus also issued his own *Institutes*. Best described as an "extremely detailed annotated bibliography," the work also offers poignant testimony to the collapse of learning around him.[15] Cassiodorus warned his monks that books would have to serve "in place of a teacher." Broken links with Roman culture's oral tradition meant that "you have masters of a bygone generation to teach you not so much by their tongues as by your eyes." He told them to leave blank sheets in codices in anticipation of recovering works then lost, and to preserve Greek manuscripts even though in this Latin world there were hardly any Greek-speakers left. "Consider the nature of the cause entrusted to you," he enjoined them, "the serving of Christians, the guarding of the Church's treasure [its books], the lighting of souls."[16]

Among the first to perceive the monastery's potential for sustaining ancient knowledge, Cassiodorus also illustrates the limits of viewing the institution primarily as a vessel for its transmission. Neither the monastery at Vivarium nor its library left any trace after the lifetime of its founder; only Cassiodorus's *Institutes* survived, more as a textbook than anything else. Scholars today look back at the period from the sixth to the ninth centuries as a bottleneck through which only a trickle of classical texts passed. The vast majority of surviving manuscripts from before 800 contain either biblical and liturgical texts or the writings of Christian theologians, predominantly Augustine, Jerome, and Gregory the Great. True, a few pagan treasures were tucked away for the ages. A copy of Virgil's *Aeneid* spent eight centuries at Bobbio before Italian humanists rediscovered it in 1467. But most classical works were clearly judged irrelevant. Only 10 percent of manuscripts dating between 550 and 750 are *not* concerned with Christianity, and all but one, a fragment of Lucan, have some utilitarian purpose, chiefly legal, medical, or grammatical.[17] Many works now considered priceless were simply not worth the parchment they were written on. They survive today only because the writing surface was recycled—either erased and written over or turned into scraps for bookbinding. The sole extant copy of Cicero's *Republic*, for example, was discovered in the nineteenth century beneath a transcription of Augustine's commentary on the psalms. We have the work only because the monks at Bobbio failed to scrape off the parchment completely before reusing it.[18] In the early Middle Ages, Christian scripture, and the commentaries necessary to interpret it, always and everywhere trumped Cicero.

With social and political instability a constant threat to life and property in this period, books, the time to transcribe them, and the parchment on which to write were all rare luxuries. Difficult choices had to be made. Yet, paradoxically, some of the best monastic scriptoria could be found in the poorest areas most remote from the former Roman Empire. North of Hadrian's wall, in places that had never known Roman rule, the Latin language and classical culture were alien imports. Monasteries and Christianity were one and the same in a largely pagan society, and so religious devotion and Latin education overlapped. Irish monks in particular became known both for their learning and for their austerity, and they went to the continent to found and reform monasteries in Gaul and Italy. It was in frontier areas like Ireland and northern Britain that the Bible first became a cult object, a Holy Book brandished to convince and awe the illiterate unbelievers huddled outside monastery walls.

The Lindisfarne Gospels, among the world's most lavishly illus-trated and ornamented books, were the work of monks living around 700 CE on a windswept island off northern England. Even today, Lindisfarne is accessible only by a causeway flooded twice daily by the incoming tide.

From Vivarium at Italy's toe to Iona on the British coast, monasteries almost alone preserved written culture in the West from the end of Rome in the fifth century, through the intellec-tual trough of the seventh, until the rise of the university in the twelfth. But more was at work here than the passive transmis-sion of learning, more even than the active program of copy-ing and storing that Cassiodorus envisioned. The dedication of monks to specific texts—and their lack of concern for others—depended on how suitable these texts were to the crafting of lives in an ascetic community. Scholars since the Renaissance have often faulted monks for their selectivity in preserving the her-itage of the past. But this was merely the flip side of a program of monastic reading and writing that was always oriented toward the present and the future. To understand the deeper rea-sons that monks filled so many days and years in scriptoria, we have to turn to the larger devotional regimen of which books were a part, shifting the focus from which books were lost or survived to the kinds of new writing these desolate centuries pro-duced. This reveals how monks used texts not merely to orient individuals during their time on earth but to sustain the wider monastic community itself over generations.

TEXTS AND TIME IN THE BENEDICTINE RULE

The Rule attributed to Benedict of Nursia has literally provided a handbook for life for more than fourteen centuries of monks, who follow its instructions on a daily basis, refreshing their understanding of the text as needed. One could find in it a program for virtually every minute of a monk's life. On Sunday, for instance, "The brothers will arise earlier than usual . . . After the six psalms and the versicle have been sung . . . the brothers will sit down by order of seniority. When this is done, one brother should read four lessons and responsories from the book. After the completion of the fourth responsory the cantor should sing the *Gloria* and all will rise in reverence. After this, six psalms with antiphons and versicle will follow as before, and a further four lessons with responsories will be read. The abbot will choose three canticles from the prophets to be chanted with *Alleluias*." And so on. This is the way Sunday morning prayers were to be followed throughout the year, except when "the monks—Heaven forbid—arise late."[19] Time discipline, as we will see, was utterly central to the Rule.

The Benedictine Rule was condensed in the sixth century from the much longer, unwieldier Rule of the Master and drew as well from Cassian's *Institutes*.[20] By the ninth century, particularly under Charlemagne's sponsorship, it had become the dominant program of monastic life in Latin Christendom. By no means the only rule for monasteries, nor the oldest, nor the most innovative, it nevertheless achieved authoritative status on account of its simple practicality and realistic expectations of the average monk's capacity for ascetic discipline. Crafted for spiritual use, tested by time and repetition, and propagated by anonymous scribes, it bears a certain resemblance to the Christian scriptures themselves. Adhering to such a text enabled communities of monks to survive and thrive despite the personal quirks and transient lifespans of individual members. In Benedict's ideals and their development in practice we see how monastic time played upon cycles of days, weeks, and years, endlessly repeating, to ensure the survival and stability of the monastery and of learning itself.

Outside the Rule, Benedict of Nursia (ca. 480–547) is known only from the account of his life attributed to Pope Gregory the Great. Though an exact contemporary of Cassiodorus and nearly his neighbor, Benedict seems to have taken a less scholarly approach to the monastic vocation. At no time in his life is Benedict shown reading, studying, or explicating texts, even scripture. Instead, like Antony, Benedict renounced an urban education in the liberal arts to devote himself to God in the wilderness. Gregory puts him in the caves and hills of central Italy, struggling to reform fellow monks and performing assorted miracles: reviving a dead boy, for example, or shattering a poisoned glass of wine with the sign of the cross. But the Rule itself tells a quite different story from Gregory's biography, for it enshrined reading—personal reading, listening together to texts read aloud, communal singing of scripture—as part of the daily routine of monastic life. Shorn of all the details of time, place, and culture that made Benedict's life story so inspiring to monks, the Rule offered spare and distilled common sense, proving itself supremely well adapted to any community of monks who came upon it and took it up.[21] Women in particular could follow and adapt the Rule, making the monastery the principal haven for literate, educated women until the Republic of Letters, and much later the laboratory, conceded them a modicum of gender equality.

In the prologue to the Rule, Benedict describes the monastery as a "school for God's service," a training ground for the renunciation of personal will and utter devotion to God. Seventy-two "instruments of good works" enumerate the goals of life in the cloister, beginning with "To love the Lord God with all our heart, soul, and strength." Then come more concrete precepts, among them to love fasting, to visit the sick and comfort the sad, to resist returning an evil for an evil, to fear Judgment Day, to enjoy holy reading, to honor the elderly and love the young, and never to despair of God's mercy. A number of the Ten Commandments appear in the list, as do warnings against petty faults that might, unchecked, cascade into sin. Numbers 37 through 40 enjoin the monk, respectively, "not to love sleep," "not to be slothful," "not to murmur," and "not to slander." Private property too is singled out as a vice to be "cut out at the roots." Monks' personal effects should be limited to what the abbot would provide, "namely, cowl, tunic, stockings, shoes, girdle, knife, pen, needle, towel, and writing tablet." Humility is the architect and guiding principle for all the rest: the basis for obedience to the abbot, for silence in the cloister whenever possible, for the surrender of one's habits of mind and body to the will of God, and ultimately for salvation. Benedict enumerated twelve stages of humility, together likened to Jacob's ladder ascending to heaven. Emptying the mind of worry, freeing it from material cares, minimizing the risk of deviation from total devotion, and legislating equality in the collective striving for God—rung after rung, the Rule gave the ladder of humility a stable structure.

The genius of the Rule lay in the recognition that monks needed a specific regimen to make this spiritual goal an attainable reality. It was one thing to declare that the entirety of one's life, every moment, was to be devoted to God, another to know precisely what to do during all the minutes that followed sunrise, day after day. Thus Benedict spelled out exactly what to eat, when to eat, where to sleep, when to rise, what to wear, even down to variations for different climates and seasons. Bedtime came as early as 6:30 p.m. Monks should sleep in separate beds, if possible in one room, "in their robes, belted but with no knives, thus preventing injury in slumber." About eight hours later, in the middle of the night, monks arose. Then began a cycle of prayer, alternating with periods of reading, work, and meals, lasting throughout the monks' time awake. There was no breakfast, and during the darker months of the year only one meal a day. Taking the Lenten season as a benchmark, a typical twenty-four-hour period might unfold as follows:[22]

2:00 a.m.	Rise
2:00–3:30 a.m.	Vigils

3:30–4:30 a.m.	Meditation
4:30–5:00 a.m.	Matins
5:00–9:00 a.m.	Reading, with Prime at 6:00 a.m. (sunrise)
9:00 a.m.	Terce
9:15 a.m.–4:00 p.m.	Work, interrupted by Sext at 12:00 p.m.
4:00 p.m.	None
4:30 p.m.	Vespers
5:00 p.m.	Meal
6:00 p.m.	Compline
6:30 p.m.	Sleep

Every two or three hours, then, a bell would sound calling the community to prayer. Monks must "rise at the signal and hurry" but "make haste with gravity and modesty."[23] A familiar children's song amiably chides the brother (Frère Jacques) who slumbers through morning bells. Not without reason has the monk, whose schedule is always full, been called the West's first true professional.[24]

The Latin terms in this list are the canonical hours of the monastic liturgy, the focal points of the day: times for collective reading, prayer, and ritual. Known collectively as the Divine Office or simply the Hours, this perpetual cycle governed time in the cloister. At its heart lay the singing of the 150 psalms from the Old Testament. Psalmody had been a defining feature of monasticism, recognizable to outsiders, ever since the days of the desert hermits. The earliest monks in Egypt performed the psalms from memory as a meditation device; some, undertaking feats of ascetic athleticism, would pray the entire psalter in one evening.[25] Benedict prescribed a repetitive cycle that was still comprehensive yet less herculean in its demands. Psalms were spread across the week and assigned to specific daily prayers, making the weekly program not only more feasible but more conducive to meditative understanding of the psalter's words. Later monks were encouraged to ruminate on the psalms, *ruminatio* evoking the rustic image of a cow chewing its cud many times over.[26] Voicing the psalms aloud and in community would bring monks closer to God. The sound of their industrious mumbling was often likened to the buzzing of a bee.[27]

Reading was commended to monks even outside the liturgy. All common meals were to be accompanied by edifying reading. The time after supper and before bed was also to be filled with reading rather than talk. The extra dark hours after matins in winter were to be used "to practice psalms or for reading." The chapter in the Rule labeled "Daily Manual Labor" says less about the tasks a monk might be assigned than about the reading he should do whenever unoccupied with them. Reading filled the interstices of the day, especially in winter, when there was little work to be done in the fields. On Saturdays "all shall read," and anyone too lazy to do so "will be assigned work so as not to be idle." More than an antidote to idleness, however, reading was a component of spiritual discipline. During Lent, Benedict says, when "we conduct our lives with the greatest possible purity," we "devote ourselves to tearful prayer, reading, contrition, and abstinence." For this reason, as the Lenten season commenced, every monk was to receive a book from the monastery's library, for him to read "cover to cover." Monasteries in time became the first sites in the Western tradition where silent reading was the norm: even the greats of antiquity had mumbled to themselves when reading alone.[28]

In Benedict's model monastery, the written word entirely dominated the spoken word. The Rule consistently prefers silence to speech. For just as reading is a kind of labor, talk is a species of idleness. Monks eventually designed a system of sign language—118 hand signals were recorded at the eleventh-century monastery of Cluny—to request food and clothes and coordinate participation in the Divine Office.[29] Many inducements to sin, diversions from God's path, are inherent in speech: gossiping, complaining, joking, expressing anger, pride, or jealousy. Hence the great virtue of reading at communal gatherings, when chatting might otherwise fill the silence: one man read while the others listened, preventing their minds from straying by training their ears on the words, their tongues still. Reading aloud gave voice to the written word, to be sure, but this was not speech. It was edifying but inert; not a dialogue but a monologue, whether one person read or many sang in unison. At meals, "no one is to ask questions about the reading . . . unless the superior wishes to speak briefly for their moral improvement."[30]

Writing became even more dominant as Benedictine practice developed. By the tenth and eleventh centuries, when Europe's reviving economy drove the founding of new cloisters, hordes of new texts were being produced to regulate monks' lives in community—and nuns' as well. The Divine Office became ever more elaborate as monks strove for greater discipline and perfection. Lectionaries (excerpting scripture), hymnals, missals (for the mass), and collections of saints' lives, read on the saints' days strewn throughout the year, joined psalters among a growing library of liturgical books. The singing of the psalms evolved into what we now call Gregorian chant, with monks devising the West's first systems of written musical notation and the librarian, not the cantor, acting as master of ceremonies.[31] Rosters of monks and nuns, living and dead, were drawn up so that they could be named in liturgical prayer. These helped form the monastery's sense of its own history, as did archives of written charters recording past land grants from wealthy donors.[32] Finally, detailed "customaries" arose to codify local embellishments to the basic Rule laid down by Benedict, including those making special accommodations for women. Customaries might specify rituals to tend the sick and bury the dead, spell out precise movements for processions through Romanesque churches, provide instructions for the keeping of relics, offer statutes for the governance of the cloister, or—not least—describe the ways in which books should be consecrated for liturgical use. Customaries functioned not merely to record monastic practice but actually to *reform* it—to introduce tighter discipline where observance had become lax.

They show how assiduously medieval monks and nuns followed the written word.[33]

Benedict's Rule had been intended not as a guide to learning, like Cassiodorus's *Institutes*, but as a guide to life. Benedict mentions few works by name, preferring familiar categories such as "the lives of the saints" and "commentaries by famous and orthodox Catholic fathers." Just as he presumes the existence of a library without prescribing its contents, he speaks of pens and writing tablets but says nothing about copying manuscripts. No mention is made of schools to assure the literacy the Rule obviously requires. More detailed attention is given to the kitchen and service at table than to books. Benedict's was a spiritual, not an educational, program. Yet such was the power and clarity of Benedict's spiritual vision that an entire program of learning followed in its wake. Having founded a life in common upon the sacredness of their time together, monks and nuns then produced the texts to fill it up. In the practices of true scholarship that thereby became possible, monks made their most lasting contribution to the wider world's understanding of time in its broadest cosmic sense.

FROM THE LITURGICAL YEAR
TO THE MILLENNIAL WEEK

The monastery persisted for so many centuries, surviving in a world of so much travail, because timelessness was a cardinal aspect of the monastic ideal. In the Christian worldview, both time and the world were God's creations. *Saeculum* meant both "the world" (hence our "secular") and an "age" (hence the French *siècle*). And one day God would bring both to an end. The Christian monastery was an otherworldly place on earth with its own sense of time, grounded in the endless cycles of the Divine Office. The whole point, from Antony's withdrawal to the Egyptian desert to the spread of Benedict's Rule over Western Europe, was to abandon the vicissitudes of the world and to devote the entirety of one's life to God, timeless and eternal. For many, if not most, monks and nuns, this was virtually the only life they had ever known. Children as young as seven years old entered the cloister as oblates, "offerings" to God from their families, and became habituated to the Rule and trained in Latin practically as a mother tongue.[34]

But monks and nuns could never withdraw entirely from the world surrounding them, precisely because they depended so heavily on donations from it—of oblates, of land and resources, and of political and military protection. Monasteries were attached to the core tenets of Christianity, not to deviant or fringe beliefs, and had a critical role to play wherever society embraced Christianity and held its values as central. At certain times of the year, feasts such as Easter brought all of Christendom together in simultaneous remembrance of Jesus' passion (crucifixion) and resurrection. Easter above all became the occasion for the best monastic minds to raise up their vision from the days and months of the liturgical year to the contemplation of God's time over centuries and millennia.

The liturgical year, common to both monks and laypeople,

formed the heart of Christian unity. Feast days gathered believers not only to recollect the milestones in Christ's life and death but also ritually to relive them: to bring the past into the present. Two holiday cycles dominated the liturgical year, one focused on the anticipation and birth of the Savior, from Advent to Christmas, the other on preparation for his resurrection on Easter Sunday, the holiest day in the Christian calendar. Christmas had long been fixed to the winter solstice in the Roman Julian calendar, December 25, and it has remained there ever since. This made it relatively simple to calculate backward to the beginning of Advent. Easter, by contrast, was a movable feast, falling on a different day each year and yet the center of some sixteen weeks of liturgical celebrations, before and after, linked directly to it. Lenten fasting, for example, commemorated Jesus' forty days in the desert, Holy Week the sacred drama of his last days on earth, Pentecost the fiftieth day after his resurrection, when Christ's disciples were filled with the Holy Spirit.[35] All these dates had to be established well in advance to prepare the requisite festivals. In late antiquity the pope had simply announced each year when Easter would come. But as communications deteriorated with the collapse of Rome, it became critical for local congregations to celebrate with confidence even in isolation.[36] Rosters of Easter dates decades into the future had to be laboriously tabulated, and monks were the only learned men available to revise and update the calculations periodically.

The correct calculation of Easter ranks among the most vexing and complex mathematical problems in history. Evolving out of the Jewish Passover and then deliberately fixed so as never to coincide with it, Easter falls on the first Sunday after the full moon following the spring equinox. Its precise calendar date therefore depends on no fewer than four different cycles: that of the seven-day week, from Sunday to Sunday; that of the moon, lasting 29.53 days from one full moon to the next; that of the sun, lasting 365.2422 days from spring equinox to spring equinox; and that of the calendar year, lasting 365 or 366 days according to the system of leap years initiated by Julius Caesar.* Two of these—those pertaining to the sun and the moon—can be reconciled by calculating how many solar years it takes to accommodate a whole number of lunar cycles; Alexandrian computists, heirs to Hellenistic astronomy, established this number as 19.† The other two cycles—those for the week and the calendar year—repeat every 28 years.‡ Multiplying 19 by 28 yields

---

*Caesar fudged a critical problem in taking the length of the solar year as precisely 365.25 days—an extra quarter day to be made up every four years with a leap day—instead of 365.2422. Over centuries this caused the calendar date to creep backward relative to the solar date. This explains why the original winter solstice, coinciding with Christmas Day, later migrated to December 21 or 22. Today we solve this problem by ignoring leap years (those divisible by 4) when they are divisible by 100, unless they are also divisible by 400. Thus the years 1800 and 1900 each had no February 29, but the year 2000 did. This means that after about 8,000 years our own calendar will still have "lost" a day.
†Multiplying 19 by 365.2422 and dividing the result by 29.53 yields 235.001, close to a whole number.
‡The product of 4 (the frequency of the leap year) and 7 (indicating the quadrennial progress of the leap day through Sunday, Friday, Wednesday, Monday, Saturday, Thursday, and Tuesday), this number specifies how often the same matchings of calendar dates to days of the week can be reused.

an overall cycle of 532 years, the shortest span of time in which the entire sequence of Easter dates, as identified by Julian calendar month and day, begins to repeat itself.

It took centuries of blistering argument and tricky mathematics (not easy in the days of roman numerals) before computists even arrived at the 532-year figure, much less understood why it worked. As late as the sixteenth century, Christians were still refining their calculations by using cathedrals as giant astronomical observatories, poking holes in vaulted ceilings to trace beams of sunlight across marble floors.[37] Rather than settling on any mathematical compromise (or fudge), Christians have always exhibited what to outsiders may seem a fanatical insistence on getting the date exactly right. A system that accidentally permitted Easter to fall before the actual spring equinox, for example, might cause the Resurrection to be celebrated before daylight has in fact triumphed over winter night, sending entirely the wrong theological message to the faithful.

An elaborate bundle of techniques called computus therefore developed around Easter calculations. Computus formed the centerpiece of "scientific" education in the monasteries. Just as devotional reading (*lectio divina*) had absorbed and replaced the Roman humanistic trivium, so computus was cobbled together from the remnants of the mathematical quadrivium (arithmetic, geometry, astronomy, and music). The West's first true applied science, computus progressively organized educated monks' entire understanding of the natural, human, and divine worlds around the guiding principle of time. Much like popular almanacs in the modern period, computus manuscripts became "filing cabinets" for anything and everything relating to time and periodicity, whether drawn from music, navigation, climatology, agriculture, prosody (rhythmic speech), or even medicine (whose therapies were correlated with astronomy and the seasons).[38] Not surprisingly, saints' (and particularly martyrs') days filled up the calendar, but so too did marginal notations on local weather events, famines, eclipses, and, most notably, politics. From these year-by-year annals developed some of Europe's first narrative historical chronicles.

Above all, computus accustomed monks to thinking about epochal spans of time, ultimately stretching back to Creation itself. It thereby prepared them to confront the wider Christian population's greatest unsolved mystery with respect to time: when it would end, when their suffering would cease, when Christ would return.

Popular speculation about the precise date of the Second Coming has formed a powerful undercurrent in Christianity from its earliest days as an explicitly messianic movement. Church leaders feared this as a potential license to riotous indiscipline and moral laxity, yet nonetheless engaged in a complex dance with millennial expectations. Augustine, that architect of orthodox opinion, conceded that the world lived in an age of senility but vehemently insisted that no one could know the precise date of its death. Those who nonetheless sought such a date in scripture latched onto II Peter 3:8 ("With the Lord a day is like a thousand years, and a thousand years are like a day") to develop a theory of the "millennial week." Reasoning that if the Lord created the world in six days and rested on the seventh, and each day is for him a thousand years, then in the year 6000 will come a day of rest, a new millennium heralded by Christ's return.

Early Christian chronologists unintentionally offered more grist for the mill. Working through the famously detailed genealogies of the Old Testament, they had fixed the world's creation at 5,500 years before Christ. When they wrote, in the third century CE, this located its end comfortably outside anyone's lifetime. But with the collapse of the Latin West in the 400s, the *anno mundi*—AM, the year of the world—entered the perilous 5900s. At this point, the establishment quite literally procrastinated. Scholars ransacked their Bibles and rechecked their calculations to redate Creation to around 5,200 years before Christ, thus rejuvenating the world by some three centuries. Still, this merely planted another time bomb, inviting those 300 years in the future to speculate again that the end was just around the corner.[39]

It was a Northumbrian monk, Bede (ca. 672–735), who finally defused the bomb and in the process changed the way we think about time. Bede's *The Reckoning of Time* became the most influential computus textbook of the Middle Ages. Synthesizing liturgical, historical, and astronomical conceptions of time, it covered, besides Easter, everything from fractions and finger-reckoning (a means to perform basic arithmetic on one's hands) to tides and shadows to Antichrist and Judgment Day. Bede had no truck with "rustics" who badgered him to reveal when the millennium would come. Writing in the 5900s of the then current *anno mundi,* he pieced together the Bible's many "X begat Y" formulas to revise the date of Incarnation downward again, this time dramatically. When he announced to contemporaries that Jesus was born in 3952 AM and that they were nowhere near the seventh millennium, it was a bitter setback to the apocalyptically minded.[40]

In his other major work, Bede showcased a more properly Christian attitude toward historical time. The *Ecclesiastical History of the English People* depicts how history revealed God's special mission for his native England. It is also the first major Western work to introduce *anno Domini* dating, a practice that has effected a subtle revolution in our consciousness of time. Monastic life was a life of dogged patience and the wider Christian life was one of eager anticipation, but the two opposing attitudes toward time could finally be reconciled in this new system of chronology. Pegged to Jesus' incarnation, *anno Domini* folded remembrance of Christ into the enumeration of the years, tallied one by one into a redemptive future stretching indefinitely before us. A universal index of history's progress, it superseded a hodgepodge of alternatives—Greek olympiads, Roman emperors' regnal years, fifteen-year tax cycles, and the Hebrew lunar calendar. Bede's uniform time scale enabled him to adorn his narrative with numerical reminders of the Incarnation, in each instance underscoring the profound interconnectedness of all the diverse phenomena in God's otherwise inscrutable master plan. History does guarantee salvation, in short, but as individuals and even as nations we can play our part only by following Christ's example diligently in the here-and-now. Writing in the opening pages of the *Ecclesiastical History*, Bede explained how his own lifetime of work had in a sense begun with his oblation at seven years of age: "From then, I have spent all my life in this monastery, applying myself entirely to the study of the Scriptures; and amid the observance of the discipline of the Rule and the daily task of singing in the choir, it has always been my delight to learn or to teach or to write."[41] A clearer encapsulation of the humble monk's relation to texts and time could scarcely be imagined.

CODA: A.D. 1000 VS. THE *KALIYUGA*

Anno Domini of course did little to quell apocalpytic expectations in the wider Christian populace. As A.D. 1000 approached, many simply fastened upon Revelation 20:2–10 to argue that the devil, after a thousand years of captivity following Jesus' birth, would soon unleash the Antichrist upon them. In 982, the famed computist Abbo of Fleury—the monastery that housed Benedict's bones—issued a revised calendar to persuade people that the year was not 982 but 1003 and that the dreaded moment had already passed without incident.[42] He was unsuccessful. Even the recent turning of the second millennium revealed an abiding fascination with the possibility of apocalpyse; witness the *Left Behind* book series. The Y2K phenomenon too, while born of legitimate anxiety about our dependence on technology, was tinged with doomsday expectations. Popular anticipation of the world's end is a common (if usually heterodox) feature of all the Western religions—Christianity, Judaism, and Islam. It also figures prominently in Buddhism, particularly in China, where belief in the imminent appearance of the Buddha Maitreya has often fueled huge rebellions.

For a revealing contrast with the millennarianism of the Latin West, we must therefore look to India, where by 1000 CE Buddhism was dying out in the land of its birth and Islamic conquest was in its very early stages. In the Sanskritic tradition, the cycles of time were so astronomically huge and seemingly precise that there could be no expectation of epochal breakthrough, only ceaseless repetition. The *kaliyuga*, our current era of decay and degeneration, will indeed culminate in a rolling series of global catastrophes. But it is slated to last fully 432,000 years from its inception in our 3101 BCE. Then the world will be reborn in another cycle, comprising but one day in the life of Brahma the Creator, ten *kaliyugas* or 4.32 million years in length. And this is nothing compared to the duration of the universe itself, over 311 trillion years by some calculations. The Muslim traveler Al-Biruni, who visited India in the early years of the second millennium, explained how such huge numbers helped Indian astronomers accommodate the cycles of stars and planets (in somewhat the same way that 532-year cycles did for Easter). But he found the Indians completely lacking in what he, as a westerner, considered historical sensibility: they were careless about the chronology and sequencing of past events.[43] Personal, historical, and cosmic time unfolded on radically different scales in India, with no divine providence or dynamic of salvation to bring them into synchrony. Endless reincarnation and ultimate release (*moksa*) simply dissolved the individual in a universal process of unfathomable duration.

Sanskrit learning as a result emphasized timelessness, not time, and textlessness, not texts. India, uniquely among world knowledge systems, held oral transmission and recollection a more authoritative guarantor of permanence than transitory writing on palm leaves or tree bark. Sanskrit was literally the eternal speech of divinity, not, like Latin, a practical conduit for God's word. Gurus made their disciples memorize, not copy, the Vedic scriptures and verbalize them precisely, so the magical power of their mantras could not be diluted or misdirected. Sanskrit grammarians devised nearly four thousand rules to buffer the spoken language against change and degradation. As a consequence, what manuscripts we do have are extremely hard to date based on literary style or vocabulary.[44] Authors of learned treatises deliberately stripped concrete historical details from their texts to imitate the eternal quality of the Vedas and associate their works with the cyclical, repetitive, time-transcending ritual of Brahmin liturgical utterances.[45]

Small wonder, then, that the great Indian monastery at Nalanda, where the voices of ten thousand students once filled the courtyards with debate and discussion, today stands mute in stone ruins, and that our best written account of it stems not from an Indian but from a Chinese visitor. The giant temple/dormitory/lecture hall complex at Nalanda flourished from the fifth century until it was sacked in the twelfth century by Muslim Turks. A product of Buddhism, the world's other great monastic religion, Nalanda hosted Buddhists and non-Buddhists alike, who studied both scripture and secular topics, with water clocks and gongs marking the hours of regular monastic life. Theirs was a profoundly oral culture, not a written one. "The day is not sufficient for asking and answering profound questions," in the words of the seventh-century pilgrim Xuanzang, from China; "From morning till night they engage in discussion."[46] None of the European monasteries ever approached Nalanda in size, scope, or dedication to knowledge. Christian ascetics had long since traded talk for silence, forsaking vocal interaction for patient devotion to texts. They might outlive Nalanda, though they would not necessarily outshine it. We have to look beyond the monastery to understand where and how the spirit of scholarly dispute revived in Europe, to an entirely new institution of learning that took root there: the university.

3

The University

1100–1500

EUROPE'S MEDIEVAL REVIVAL GENERATED GREATER
MOBILITY, NEW TOWNS, MORE CONTACTS BEYOND
CHRISTENDOM—A RECONFIGURATION OF SPACE
DEMANDING A REORDERING OF KNOWLEDGE.

THIS CHAPTER, on the university, must begin by dispelling some anachronistic misconceptions. It traces the origins of the contemporary world's dominant intellectual institution, and it is tempting to view the past as simply containing the seeds of the present. To avoid making the university sound either inevitable or unchanging, let us start by noting three things that made the medieval universities profoundly different from our own.

First, the earliest universities, in the twelfth and thirteenth centuries—at Bologna and Paris—were not deliberately founded; they simply coalesced spontaneously around networks of students and teachers, as nodes at the thickest points in these networks. Later European universities, like American universities, were of course deliberately established, but only after the model had emerged (twice) on its own.

Second, virtually all European universities are urban phenomena. This follows from the first proposition, for when teachers and students began to assemble, they needed to do so in places with infrastructure and amenities: lodging and stationers, taverns and, yes, brothels. Most universities in Europe are still identified by the cities where they coalesced (Oxford and Cambridge most notably) despite almost never having been founded by town leaders. By contrast, American universities are as likely to be named for people (like John Harvard and Eli Yale) or larger territorial units (like Michigan and California) and located in idyllic rural settings (like Ithaca, New York, and Grinnell, Iowa).

Third, and perhaps most surprisingly, universities originally had no campuses, no buildings, no bricks and mortar. The term *universitas* referred to a group of people, not to a physical place. Nor did it betoken "universality" in the sense of all-encompassing knowledge, as we might think today. Instead, *universitas* was a concept in ancient Roman law referring to a sworn society of individuals. By the thirteenth century, it could refer to any association of merchants or craftsmen—a guild, in short—brought together for mutual support and collective bargaining against those who did not belong to the guild. Soon enough, the *universitas* of scholars was being compared to guilds for everyday occupations like clothier and tanner. Like them, it had masters (professors), journeymen (or "bachelors," as we still call them), and apprentices (students).*[1] And like them, it aimed in the first instance to provide vocational training, originally for preachers,

---

*Medieval people at first used a different term, *studium generale*, to refer to what they later called universities. *Generale* referred not to the multiplicity of subjects taught but to the superregional breadth of geographical recruitment, to contrast with a *studium particulare*, which drew its students exclusively from a particular locale.

lawyers, and doctors, and in our own time for businessmen, journalists, and engineers. Disinterested scholarship, academic freedom, liberal education, impractical idealism—all the staples of today's graduation speeches—came only as unintended by-products of the clustering of scholars, expressions of the proud guild spirit of the *universitas*.

If the monastery was a viable institution for organizing knowledge in a world dominated by Christianity, how did this guild of students and teachers come to displace it? Why did the monastery not continue as the predominant home of scholars and their books until Christianity as a unifying ideology was challenged by the Reformation? The answer to the latter question is of course that the monastery, as a place of withdrawal from the world, did and does persist, up to the present day. In the twelfth century in particular it experienced a period of genuine efflorescence. If the university did not emerge as an answer to monastic stagnation, why did this new institution of knowledge emerge while the old one was still thriving?

Put simply, Europe finally recovered from the blows dealt to it in the waning days of Rome. Throughout the eleventh century and culminating in the twelfth, Europe's economy rebounded dramatically. Agricultural productivity improved, the population boomed, commerce and trade flourished, cities and towns took shape, church and state bureaucracies spread their tentacles throughout society, and people began to interact more through money and contracts and less through oaths and traditions. Above all, people took to the road. Pilgrims, merchants, soldiers, troubadours, preachers, and crusaders dispersed across Christendom and beyond. Many young men took advantage of the new prosperity by traveling in pursuit of knowledge. "Academic peregrinations" took Germans to Paris to learn theology, Poles to Bologna to study law, Englishmen to Toledo to translate Arabic scientific texts. Townsmen provided them with bed and board, pens and parchment. Teachers soon won the right to take their credentials with them, to lecture at any school in Christendom.

Prosperity eventually did wane, amid famine, rebellion, war, and heresy, before the Black Death of 1348 paradoxically revived it, clearing the slate for economic opportunity as the survivors rebuilt. By then, the university as we know it had taken shape. The reconfiguration of space in that first period of mobility accounts for the reordering of knowledge accomplished by the university. Pouring into the towns, fanning out over the continent, and reestablishing contacts with the Mediterranean world beyond Latin Christendom, scholars came together in the same centuries and for the same reasons that Europe itself began to coalesce.

ABELARD'S LOVES

No one better exemplifies the newfound ferment and mobility in medieval Europe than Peter Abelard (1079–1142), the combative roving scholar immortalized by his tragic love affair with Heloise. Abelard hailed from Brittany, on France's Celtic fringe near the Atlantic coast. He gained early notoriety in a series of urban cathedral schools clustered between the Loire and Moselle rivers. Dissatisfied with the plodding, meditative instruction offered by even the most respected scholars, Abelard cast himself as a knight errant, armed with logic, ever ready to joust with his masters. On one occasion he boldly offered to interpret the Book of Ezekiel after a single night's preparation, rejecting the panicked entreaties of wide-eyed fellow students that he allow himself more time for such a difficult text. This episode is one of many recounted in Abelard's *History of My Calamities*, a classic morality tale of scholarly machismo. Again and again, having incited the jealousy of lesser minds (as he sees it), Abelard is forced to decamp to another locale, even as the sheer vigor of his intellect pulls admirers in tow: "I was so carried away by my love of learning that I renounced the glory of a military life, and withdrew from the court of Mars in order to be educated in the lap of Minerva. I preferred the weapons of dialectic to all the other teachings of philosophy, and armed with these I chose the conflicts of disputation instead of the trophies of war."[2] Virtually all who congregated around him were men, free to pack up at will, braving highwaymen and hardship. (Unlike monasteries which catered to both sexes and occasionally even mixed them at the same site, the cathedral schools where they met excluded women.) Together they set about questioning, sparring, reasoning, disputing. In the frissons of these verbal "dialectics," Abelard and his students pioneered a new, very masculine style of learning later institutionalized in the universities.

Abelard's best student, though, was a woman. Well born

and extraordinarily intelligent, a teenager over two decades his junior, Heloise (1101–1162) became the object of what Abelard described as a calculated seduction. They conceived a son, whom she named Astralabe, after the Greco-Arabic stargazing instrument. At Abelard's insistence they married in secret, though Heloise resisted, holding that "pupils and nursemaids, desks and cradles" have no place together. Her uncle effectively settled the issue by ambushing Abelard in the night and castrating him. Abelard packed off Heloise to a cloister, transforming her overnight from student into nun, though she later became a distinguished abbess known for her learning. Abelard himself faced a second castration of sorts when uncomprehending detractors condemned his book on the Trinity and forced him to burn it. He took refuge in a series of monasteries but was again thronged with visitors and eventually returned to teaching, writing, and philosophizing.

"From the treasures of your philosophy," Heloise once wrote to Abelard, "I often come with parched throat longing to be refreshed by the nectar of your delightful mouth." Her fate symbolizes women's wider exclusion from learning in the shift from monastery to university. Before his castration, in their secret love letters, she implored him to view *amor* (romantic passion, lust) as a path to selfless devotion (*dilectio*) and divine love (*caritas*). After his castration, he saw things in starkly different terms: "I took my fill of my wretched pleasures in you, and this was the sum total of my love."[3] Treating her now only as his sister in Christ, he mentored her from afar; she asked him to help her

84

adapt the Benedictine Rule for cloistered women. Abelard had turned his mind from the passionate dissection of feeling to the sexless logic of faith. For the next two decades he wrestled with the logical puzzle of how God could be one yet three—Father, Son, and Holy Ghost—and likened the last of these to Plato's World Spirit. In *Sic et Non* ("Yes and No") he combed the works of the church fathers for excerpts shedding light on more than one hundred difficult questions, from whether God is a substance to whether a man can dismiss a fornicating wife and remarry. The more contradictory and divergent these "authorities," the richer the intellectual feast. Abelard even coined a new word, "theology," to describe how rational argument could be used to sort through the knottier points of faith. A new dialectical, dialogic form of knowledge had arisen alongside monastic copying and devotional reading, and it was now exclusively the province of men.

Abelard's probing intellect, which made questioning and disagreement the royal road to God's truth, only incited more conflict and humiliation. Among his many enemies, Bernard of Clairvaux (1090–1153), Christendom's star monastic intellect and reformer, became Abelard's most emphatic opponent and the architect of his undoing. Bernard led the Cistercians, a new order aiming to restore monasticism to the devotional, the spiritual, and the ascetic. Cistercians abhorred the temptations of flesh and spirit that they found in the cities—and in the increasing wealth and worldliness of existing rural monasteries—and so set off for the wilderness. They prized manual over intellectual labor, clearing and developing so much new land on the under-populated medieval frontier that they became rich despite them-selves. (Today the vineyards first cultivated by Cistercians in Burgundy rank among the most lucrative real estate in the world.) Bernard brought the incipient rift between rural cloister and urban school to a head. "Flee this Babylon and save your souls," he exhorted. "Fly to the monasteries of the wilderness where solitary rocks and forests teach more piety than mortal masters." Abelard he charged with "sweating to make Plato a Christian"; theology he mocked as "stupidology."[4]

Bernard was not a bigoted man, nor uneducated. He simply held knowledge acquired by mystical devotion and contempla-tion preferable to the argumentative, hair-splitting logic that had made Abelard famous. Bernard's sermons on the Song of Songs, the most erotic book of the Bible, are a masterpiece of Christian mysticism. A difficult passage—"Let him kiss me with the kiss of his mouth"—became the basis for a spiritual vision of Christ as bridegroom, the human soul his bride, and salvation a passion-ate marriage with divinity. If Heloise saw erotic love as spiritual, Bernard saw spiritual love as erotic (and Abelard simply put them in different analytical categories). Mystics for centuries thereafter—particularly learned women, denied an outlet in the schools and universities—wrote in much the same terms. The Benedictine abbess Hildegard of Bingen (1098–1179), for example, is still beloved by New Agers for her ethereal musical compositions, holistic medical therapies, and hallucinatory visions of a divine "living light."[5] Because God talked to her only in the most theologically orthodox terms, Bernard reluctantly condoned her prophetic writings. But he could not leave the seductions of Abelard's logical philosophy unchecked. When Abelard wrote another book on *Theologia*, Bernard contrived to silence him once and for all, arranging to have him—not just the book—condemned for heresy. Abelard took refuge with the powerful Benedictines of Cluny, who, when he died soon afterward, sent his corpse for burial to Heloise.

A TALE OF FOUR CITIES

Bernard won the battle but could not win the war. The virtues of the wilderness were ultimately outweighed by the charms of the cities, which soon became magnets for hordes of aspiring scholars. The biggest network of these lay precisely in Abelard's old stomping grounds, in the cathedral schools at Chartres, Laon, Rheims, and Paris—including at Notre Dame, the architectural emblem of Europe's Gothic revival. By 1200, long before it became the capital of a powerful nation-state, Paris was renowned as the international center for theology.

Other scholarly pilgrimage sites developed their own academic schools and specialties, or "faculties," which soon came to be standard features in almost every university: Bologna for law, Salerno (among others) for medicine, and (much later, in imitation of Paris) Prague in the liberal arts. Each center of learning crystallized from a separate regional economy of scholarly mobility. Each exemplifies a feature of university life soon common to all the rest, whether the housing of students in colleges, the development of legal protections for scholars, the *viva voce* (oral) style of learning, or the need for liberal arts training as a prerequisite to vocational study. What united their disparate efforts was a new form of pedagogy, later dubbed "scholasticism," after the schools themselves. In a nutshell, scholastics posed questions of the canonical texts in their respective fields and painstakingly enumerated their points of agreement and disagreement—the same procedure Abelard followed. Then, extending the method of *Sic et Non*, they reasoned out resolutions to those questions. The dialectical method was both a tool for teaching and a means of advancing knowledge. Herein lay the universities' claim to provide rationally trained preachers, lawyers, and doctors for a growing society.

Theology at Paris

In 1200 the scholars who had been swarming in and around the Île de la Cité in the heart of Paris made their collective economic power felt in the most dramatic way. In an isolated incident that grew into a citywide fracas, a German student bilked out of some wine by a tavernkeeper returned with friends to beat him up. The tavernkeeper summoned the royal bailiff, whose attempt to enforce justice resulted in a violent melee at the German students' hostel. The Paris masters, siding with their students (who numbered in the thousands), threatened to pull up stakes and leave town. The king himself then interceded and, shockingly, imprisoned the *bailiff* for life, offering his henchmen the choice between trial by ordeal (and possible hanging) and permanent exile. Apparently no one thought of punishing the unruly German students. Students were already immune from civil justice as clerics. Tonsured and robed, sometimes bearing arms, they roamed about town like Jedi knights. And in 1200 they won a royal charter guaranteeing the right to be tried by their own masters. Though after 1215 secular authorities gained jurisdiction over such crimes as murder and rape, the Parisian *universitas* otherwise formed a law unto itself.[6] When another riot erupted in 1229 (again over wine, this time during Carnival), even the king's indulgence was overtaxed, and a "great dispersion" led emigrating scholars to found entirely new universities at Angers, Orléans, Toulouse, and elsewhere. Some, crossing the Channel, augmented those already forming at Oxford and Cambridge, where their theological acumen put these towns on the intellectual map of Europe permanently.

In the meantime, colleges had been established to provide more structure, discipline, and support for students away from home, many of whom were as young as fourteen when they began formal study. A college, unlike a university, was a physical building where students and their masters resided together. Many colleges originated as charitable foundations set up to provide room and board for needy but promising young men. The Sorbonne, now almost synonymous with the University of Paris, originated as just one of its colleges, endowed by Philip of Sorbon in 1257. Colleges contributed considerably to better town-gown relations, since students were housed in them under their masters' watchful eyes. Drunkenness and violence were channeled into more socially acceptable entertainments, culminating much later in the sherry hours and intramural athletics of the Oxbridge colleges, with their Gothic spires and quadrangular lawns.

The earliest and most important Parisian colleges were those of the newly established mendicant orders, the Dominicans and the Franciscans. Like the Cistercians before them, the mendicants represented another religious response to the challenges of mobility in twelfth-century Europe. Dominic Guzmán, of Castile, established his order to combat heresy in urbanized Italy and southern France, specifically among the Cathars, who practiced a radically antimaterialistic Christianity possibly transmitted from Bulgaria. The aim was to lure back parishioners cast spiritually adrift by an increasingly wealthy, distant, haughty church hierarchy. Acting on much the same impulse, Francis of Assisi preached to the swelling ranks of the urban poor in Italy. Both types of friars (as they were called) lived according to a rule and took vows of obedience, chastity, and especially poverty and as such resembled monks. But they refused to be tied down by cloisters and property ownership, moving about, begging for a living (hence "mendicants"), and preaching, especially in the burgeoning towns. Within four years of their establishment in 1216, the Dominicans had opened a theology college at Paris, and they soon did the same at Bologna. The Franciscans overcame their founder's hostility to scholarship and arrived in force in 1218. And while relations among friars, traditional masters, and town and royal authorities were not always smooth, the mendicant orders healed the rift that had developed between scholastics and monastics, logic-choppers and spiritual seekers, at the time of Abelard's conflict with Bernard.

This rapprochement also laid the basis for the systematic elaboration and practical application of theology initiated by Abelard. Friars had a crying need for thematic sermons: topical lectures to minister to restless urban parishioners, often in the open air, and to enable roving preachers to touch the hearts and souls of the laity. Sermon material was collected in compendia of biblical "distinctions," variant usages of a given term culled from biblical texts. References to dogs returning to their own vomit (2 Peter 2:22) or overeating (Isaiah 56:11), for example, provided concrete images to illustrate a deeper symbolic point about the sin of gluttony.[7] By the early 1200s, the Bible itself had been transformed from a series of discrete books into a giant, portable bound volume, the books themselves conveniently divided into chapter and verse. "Concordances" indexing diffi-cult passages and directing users to their contexts replaced cum-bersome marginal and interlinear glosses, favored by monks, as the primary means whereby scholars interpreted texts. Though created to serve practical purposes, these and other finding aids also represented a subtle intellectual breakthrough. Alphabetical order not only facilitated quick and easy referencing but, more deeply, allowed each reader of a text to use his own reason to piece together a moral lesson from scripture, one that was both compelling and doctrinally sound.[8]

Freelancers like Abelard courted disaster in taking this liberty. But in the rigorous theology curriculum that evolved at Paris, the unabashed pursuit of rational inquiry was institutionally yoked—and subordinated—to the task of instructing society on what it means to be a Christian. Handy preaching aids simply stood at one end of a continuum whose opposite extreme was full-blown scholastic theology. There was nothing showy or sensational about the corpulent Parisian Dominican Thomas Aquinas (1225–1274), who took on questions like "Can God do what he does not, or not do what he does?" Meticulously weighing the objections and counterobjections to each proposition and arming himself with the philosophy of Aristotle (newly rediscovered through Muslim mediation), Aquinas produced the greatest summary of Christian theology yet devised, the *Summa Theologica*. In Aquinas's thought, pure (Abelardian, Aristotelian) and applied (Dominican, Franciscan) conceptions of knowledge meshed with and mutually reinforced each other. After all, both were in different ways the products of mobility and urbanization, two responses to a new hunger for knowledge in a rapidly changing society.

Soon enough the Dominicans had to admonish university graduates not to make their own sermons for lay audiences sound like academic disputations.[9] University education had begun to foster an ivory-tower mentality. Physical concentration, royal protection, and safety in numbers enabled scholars to work solely for the sake of knowledge. Yet what made this academic freedom possible was the very stringency of Christian doctrine. Orthodoxy, which we now take as a sign of intellectual strangulation, functioned in the Middle Ages as an agent of intellectual coherence and standardization. The pope himself guaranteed the right to teach anywhere in Christendom (*ius ubique docendi*). Local bishops had been extorting bribes from qualified masters (itself a sign of an increasingly monetized economy), and cliquish faculties were closing ranks against competition from outsiders.[10] The pope therefore determined to pry open the system by cracking down on such abuses. Papal sanction enabled scholars to wander physically at the same time it set an outer limit on their tendency to stray doctrinally. When scholars could take their knowledge anywhere, universities all over Christendom came to share the same curricula, the same textbooks, the same methodologies. Even before the advent of formal degrees on sheepskin parchments, this practice made university learning, with theology as its capstone, Europe's first individually portable, internationally recognized form of knowledge.

Law at Bologna

By some accounts, Paris was actually the second university to form. The other claimant to priority is Bologna, in northern Italy, less well known today but originally more popular, with 10,000 students at its thirteenth-century peak to Paris's 7,000—both huge numbers for the time.[11] While Paris was known for both theology and liberal arts, Bologna was the preeminent school of law, both civil and canon (the law of the church). Men went there mainly for practical, utilitarian reasons. Law, especially in the Italian city-states, paved the way to a rewarding career in the courts, diplomacy, civilian office, or the service of a bishop—even the papacy itself. Arriving in Bologna as foreigners, scholars lacked roots, relatives, and rights—the appurtenances of local citizenship. If an English student skipped out on an unpaid debt, for example, city-dwellers might confront his innocent countrymen and demand its repayment, a practice known as reprisal. Without basic legal protection, scholars had to band together in defense of common interests, such as rent control and tax exemptions. In so doing, they simply took part in the great legal and social mania of the age: spontaneous self-organization in corporations.

Bologna, like other northern Italian cities, enjoyed a robust commercial economy but suffered from the power vacuum prevailing in the peninsula. The Holy Roman Emperor Frederick Barbarossa, who resided north of the Alps, in Germany, with most of his territories and retinue, lay claim to large swaths of the region, particularly the wealthy cities of Lombardy. But he had little means actually to govern. In a gambit to gain the loyalty of "all those scholars who wander for the cause of study," Barbarossa extended his protection to "those made exiles for the love of knowledge." An 1158 decree, by some estimations the Magna Carta of the European university, granted them safe travel on the road (not that the emperor had constables to enforce this), freedom from reprisals when in town, and the right to be tried not by civil authorities but by their own masters. Four of Bologna's most famous jurists assisted in drafting it. But lacking an archive in which to deposit the decree—this was before government bureaucracy existed—they simply inserted it at the relevant place in the Justinian Code. This ancient Roman lawbook, long since lapsed, was treated as a living ghost in Italy by scholars (for whom it provided codified answers to many legal problems) and the shrewd German emperor (whose *imperium* it seemed to legitimate).[12] In the absence of legal infrastructure, they necessarily trusted in the authority of a legal idea, kept alive in a written textbook and in the minds of the scholars who studied and transmitted it.

The revival of Roman law marked one of the great intellectual movements of the twelfth century, and in its Italian homeland it overlapped especially potently with the German law brought centuries before by Lombard invaders. Whereas Roman law was rational yet individualistic, Germanic custom, however fuzzily, put great stock in community spirit. In their synthesis lies the origin of the *universitas* as legal concept and social reality. Among its first beneficiaries were the true political powers in the region, the cities. Reacting to the chaos and tumult attending the absence of larger jurisdictions, urban clans of noble families organized to erect towers, stake out neighborhood turf, and protect themselves by force of arms.[13] Self-governing "communes" were the result. The feuds of the Capulets and the Montagues in *Romeo and Juliet* depict this world fictionally but fail to convey how, amid the violence, vendettas, and partisanship, the culture of active citizenship first took root in these urban institutions. Soon middle-class merchants and property owners dubbed the *popolo* (the people) challenged nobles for civic leadership by creating their own organizations, at times dominating the government of the communes. It was not long before the impulse reached down to craftsmen, giving rise to specialized trade guilds.

Corporations in all these forms were another product of the mobility and fluidity of medieval society. Medieval people created them "like children blowing bubbles," treating not only town communes and craft guilds but also cathedral chapters, kingdoms, and even the empire itself as *universitates*.[14] As paradoxical as it sounds to modern ears, they expressed their individuality by folding themselves into groups, for only in this way could an expanding roster of new social roles, from friars, to scholars, to citizens, to merchants, protect and assert themselves. The scholars' *universitas* was clearly but one expression of this much larger phenomenon.

Bologna actually had two rival *universitates*, one for masters and one for students, but economics and politics decidedly gave students the upper hand. Teachers lived on student fees virtually everywhere at this time. But at Paris, many theologians enjoyed ecclesiastical sinecures, called benefices, which granted them economic independence. Their students, moreover, tended to be both poorer and younger and thus better inclined to heed their masters' wishes. In Bologna the situation was reversed. There the student guild had the collective spending power, maturity, and bargaining muscle to hire and fire teachers and even strike for better conditions. Masters were fined for starting class even a minute late and had to issue prorated refunds for any lectures left uncompleted at the end of the term. They also had to post bail in order to leave town on vacation. One statute even prescribed the death penalty for anyone conspiring to transfer the university to another city.[15] Perhaps most decisive was the students' natural alliance with the *popolo*: both groups lived in the urban marketplace, buying and selling goods and services; their lives were governed more by monetary transactions than by feudal, ecclesiastical, or generational hierarchies.[16] By the late thirteenth century, Bologna's masters had become salaried employees of the commune itself.

If students' power reduced their masters to a subordinate position locally, Bologna's law faculty nonetheless enjoyed unimpeded renown on a regional and international level. This was particularly true in canon law. What scholars call a commercial revolution in the northern Italian cities—not so much in Bologna as in Genoa, Pisa, Florence, and Venice—created high demand for a new class of scholastic services to address the needs of a growing economy. One pressing issue was usury. Long-standing church doctrine condemned any financial transaction in which a lender charged interest on a loan. Substantial penalties ranging from fines to excommunication and legal infamy attended those who did. Dante relegated usurers to the seventh circle of hell. Jews became prominent—but also resented and persecuted—as moneylenders in medieval Europe because they recognized no such restrictions. Faced with this situation, canon lawyers reacted with typically scholastic casuistry. Excavating the relevant Roman case law, they found a principle holding that a lender might very well charge a *penalty* for money not returned. The difference between the original amount and the principal plus penalty was called "what is in the middle," *quod inter est*. The canonist Azo of Bologna (ca. 1150–1230) was the first to shorten this and make it a noun, "interest," now reconceptualized as compensation for real *or* imaginary delinquency in repayment.[17] Many similar aspects of the modern world's financial and corporate structure were first formulated in this way.

Interest is just one example of the complexities people everywhere confronted in twelfth-century Europe and of their practical creativity in devising solutions. The title of the greatest Bolognese compendium of canon law, Gratian's *Condordance of Discordant Canons* (ca. 1120–1150), gives some idea of the problems lawyers faced and the method they used to solve them; like Abelard and Aquinas, they inherited droves of contradictory texts needing rational order and resolution. In a clearer way than is perhaps apparent with theology, though, scholastic law aimed not only to resolve old contradictions but to develop new legal concepts for an ever-changing society. The corporation (*universitas*) itself is founded on the notion, bizarre to nonwesterners, that a group can form itself as a "fictional person," buy and sell property, govern its own members, and even be sued in court. Yet it ranks among the greatest medieval contributions to modern economic, social, and political life. Law, in drawing on past precedent to regulate new ways for groups to interact, shows how reason could serve not merely to reconcile authorities but to become an authority in its own right. Small wonder that the university's own authority arose when scholars trained their legal minds on their own predicaments. Its autonomy as an independent corporation is another building block of academic freedom.

Medicine at Salerno and beyond

Why does light shining redly through urine indicate, by infallible trial, a disease of the spleen? Why does the gaping wound accuse and show who was the criminal when blood oozes from it in the presence of a murderer? Why do beans, whose nature is cold, increase the venereal powers and the *agnus castus* (chasteberry) decrease them? Why does cheese quickly putrefy if its maker gratifies a secret passion?[18]

Scholastic medical doctors never produced an Aquinas or a Gratian, a logically ordered *summa*, or a systematic distillation of the myriad human sufferings, natural oddities, and occult phenomena forming their ambit of study. For this they had to consult Ibn Sina's *Canon*, the Bible of medieval medicine, written by a Muslim. Medieval diagnostics and therapies strike us today as quaint at best, folly at worst. But scholastic medicine did produce scores of questions, rhymed in hexameter for students to memorize, transposed into didactic adages for handy bedside application, and debated and discussed in learned forums for half a millennium. Those above derive from twelfth-century Salerno, Europe's first scholastic medical center and a

key portal for the thriving multicultural science of the Arab
world.

Documents from as early as the 900s attest to the renown
of this southwestern Italian town as a health spa on the Mediterranean coast. Azure skies, ocean breezes, and palm trees
undoubtedly attracted the infirm and dispirited and stimulated a
community of healers to care for them. Scholarly physicians
rubbed shoulders with lay practitioners peddling folk and herbal
remedies, and also with learned women. Trotula, the famous
"Lady of Salerno," may actually have been a composite of several female (and male) medical specialists, but their precious
gynecological wisdom, such as a treatment for uterine flatu-
lence, was later imparted to male readers from Glasgow to
Wrocław through the Salernitan *Trotula* texts.[19] No umbrella
school or corporate organization existed to credential or protect
Salerno's multifarious healers, at least in the early centuries.
Instead they all competed with each other. The vitality of this
medical community was another testament to the urban openness and dynamism that preceded universities' formal institutional coalescence.

Muslims, Jews, and Christians (Orthodox and Roman
Catholic) all crossed paths here on land and especially at sea.
"Salerno's physicians dream of a time when practitioners of all
kinds of medicine, from all peoples, might work together,"
wrote Benjamin of Tudela, a twelfth-century Jewish traveler.[20]
(Benjamin also noted that many Christians ignored Bernard of
Clairvaux's injunction to accept disease as punishment from

God.) Contacts beyond Christendom and outside Christian learning gave Salernitan masters access to the Greek texts of Hippocrates, Aristotle, and Galen, themselves given new life by Islamic continuators. The first great translator of these texts, Constantine the African (died ca. 1087), worked just a stone's throw away from Salerno, having emigrated from Qairawan, in Arab Tunisia, to the venerable monastery at Montecassino. But there were other points of entry as well. Muslim-dominated Sicily and southern Spain were such beehives of medical and scientific knowledge that Latin Christians moved to them from as far away as England. Together these locales define an arc of coastal cities reaching up the Italian coast from Salerno, around to Montpellier (now in France, then aligned with the Spanish Crown of Aragon) via Barcelona, and down to Valencia. When Salerno faded from glory, Montpellier replaced it, becoming the site of Europe's first organized university medical faculty. In all these towns, medical practitioners benefited from proximity to the superior scientific tradition of the Islamic Mediterranean.

It is easy to mock Greco-Arabic medicine for its pseudo-scientific rigor: its four humors (blood, phlegm, black bile, and yellow bile), the four temperaments their circulation creates in each person (hot, wet, cold, dry), and the like. But to medieval scholastics, such theoretical schemas raised medicine up from an *ars,* a skill, a bundle of empirical therapies and rules of thumb, into a true *scientia,* a form of abstract knowledge recorded in written treatises. The surgeon Henri de Mondeville (1260–

1320), who taught at both Montpellier and Paris, argued that scientific medicine placed its practitioners a cut above the "illiterate barbers, fortunetellers, alchemists, old women, converted Jews, and Saracens" (Arabs) with whom they had to compete.[21] Competition was keenest in Spain, where different faiths and traditions coexisted for a long time under Muslim rule. Jews in particular, even in Christian kingdoms like Aragon, enjoyed great success as court doctors and private practitioners. The bearers of a sophisticated and well-developed Hebrew medical tradition and often fluent in Arabic, Jews also acted as conduits of Islamic learning and Mediterranean sophistication. But by the fourteenth century Jewish doctors were foresaking Arabic and sometimes Hebrew to learn Latin and even study (until their expulsion in 1394) at Montpellier.[22] Their shift in ambitions provides indirect evidence of European scholastics' competitive triumph, the result not of better theories and texts but of countless bedside ministrations.

Laypeople, not scholars, took the initiative in establishing the superiority of Christian university physicians over rival healers. Kings hired court doctors and often consulted them on political affairs; towns hired their own physicians; criminal courts relied on them for forensic testimony; church officials needed them to certify impotence in petitions for marital annulment.[23] Much like preachers and lawyers but even more so, medical doctors rose to influence in a world dominated by illiterate but otherwise powerful and intelligent courtiers, parishioners, clients, and patients.[24] In each of their roles, academic physicians had been trained through the scholastic method of ceaseless verbal questioning to think on their feet and impress laymen with their knowledge.

Viva voce learning, pedagogy through the "living voice," was standard practice in medicine, as in every field. After the dictation of introductory texts in lectures, the real heart of teaching was the disputation, a staged debate between master and master, student and student, or master and student. In so-called *quodlibets* ("whatever you want"), a question was posed and a master took on all comers. A master might even dispute himself, in person or in a written treatise or commentary. These virtuoso performances were like knights' tournaments for scholars. Disputations represented the direct continuation and institutionalization of Abelard's dialectical warfare, not on account of his personal influence but instead owing to the culture of aggressive masculinity they shared.

Debating questions may seem quite ill-suited to medical diagnosis, therapy, and hands-on practice, even if it makes perfect sense for theology and law, whose practitioners lived and breathed the written word. But it was precisely because *scientia* founded its superiority to *ars* on the disputation of texts that the scholastic method triumphed even in medicine, the most applied field of university endeavor. Indeed, it was by borrowing from the dialectical methods of nearby theology and law faculties that new medical schools at Paris and Bologna managed to rival and eventually surpass Salerno and Montpellier. The Bolognese doctor Taddeo Alderotti (1223–1295) and his school debated hundreds of questions on conditions ranging from epilepsy to kidney stones. Alderotti conceded that it is often better to be "armed with the scythe of authority and not vacillate in sophistical appearances." Experienced clinicians might know more about curing fevers, for example, than textual scholars did. But he defended disputation as the preferred method for both practical training and theoretical inquiry. When this same physician could be found arguing about whether "eyesight is by the emanation of rays from the eye to the perceived object or vice versa," we are indeed far removed from the realm of direct clinical application.[25]

Medicine's embeddedness in wider questions of science and philosophy was typical of the Greco-Arabic contribution to university learning. In an epoch when medicine had very little power to cure and to heal, merely the ability to diagnose and to explain disease exerted a palliative effect, and this is precisely what *scientia* offered doctors and their patients. The prestige of this tradition only increased as translators—notably of Aristotle, then, by the Renaissance, of Plato and others—kept injecting new texts into a scholastic world hungry for better, more philosophical answers to their questions. That medicine alone among the Mediterranean sciences achieved formal institutional status again shows that universities succeeded only by straddling an often precarious boundary between pure scientific curiosity and practical clinical use. For medicine, as for theology and law, social utility formed the precondition for intellectual exploration. University faculties of all sorts enjoyed autonomy as enclaves within society only because they ultimately served the world surrounding them.

Arts at Prague

Prague was the first scholarly foundation east of the Rhine and north of the Alps, and the last of the truly international universities. Located in the capital of the Czech lands (Bohemia and Moravia), it mainly served students from the German-speaking areas of the Holy Roman Empire. Emperor Charles IV established it in 1348, the year of the Black Death, which spared a thriving Bohemia. Prague seemed poised to make Slavic Europe a new center in the continent's intellectual landscape. But within decades of its foundation, Prague's university was ripped apart by Czech-German ethnic tensions. Its one-time dean of arts, the Czech Jan Hus (ca. 1369–1415), defended a heretical theology aligned with protonationalist aspirations. Through a tortuous series of events, this European university professor wound up being burned at the stake.

There was nothing innovative about Prague's curriculum: Charles intended expressly to replicate the best of both Paris and Bologna. Its arts faculty in particular functioned as such faculties did everywhere else, as routine preparation for advanced professional study. Instruction was given in the standard trivium (grammar, rhetoric, and logic) and quadrivium (arithmetic, geometry, astronomy, and music). Together these seven liberal arts, inherited from ancient Rome, are still nominally recognized in the bachelor's (B.A.) and master's (M.A.) degrees used today.

And as at other European universities, the Prague arts faculty thrived on verbal learning. *Quodlibets* were standard fare, with masters adopting pseudonyms for disputation. Impersonating Socrates and Plato, Cicero and Seneca, even the Muslim philosophers Avicenna (Ibn Sina) and Averroës (Ibn Rushd), they presided over a very cosmopolitan intellectual center.[26] As the "lower" faculty feeding into the three "higher" ones (theology, law, and medicine), the arts faculty was a place where an unusual degree of intellectual freedom could be had. But this was only because the liberal arts had so little relevance to career training in real-world occupations, a fact the Czechs well knew.

Like those at Paris and Bologna, Prague's student body was grouped by place of origin into formal "nations." Usually there was little correspondence with any meaningful ethnic divisions, much less modern national ones. At Paris, the "French" nation included Italians, Greeks, and Spaniards; there were separate nations for Normandy and Picardy (both now parts of France), and an "English-German" nation took in everyone else. Bologna simply had two, one for each side of the Alps. In Prague, however, German-speakers dominated three of the four nations (the Bavarian, the Saxon, and, surprisingly, the Polish). The Germans thus outvoted and increasingly outnumbered the Czechs in their homeland. Most of Prague's masters in arts, moreover, were simultaneously enrolled as bachelors in theology, teaching in the lower faculty to finance advanced religious study. And most of them were Czech. As up-and-comers, they resented the haughtiness of the sophisticated Germans who dominated the theology faculty.[27]

To the Czechs' sociologically rooted grievance was soon added theological fuel. In travels to faraway England, Bohemians copied and brought back the writings of John Wyclif (ca. 1324–1384), the heretical Oxford theologian who led a movement demanding a purer, more decentralized, laypersons' religion. Wyclif argued that no human institution, even and especially the Roman Catholic hierarchy, could embody the spiritual perfection required of God's one true church (those predestined to be saved). The messy business of administering Christianity must therefore revert to secular powers. What Wyclif called "political religion" furnished a well-developed philosophical justification for Czech theologians' logical next step: advocacy of a national church. Matters came to a head when, in 1408–1409, the Czech nation seized voting power from the (anti-Wyclif) Germans, who then emigrated en masse, 1,200 of them, to found a new university in Leipzig. Charles's son and successor, King Wenceslas IV (not the "Good" one), ratified the Czechs' new privileges. Prague became a territorial university, recruiting from a circumscribed region under the patronage of secular rulers, which became the standard model in centuries to come.

John Hus, meanwhile, had been preaching in Czech, to Czechs, for a Czech church, at Bethlehem Chapel in Prague. Prague citizens had endowed scholarships for university students and even established a college for them connected with Bethlehem Chapel. These moves to vernacularize Christian practice and nationalize university teaching could not have come at a worse time. During these same years, the Roman Catholic

Church was itself in schism, with two giant rival European power blocs supporting separately elected popes reigning from Avignon and Rome. Wenceslas was himself challenged by an anti-Emperor. No potentate or institution, religious or secular, spoke for the whole of Latin Christendom. So university academics stepped forward as the sole remaining universal authority.[28] A council was summoned at Constance to put the church back together. Its legal and theological claim to adjudicate between rival popes (conciliarism) was yet another outgrowth of the corporative thought that made the leader of a body beholden to its members. In such a climate, it was clear that Hus and his followers represented a profound threat to the reestablishment of Christian unity. After a series of backhanded dealings, Hus was imprisoned without trial or (like Abelard before him) any opportunity to defend the orthodoxy of his views. He was executed at the Council of Constance on July 6, 1415.

Theology could provide the basis for Europe's intellectual standardization, but embedded as it was in the continent's fractious political and social geography, it could also tear it apart. To understand how Europe's scholarly world could coalesce again into an interdenominational "Republic of Letters," we must first examine how a rival geopolitical religion, Islam, cohered entirely without the benefit of credentialing institutions.

CHRISTENDOM VS. DAR AL-ISLAM

Dar al-Islam, the domain of Islam, not only hosted an international community of scholarship in these same centuries; it

was one. What religion meant, how law and life should interact, what knowledge was for: all were ultimately decided not
by any patron state, church hierarchy, or even professorial
guild but by the *ulama,* a body of scholars that has thrived
without formal institutional definition to this day. Almost
from its inception, Islam was divided—but not disunited—by
antagonistic religious blocs, primarily Sunni and Shi'ite, but
also many subdivisions within these. Successive and at times
rival caliphates eventually lost their claim to exercise secular
jurisdiction as universal Muslim empires. Amid such doctrinal
and political fragmentation, learned men (rarely women)
became the true bearers of religious identity. Typically hailing
from prominent local families known for their learning and
piety, the *ulama* resembled the Chinese scholar-gentry and
the Brahmin castes in India. (Only in Europe, where warriors,
not scholars, first peopled the aristocratic elite, did they
have no analog.) More than in any of these other knowledge
traditions, however, *ulama* derived their power and influence
from Islam's rootedness in an already highly urbanized region
of the globe.

Dar al-Islam's original core territory encompassed the oldest
civilized, most continuously settled, and most historically
learned parts of the ancient world. Scholarship had flourished
there more or less uninterruptedly for centuries. No monasteries
were needed to spread religion or conserve texts in barbarous
wilds. The diffusion of ideas and the movement of scholars
instead relied on long-standing routes of trade and travel only

made easier and more secure by the breathtaking series of campaigns that brought Islam out of the Arabian desert and with remarkable speed extended peace and stability from Spain to Samarkand. Face-to-face teaching and transmission of ideas simply never suffered the ruptures of civilized life that made the preservation of writing and the laborious reconstitution of knowledge necessary in monastic Europe.

We have already encountered one consequence of this in the context of Greco-Arabic medicine: Islam became the greatest heir to and continuator of the Hellenistic library. Alexandria's Museum may have been largely defunct when the Muslims found it—and Caliph Omar's book-burning dictum only finished the job—but other centers of Islamic higher learning built on the Ptolemaic precedent for royal patronage. Abbasid Baghdad became the new Alexandria. Its House of Wisdom, founded around 800 CE through the caliph's largesse, gathered a multicultural scholarly community to translate all known exemplars of "foreign" wisdom into Arabic.[29] Christians, Jews, and even the stargazing pagans of Harran (in what is now Turkey) worked there alongside Arab Muslims. Greek, Syriac, Persian, and Sanskrit texts and terms were all appropriated, and Arabic itself became a far richer and suppler language, and above all an international one, as a result.[30] Collation and translation, as before, remained the gateway to synthesis and discovery. Alchemy (*al-kimiya*), a precursor to chemistry but also a spiritual discipline, drew upon Egyptian and Mesopotamian sources, and algebra (*al-jabr*) developed from Hindu mathematics. (What we call

arabic numbers, including zero, actually originated in India.)
Nourished by multiple sources, Islamic learning brought the
Greek and Indian exact sciences to a far higher degree of technical refinement than either had attained independently.[31] Later
Muslim astronomers came within a hair's breadth of replacing Ptolemy's geocentric universe with a sun-centered one, for
example.[32]

It is unfair, though, to measure Arabic knowledge simply by
the yardstick of its reception, transmission, and refinement of an
ancient heritage. Islam also possessed an indigenous scholarly
tradition independent of Greece and paralleled only by Judaism in its synthesis of religion and law, written text and oral
recitation. Arabic, the holy language of the Quran, was, like
Hebrew (another Semitic language), originally written without
vowels, or at best with ambiguous diacritical marks as substi-
tutes. Only in being voweled and voiced did the word of God
become real and unambiguous meaning emerge. Recitation, repetition, and eventual memorization of the Quran lie at the very
heart of Muslim religious practice. The creative spark to scholarly interpretation thus consists in elaborating in speech what
must remain latent and incomplete in writing. The Quran itself
gives the best illustration of this. While it quickly achieved a
fixed, canonical form as a written (but orally recited) text, it did
not provide infallible guidance for every human predicament.
The text of the Quran instead had to be supplemented by the
sayings of Muhammad and the oral reports of his Companions,
the *hadith*. New *hadith* were always being discovered in Islam's

early centuries, and each such claim had to be scrutinized for authenticity and integrated with all other knowledge.

It was the need for guidance among new (or newly converted) Muslim communities far removed in space, time, and culture from the Mecca and Medina of the Prophet that drove the search for more authoritative *hadith*. In an iterative process of question and answer, new believers brought new problems to the *ulama* for resolution. Islamic thinkers developed their own version of the scholastic method in response, progressively amalgamating and smoothing out differences in interpretation. Dozens of informal schools of religious law competed in Islam's early centuries, sometimes violently. But the search for consensus among the *ulama* steadily reduced this number to only four, the same four schools still ascendant within Sunni Islam today, each dominant in different parts of the world but more or less coexisting.[33] (Shi'a Islam has its own jurisprudential tradition.)

Muslim learning continues to expand by applying the Quran and the *hadith* to the myriad conflicts and complexities of daily life and augmenting them with appeals to analogous past cases and the standard practices of the Muslim community. Thus a twentieth-century legal ruling on artificial insemination drew on an ancient precedent in which a woman, soon after intercourse with her husband, unwittingly impregnated her lesbian lover, a slave girl, through the transfer of bodily fluids.[34] (We cite this case not to indulge stereotypes of a hypersexualized Orient but to point to the surprising worldliness of Islamic law at a very early date.) In all these cases, innovations in scholarly interpretation must be shown to rest on the assumed truth of past wisdom recorded unerringly in recited texts. Every copied text in Islam attains clarity and completion only in the commentary that the scholar provides, quite often by literally interpolating new words in red ink in original passages written in black.[35]

Despite the proliferation of texts, commentaries, and schools of interpretation, however, the intimate bonds of face-to-face transmission always remained the preferred mode of transmitting learning in Islam. In the best case, a Muslim scholar, as freely as any pilgrim to Mecca, could and would travel huge distances and visit multiple sites to acquire knowledge orally, as close as possible to its original sources. Alternatively, he could learn from hearing a written text recited, but only from someone formally certified to impart it to him. Having been dictated a manuscript, a student would copy it, memorize it, and recite it back before being issued a license, or *ijaza,* to reproduce it still further. In effect, the *ijaza* constituted an authorization one scholar issued to another to teach a specific text. (Even women, despite being barred from official scholarly positions like judgeships, could accumulate *ijazas* in this way.)[36] Every hand-copied written manuscript circulated in Islam thus included, in addition to the body of information it conveyed, as complete a list of prior copyists and commentators as possible, ideally going back to its original author. The concern to build a "golden chain" of authentic, reliable, documented oral transmitters accounts in large part for the Islamic world's long-standing resistance to the printing press, despite its very early adoption of paper from

China.[37] Over a lifetime of study, seekers of knowledge accumulated a satchel of licenses rather than a handful of degrees; the
transmission of knowledge was from person to person, not in
schools organized as formal corporations as in medieval Europe.

Islam did of course develop an analog to the university in the
form of the *madrasa,* an endowed residential center of study in
religious law. This institution of learning originated in Iran,
which antedates Greece as a center of urban civilization. After
Iran converted to the Muslim faith, between the seventh and
tenth centuries, Persian *ulama* provided much of the learned culture that the Arabian desert tribes originally lacked. Iran's cities
eventually became victims of their own success, however, as
their rapid growth outstripped the resources of their agricultural hinterlands. Their decline, capped by the depredations of
thirteenth-century Mongol invaders, fueled a diaspora of cultured Persian *ulama* who fled the cities and fanned out across
Dar al-Islam. Spreading their knowledge by founding *madrasas,*
they helped to further homogenize understanding of what it
meant to be a Muslim. This scholarly dispersion coincided in
time with Latin Christendom's revival but was fueled by the
opposite economic trend: Iran's deurbanization and economic
contraction.[38]

Contemporary critics of Islam charge that the *madrasa* subordinated higher learning to religious doctrine and eventually
stagnated, whereas European universities integrated Greek philosophy into their curricula and ultimately gained intellectual
freedom. True enough, but the analogy is misleading. As chari-

table residential endowments, *madrasas* resembled colleges and not universities.[39] Moreover, since religion developed in partnership with law in the *madrasa*, not with philosophy as in Christian theology, philosophy profited by its very isolation, as the odd one out. *Falsafa* was in fact regarded as the queen of the "foreign sciences." Flourishing for centuries, largely under traditional Mediterranean court patronage, it extended the legacy of Aristotle. The *Canon* of Ibn Sina (ca. 980–1037), as we have seen, furnished a fund of medical and scientific knowledge to Latin Europe. And in Ibn Rushd (1126–1198), Islam produced a thinker far more radical than Abelard, one who held pure philosophy to be a higher road to salvation than revealed scripture, which he cast as a crude version of the truth suitable for the masses.

Institutional marginality did condemn Islamic inheritors of Greek learning to decline after their rival, the Iranian al-Ghazali (1058–1111), successfully denigrated philosophers for their "incoherence." Yet what looks like the death of Greek learning at al-Ghazali's hands signaled, from a different perspective, a reconciliation between old religious law and new currents of mysticism never achieved in the West. Al-Ghazali, a towering figure in Islamic thought, left a *madrasa* career to become a Sufi mystic. A rough contemporary of Abelard and Bernard, he attained what they could not: a reconciliation of scholarship and spirituality. Sufism, the spiritual movement he helped to legitimate before the skeptical *ulama*, functioned as Islam's missionary advance guard. Sufi brotherhoods were largely responsible for the peaceful spread of Islam to South Asia and over the Indian Ocean. Like the *madrasas* themselves, these spiritual institutions originated in Iran, al-Ghazali's homeland. And much like Bernard's mystics, Sufis responded to the reconfiguration of urban space in Dar al-Islam not by posing theological questions but by cultivating direct understanding of the divine. By the fifteenth century, a new synthesis had been achieved. In many urban centers, the term *madrasa* could be used interchangeably with both "mosque" and "Sufi convent." The *madrasa* served not as a scholarly ivory tower but as a center of prayer, worship, Quran chanting, and other public functions, embedding it much more deeply in the city it served than was the case with universities.[40]

Whether foreign or indigenous, legal or religious, rational or mystical, learning in Dar al-Islam looked back to the time of Muhammad for its canonical texts but forward in its determination to apply knowledge to the perfection of Allah's community on earth. Rearticulating the past provided the touchstone for consensus, unity, and growth in the future.[41] Interpretive latitude found its limits in the need to recite and conserve texts while commenting on and interpreting them. Paradigm shifts might be impossible, but the unlimited accretion of new skills and insights was not. These were much the same precepts as those that medieval European scholastics held. The relevant conclusion, then, is not that universities propagated Greek philosophy whereas the *madrasas* smothered it; it is that Islamic scholarship thrived without the benefits of that philosophy, or the headaches it gave to the Europeans who institutionalized it, from Abelard to Hus. The *ulama* were an international intelligentsia defining and defined by a religious community of global aspirations, Dar al-Islam, from its very inception. Tolerance, of different religions and different religious laws, was foisted on scholars as a geopolitical imperative, since Dar al-Islam was already full of Christians, Jews, and, after the Mughals built an empire in South Asia, what we now call Hindus.

By contrast, Roman Catholic theology had difficulty accommodating even one rival, Eastern Orthodoxy (practiced in Byzantium, Russia, and elsewhere), and found it impossible to contain another, Lutheranism. When, in 1517, Martin Luther (1483–1546) nailed his ninety-five theses on ecclesiastical reform to a church door in Wittenberg, he was a theology professor at a relatively obscure German university. Like the masters Wyclif and Hus before him, he had no intention of spreading heresy or inciting schism. But Europe's combustible fusion of philosophy, religion, and politics ultimately widened theological divisions in Roman Catholicism into a permanent split during the Protestant Reformation. Lutheran ministers could have become as alien to Catholic priests, and to university culture, as Orthodox clergy. If European intellectuals were to make "Europe" into something like Dar al-Islam, something more than a geographical label, they would have to create new institutions transcending the ideological differences that so bitterly divided them. This is the story of the Republic of Letters.

4

The Republic of Letters

1500–1800

AMID CRISES IN SCHOLARLY CULTURE, CORRESPON-
DENCE NETWORKS CREATED A NEW WESTERN
INTELLIGENTSIA INDEPENDENT OF PAST INSTITUTIONS
AND RECEPTIVE TO NEW DISCOVERIES.

*In the midst of all the governments that decide the
fate of men; in the bosom of so many states, the
majority of them despotic, governed by sovereigns
whose authority extends over people and property,
there exists a certain empire which holds sway only
over the mind, an empire that we honor with the
name Republic, because it preserves a measure of
independence, and because it is almost its essence
to be free. It is the empire of talent and of thought.
The academies are its tribunals; people distinguished by their talents are its dignitaries.*

—ANONYMOUS (1780)[1]

THE REPUBLIC OF LETTERS is perhaps the only institution
listed in this book's table of contents unknown to the average
educated reader. Yet it produced or at least nurtured some of
the West's greatest thinkers—Erasmus and Copernicus, Galileo
and Descartes, Newton and Bacon. It first flourished during the

Renaissance but also thrived during the Protestant Reformation, the scientific revolution, the voyages of discovery, the rise of absolutist states, the Enlightenment—all the old chestnuts of the Western Civ. textbook. The Republic of Letters in fact helped to define what it meant to belong to "the West" after Luther showed that common religion no longer could and Columbus ensured that geographical isolation no longer would. It withstood intolerance, war, disease, hardship, and oppression within Europe's boundaries. It followed lines of global trade, overseas colonization, and missionary work beyond its frontiers.

The Republic of Letters can be defined as an international community of learning stitched together initially by handwritten letters in the mail and later by printed books and journals. The term is of ancient origin; it hearkens back to Cicero (106–43 BCE), the Roman orator who matched wits with Julius Caesar, defended the republic against tyranny, and died a violent death at the hands of Mark Antony's henchmen. When not speaking in the Senate, Cicero pursued scholarship at his country estate and corresponded with learned friends, not only to carry on the life of the mind but also to refine his oratorical and political skills. The Ciceronian ideal of a *respublica literaria* was revived imitatively when it reentered European usage in the late fifteenth century. Shorn of its political overtones in its later incarnation, this ideal inspired new practices of humanistic discourse among men (and some women) of letters.

Not only did this early modern Republic of Letters reinvent itself during a time of troubles and breakthroughs alike, but it prospered as much or more during what should have been shocks to the system. It was an institution perfectly adapted to disruptive change of unprecedented proportions. Its history raises the question of why Europe's diversity brought progress in scholarship when by rights disunity ought to have crippled it. The answer is as simple as it is radical: with existing institutions of learning in crisis or collapse, the Republic of Letters founded its legitimacy on the production of new knowledge. Real bricks-and-mortar institutions—print shops, museums, and learned academies—provided it with substance, as we will see. The Republic of Letters acted as an umbrella institution for them all. Owing to its legacy, international cooperation remains a hallmark of Western scholarship to this day.

THE LETTER

A combination of religious protest and political competition caused Europe virtually to combust between 1500 and 1700. The various Reformations and pre-Reformations—Wyclif's, Hus's, and especially Luther's—were among the prime causes. Unlike previous heresies, these movements were launched from within the universities. But they never would have succeeded if princes and politicians had not taken up the cause of religion, by either coopting or crushing the reformers. By the same token, when knowledge became politicized, the international culture of scholarship suffered.

The huge number of new universities and colleges chartered during this period almost invariably adhered to one or another confession, whether Protestant (Lutheran or Calvinist) or Catholic. Their founders usually saw them as regional or national, not international, institutions and as sources of revenue and skilled professionals. Many princes explicitly forbade native sons from studying outside their home states and taking their tuition money with them. Expanding governments needed literate men: lawyers to staff burgeoning bureaucracies and pastors to discipline wayward flocks.[2]

Never-ending religious wars drastically curtailed scholarly mobility, at least the voluntary kind undertaken for intellectual curiosity that had fueled the growth of the first universities. Early modern Europe was instead filled with different types of scholars on the move: exiles, like the unusually literate Protestant Huguenots driven out of Catholic France, and missionaries, like the Jesuits sent both overseas and to the countryside to claim (or reclaim) the world for the Roman church. Together these developments threatened a European international scholarly culture founded on the university degree. A credential first rendered portable by the ascendancy of religious orthodoxy throughout Christendom, it now functioned less as a scholar's passport than as a sign of his indoctrination in one or another, rival worldview.

A network without nodes

The Republic of Letters was a figurative polity constituted at the moment that politicized religion tore Europe apart. In conditions of crisis, it emerged as an alternative, secular institution of learning, partly rivaling, partly complementing the old universities by knitting European learning back together.

The Republic of Letters recognized no distinctions of birth, social status, gender, or academic degree. It rose above differences of language—Latin still reigned supreme as the scholarly tongue—nationality, and especially religion. It kept Protestants and Catholics in communication even when their faiths were at war, and by the late seventeenth century it welcomed Jews and deists (who believed in one God but adhered to no practiced faith). All its members were considered equal. Entrance was purely informal, though there was a clear expectation that one would acquit oneself like a gentleman or gentlewoman.

And yes, a few women belonged to the Republic of Letters. Margaret Cavendish, for example, forsook Aristotle to embrace and update Stoic natural philosophy. Her *Blazing World* (1666) ranks as one of the earliest works of science fiction. Another formidable seventeenth-century intellect, Elizabeth of Palatine, engaged in a famous exchange with the mathematician and philosopher René Descartes. An exiled Protestant princess living through the Thirty Years' War in The Hague, Elizabeth wrote to Descartes that his famous mind-body distinction was of little consolation to one whose mind and spirit found it difficult to rise above the physical and emotional distress she daily suffered as an exile. Their letters showcase the genius of a world suffused with protocols of deference and decorum. He deferred to her high-born status, she to his masculine intellect: "The life I am forced to lead does not leave me the disposition of enough time to acquire a habit of meditation according to your rules. So many interests of my family that I must not neglect, so many interviews and civilities that I cannot avoid, batter my weak spirit with such anger and boredom that it is rendered for a long time afterward useless for anything else. All of which will excuse my stupidity, I hope, to not have been able to understand [how the soul can move the body]."[3] However small their numbers, women like these do attest to the republic's openness in principle. Communication across distances made a life of the mind viable for women who were unable to travel freely or engage in the the verbal jousting dominated by males in the university disputation.

The Republic of Letters, like any republic, was governed by its citizens. But unlike other republics, its form of citizenship was anchored neither in space nor in formal laws or institutions. Unlike the urban citizenship of the Middle Ages, which granted rights in the specific town where a person lived, citizenship in the Republic of Letters was international. And unlike the guild citizenship of the medieval *universitas,* which was also international in the sense of being portable from place to place, there were no certificates, no degrees, no formal credentials of any kind: anyone who obeyed the rules of civil conduct could join. The Republic of Letters was totally unanchored in space. There were no fixed nodes, like Paris or Bologna—only the network itself.

No precise figures concerning its size exist, but during the Renaissance, the Republic of Letters numbered perhaps 600 active partipants in Italy and Germany; by 1690, more than

1,200 thrived in northern Europe alone.[4] Hamburg's state library registers 6,700 separate individuals together contributing 35,000 pieces of scholarly correspondence for the period between the Reformation and 1735.[5] Whatever its size, as one scholar wrote, "It embraces the whole world and is composed of all nationalities, all social classes, all ages, and both sexes."[6] Its members included courtiers, aristocrats, bourgeois, even craftsmen—especially master printers, whose shops formed a meeting point for academics and men of affairs. Traditional university scholars emphatically belonged too, as did members of the church hierarchy, monastic and mendicant orders, Jesuit missionaries and educators, Protestant pastors and Catholic abbés.

The republic transcended not only frontiers but generations. It was explicitly seen as a collaborative venture bringing scholars together not only across Europe but also across time. As Descartes put it, "With the later persons beginning where the earlier ones left off, and thereby linking the lives and the work of many people, we can all go forward together much further than each person individually would be able to do."[7] The belief in indefinite progress became a hallmark of the mature Republic of Letters, a key part of its legacy to modernity. It set members of this institution apart from the medieval scholastics, the first in fact to dub themselves "moderns," but, in a cliché already popular at the time, only as dwarves standing on the shoulders of past giants. Prior seekers of knowledge could at best recover ageless wisdom from the past and patiently extend it—a view shared even by scholars of the early Renaissance, who revived the humane letter from antiquity. But as scholars in this epoch of rebirth fashioned the letter into a principal mode of intellectual contact, a deeper consciousness of past and future became part of the act of letter writing itself.

Epistolary humanism

The glory of the Renaissance often blinds us to the darker side of late medieval Italy. Warfare was endemic to the peninsula's city-states, rival papacies rocked the Roman Catholic Church, and the populace had to cope with periodic waves of plague and the predations of mercenaries and tax collectors. Such hardships gave ample taste of the miseries to come in succeeding centuries. They also help explain why Italian scholars looked back to the ancient pagan world for guidance and inspiration.

Renaissance humanists aimed to recover ancient learning and ancient texts because ancient models—Cicero, most importantly —showed what it meant to have good character, to be a good leader, and to exhibit versatility and strength during times of tribulation. Scholastics caught up in logical give-and-take (recall Abelard here) often neglected to cultivate their human-ity. Humanistic scholarship resurrected classical Latin and made it an elegant language again, less bogged down by scholastic circumlocutions. To accomplish this, the humanists returned to the philological task, pioneered at Alexandria, of retrieving the best texts in the best versions and editions. And whereas the scholastics focused on Greece and especially Aris-totle, humanists emphasized Neoplatonism, the other side of the Greek tradition filtered through Byzantium, and especially the Roman writers, not only Cicero but also Livy, Lucretius, Seneca, and others.

If logic was the basis of scholasticism in the universities and grammar the part of the trivium most useful in the monastery, rhetoric occupied pride of place for humanists in the Republic of Letters. The models of classical rhetoric reclaimed from ancient texts provided a timeless set of stylistic and persuasive techniques with the unique power to put an individual's knowledge into the head of the person he or she is trying to convince. For all their love of the ancients, though, Renaissance humanists departed radically from them in the way they practiced these techniques. They revived rhetoric not as oratory—the delivery of speeches—but primarily through the art of letter writing. Letter writing stressed a very different set of virtues from the oral arguments of the Greek polis and the Roman republic. Civility, friendship, politeness, generosity, benevolence, and especially tolerance: these were the qualities of "humanity" found in the form of the letter. The letter, in other words, was a substitute for gentlemanly conversation. It, and it alone, enabled the writer to produce intimacy and immediacy at a distance, without alienating the correspondent with argument.

Justifying the use of leisure to withdraw and write letters could of course appear problematic in an age of turmoil, especially when the ancients presented themselves as such models of civic engagement. In Greece and Rome, men of real consequence invariably dictated their letters to servants; Julius Caesar could reportedly dictate as many as seven simultaneously.[8] In the interim, however, the monastery had for the first time made the physical act of writing a devotional, contemplative act, one with the potential to remove the writer from the vicissitudes of the present. Petrarch (1304–1374), the archetypical humanist, crafted a synthesis between the classical values of antiquity and the consciousness of time characteristic of the Christian monk.[9] It was Petrarch who rediscovered Cicero, unearthing a cache of previously unknown letters in a cathedral library. And it was Petrarch who found a striking new use for the genre, addressing intimate letters to the dead Cicero and other greats, like Homer and Livy. Humanists engaged in conversation across centuries, as if with real men. Petrarch even fashioned his own letters into a collection to benefit the distant future, ending them with a letter to posterity: "Francesco Petrarca to posterity, greetings. Perhaps you will have heard something about me, although this too is doubtful, whether a petty, obscure name would reach far into either space or time. And perhaps you will wish to know what sort of man I was, or what were the results of my labors, especially of those whose fame has reached you or whose bare titles you have heard."[10]

The decision, however reluctantly taken, to remain committed to scholarly citizenship as an alternative to the monastic retreat found after Rome's decline helps explain why the repeated crises of late medieval Europe prompted intellectual ferment instead of defeatism and stagnation. Letter writing held out the prospect of "thinking locally and acting globally," to invert a present-day maxim, especially when politics afforded little solace.

Scholarship across distances

As Erasmus of Rotterdam (1466–1536) defined it, "the letter is a kind of mutual exchange of speech between absent friends."[11] Communication in the Republic of Letters was indeed rarely face-to-face, and participants might correspond for decades without ever meeting each other. The letter offered a twofold benefit to its members. Not only did it revive the secular humanism of ancient pagans at a time when Christian charity seemed in short supply. As a technology of communication, it also compensated for the decrease in scholars' physical mobility.

As time went on, the Republic of Letters developed a whole culture of letter-writing practices and protocols designed to cope with distance and even parlay it into a virtue.[12] Letters were sent by regular post, diplomatic pouch, papal or imperial couriers, or simply in the hands of travelers headed in the same direction. Whether they were university students on their "academic peregrination" or other travelers, scholars relayed letters, as intermediaries, on behalf of others. Letters, though personal in style and addressed to individuals, were almost always intended for public circulation or publication, or at least for sharing with friends, so as to multiply their effect. Letters of recommendation were the first passports for scholars. They could facilitate research at a distance, as requests for book loans, manuscript consultations, or trips to local libraries or archives. Scholars would go to great lengths for each other purely on the basis of receiving such a letter. For example, they might gather data on astronomical phenomena, like comets and eclipses. Tracking Venus's movement across the night sky enlisted more than five hundred European observers across the world in 1761 and 1769. The 1761 effort alone, conducted at the height of the Seven Years' War largely through private efforts, was a testament to scholarly commitment in a time of global political conflict.[13]

The need to build trust and form judgments of correspondents' credibility and character meant that the Republic of Letters never became either impersonal or anonymous. Thus, when the Amsterdam lens grinder Antonie van Leeuwenhoek invented the microscope in 1673, the London Royal Society asked one of its trusted Dutch contacts to confirm the new development. Most letter writers, even if they had not met in person, could at least appeal to mutual friends before initiating correspondence. Letters often capitalized on chance connections and distant acquaintances to magnify webs of connectedness traversing Europe and, increasingly, the globe. Bits of information shuttled over land and sea in the Republic of Letters. "Multiplexed" correspondence carried several threads of news within a single missive, as in this 1668 example:

I have heard that there is a little book on the plan for the rebuilding of London. I should be very glad to have it.

The Florentines did not perform as many experiments as was thought. I shall not fail to let you have a copy if I can get one.

There is a physician who has performed [the experiment of] blood transfusion at Rome. His account is to be printed and when it is I shall send it to you. He only uses one ligature.

Mr. Pecquet, who is a member of the Academy, has dissected a beaver; the account is to be printed. At Caen they have dissected a porcupine.

Mr. Borel, whom you know, has the secret of coagulating fluids without spoiling them.

The two Dutchmen, of whom I wrote that they had found the longitudes, will soon be here. We shall see what they will propose.

Mr. de Beaufort, who is going to Portugal, is to take two pendulum clocks to see if use can be made of them.[14]

And so on. Letters like this increasingly dispensed with humanism's rhetorical flourishes and formality, but they honored its ideals in the breach, and testified to the dense web of informational exchange that bound scholarly friendships together.

THE BOOK

As a written genre, the letter had existed since antiquity and was also favored by the medievals—witness Cicero and Caesar, Abelard and Heloise. What made the Republic of Letters different was that it emerged simultaneously and in symbiosis with the printed book. Erasmus, for example, became Europe's first celebrity intellectual by crafting his public image in print, in particular by carefully editing and publishing his own letters.[15] Given the epochal importance of Johannes Gutenberg (ca. 1398–1468) and his printing press, we might ask, why is the book not the central institution organizing knowledge at this time? Nearly all the great scholars of early modernity gained their fame through books. But while the printing press emerged in the fifteenth century and book production exploded in short order, the book remained a mere technology of communication, albeit a revolutionary one. For all its utility in transmitting knowledge across both space and time, the book never became a reliable or comprehensive means of reinventing it. A fuller explanation of this must await the treatment of encyclopedias in the next chapter. For now, three exemplary books from the "age of discovery" illustrate the abiding importance of letters: how the conventions of epistolary humanism helped, even in print, to determine whether and how new knowledge would be recognized as such.

The rhetoric of discovery

In 1507 there appeared a book with literally earth-shattering implications, one that reshaped the way Europeans saw the world. It included a map with a bizarrely elongated landmass dubbed "America." This continent was nowhere found in Ptolemy's *Geographica*, the ancient Alexandrian treatise that for centuries had provided the definitive guide to the known world (Europe, Asia, and Africa). The German mapmakers Martin Waldseemüller and Matthias Ringmann, active in tiny Saint-Dié-des-Vosges in eastern France, had named America after the

Florentine navigator Amerigo Vespucci. Working from Vespucci's published letters, they mistakenly believed that he had reached the South American mainland (as contrasted with the Caribbean islands) before Columbus. In fact, Columbus set foot in what is now Venezuela during his third voyage, in 1498, a year before Vespucci.[16] The error illustrates a new separation of author and publisher brought about by the printing press. Those who created new knowledge were generally not those who packaged and mass-produced it. Both the Saint-Dié cartographers and Vespucci's publishers worked far from the New World. Most of Europe's early printing presses were in fact clustered in protected enclaves of the Holy Roman Empire on account of their unusual freedom to publish. Information often had to be obtained second- or even third-hand.

Why did the publishers in Saint-Dié not choose to credit Columbus rather than Vespucci? Some have suggested that Florentine patriots, tampering with Vespucci's letters, deliberately backdated their native son's American landing to precede that of Columbus, from rival Genoa. But the deeper reason was that Vespucci was the better rhetorician. Columbus had deliberately downplayed the novelty of his voyages. He died thinking that he had reached the Indies, that the Orinoco led to the Garden of Eden, and that his discovery of the Far East would prepare the way for a grand Christianizing mission that would encircle Islam from both sides. By contrast, Vespucci's letters were significantly entitled *Novus mundus* (New World). He made no bones about the revolutionary nature of his discovery: of the new lands he charted, he wrote, "the ancients had no knowledge." Vespucci's travel accounts evoked wonder and excitement at the "large green trees, which never shed their leaves" and "many sweet and delicious herbs, flowers, and roots" previously unknown to Europeans. Those who printed his letters naturally embellished them, playing up images of Caribbean islanders as cannibals (etymologically derived from "Carib"). Tropes about savages and the state of nature were common to ancient travel literature; here they only reinforced Vespucci's claim to have discovered something new and exotic yet also strangely familiar to the humanist imagination.[17]

Europeans, in other words, did not perceive the discovery of the New World as a revolution in knowledge. Instead they assimilated reports of its new plants, foods, people, and terrain to a very well-worn genre going all the way back to Herodotus's ethnography and Callimachus's paradoxography. Eager readers of the fabulous *Nuremberg Chronicle* (1493), for example, saw in vivid woodcut illustrations how Africans coped with over-abundant sunshine by hoisting grotesquely large feet as nature-made umbrellas.[18] What had changed was simply the nature of publication. Now, publishers' motives—for profit, for market reach, for appealing novelty, for attractive literary style—helped dictate how discoveries would be disseminated. Humanist rhetoric was the safest marketing technique available. From this it followed that printed books, which are often seen as ensuring the fixity and reliability of a text, could just as easily propagate and magnify error. In such circumstances, personal letters alone satisfied the criterion laid down centuries before by Socrates: that the trustworthiness of an opinion must be carefully matched to the reputation of the individual responsible for it.

Framing books with letters

One way to put a personal stamp on an otherwise disembodied and unfamiliar medium of communication was to print letters as prefaces to and endorsements of books. "Framing" letters were the ancestors of today's dustjacket blurbs. They provided entrée into the world of scholars, a familiar framework for their reception, and comfort and pride for their patrons and backers. Such letters were especially needed for books written by distant scholars and/or advancing bold new propositions. Nicholas Copernicus's *On the Revolutions of the Heavenly Spheres* was both. Its heliocentric model of the universe challenged another Ptolemaic treatise, the *Almagest*, which explained how the sun revolved around the earth. And while Copernicus's book might have remained the obscure theory of a remote Polish church official, *On the Revolutions* would become the most famous and influential scientific book ever written. Composed between 1506 and 1530, the book was not published until 1543. The letters prefacing it launched its detailed, technical findings in very gingerly fashion into the scholarly world.[19] In one of them, Copernicus's publisher, Andreas Osiander, softened the blow of proposing a sun-centered universe by proffering the book merely as a set of "novel hypotheses." In this way, "the liberal arts, which were established long ago on a sound basis, should not be thrown into confusion." In another letter, Copernicus addressed Pope Paul III to explain why he had finally decided to publish findings that he had arrived at decades before. For some time he had followed "the example of the Pythagoreans and certain others, who used to transmit philosophy's secrets only to kinsmen and friends, not in writing but by word of mouth." But his friends in the Republic of Letters had finally prevailed upon him to publish for the benefit for all.[20]

Together these prefatory items emphasize that books hardly spoke for themselves; their reception in the Republic of Letters was conditioned by the conventions of letter writing, even and especially in print. Shrewdly couched as a hypothesis with due deference to the church, Copernicus's theory gained invaluable breathing space while scholars assessed its claims. The career of the Copernican theory is in fact a perfect illustration of the republic's internationalism. From its original formulation to its culmination in the mathematical proof showing the solar system to run stably without divine intervention, its principal developers included a Pole (Copernicus himself, 1473–1543), a Dane (Tycho Brahe, 1546–1601), a German (Johannes Kepler, 1571–1630), an Italian (Galileo Galilei, 1564–1642), an Englishman (Isaac Newton, 1643–1727), and a Frenchman (Pierre-Simon Laplace, 1749–1827).

Censorship

Among these figures, it was Galileo who forced the conclusion that Copernicus's theory implied: if Ptolemy could be wrong about the number of continents and wrong about the earth's movement, then perhaps it was best to jettison the ancients and start from scratch, using empirical observation to study the natural world. The telescope, the thermometer, and plans and prototypes for barometers, microscopes, and precision clocks count among Galileo's seminal contributions to exact science. But it was his *Dialogue Concerning the Two Chief World Systems* (1632) that threw down the gauntlet to adherents of ancient texts, and by extension to Catholic church doctrine. By presenting the Copernican system as reality, not as hypothesis, Galileo famously ran afoul of the censors. Censorship is of course the greatest risk surrounding printed books. It exploded after 1500, partly because print shops, as we have seen, mass-produced books in response to profit and not propriety, but also because they enabled authorities to censor books at the source. Presses might be impounded, bookplates destroyed, printers punished; letters, however, could always be smuggled past hostile authorities or relayed through trusted intermediaries.

Nicholas Claude Fabri de Peiresc (1580–1637), the non-elected first citizen of the Republic of Letters, helped save Galileo's discoveries while the renowned stargazer was being charged with heresy and held under house arrest by the Roman Inquisition, the church body empowered to combat deviant beliefs and other threats to Catholicism.[21] Now a figure all but completely forgotten, Peiresc exchanged an estimated 10,000 letters with more than 500 individual scholars during his lifetime. Working mainly from his chateau in Aix-en-Provence, in southern France, he discovered the first nebula, organized observations of eclipses among scholars across Europe (to correct sailing maps), and made signal contributions to the study of antiquities. But Peiresc never published any books himself, lest he compromise the intellectual freedom that correspondence offered, and thus he failed to acquire lasting fame. Letters enabled him to work behind the scenes—in Galileo's case, by interceding with those close to the pope. In a letter to Peiresc, Galileo thanked his patron and friend, larding on flattery and self-effacement for the "feelings of courtesy and goodwill" that "continue to make the fortune of my misfortune appear sweeter to me." With bookstore shelves being cleared of his work, he wrote, "every effort is being made to remove all memory of me from the world." But, he continued, "if my adversaries knew how little I strive for such a vanity, perhaps they would not show themselves so anxious to oppress me."[22] Such protestations of humility might strike us as disingenuous. But Galileo knew that correspondence networks alone could sustain his ideas. Peiresc's defense of his scholarship illustrates that citizenship in the Republic of Letters was a real, not just a symbolic advantage.

Orientation toward the future

Thanks to correspondence networks like Peiresc's, authors such as Galileo, toiling in adversity, might find solace in the belief that their ideas would reach and inspire subsequent generations even if their physical books did not. And yet print did ultimately offer scholars in the Republic of Letters an advantage no other technology could: the chance to win fame in their own lifetime. For the printing press radically reinforced two of the republic's existing orientations, one toward space and one toward time. Spatially, books made widespread, uncoordinated dissemination of knowledge possible on a much greater scale than before and in a theoretically democratic way. Fanning out over the continent and across the oceans, they spoke to an indeterminate audience—those who already knew how to put scholarship in context and interpret new findings. These were precisely the skills an individual gained from citizenship in the Republic of Letters. Temporally, books spoke to posterity, potentially the largest indeterminate audience a book could address. Durable, bound artifacts, they stood a better chance of survival and suffered fewer corruptions than hand-copied manuscripts, even in small print runs. The Renaissance had originated as a rebirth of antiquity; succeeding generations, conscious of time and its cycles, saw in books a chance to match and exceed the ancients: to acquire everlasting fame for themselves.

The contrasts between monastic scribal production and book publishing are particularly instructive here. The first originated to fill the present, the second to shape the future; the first literally cloisters knowledge from the profane world, the second embraces and seeks to reform that world. Printed books, unlike manuscripts, were mechanically reproduced, and in unprecedented numbers. Products of a capital-intensive commercial enterprise quite unlike the small-scale devotional act of monastic writing, they had to find readers just so their producers could break even. These commodities, suitably adapted to the republic's practices and protocols, made it easier to address audiences unknown and generations unborn. The links thus established, not only to the present but also with the future, made Petrarch's dream of addressing posterity a technological and cultural possibility for the first time. This future-orientedness departed just as surely from the concern for transmission and authority in classical Islamic, Sanskritic, and Confucian traditions. All of these always sought to build a "golden chain" from the past to the present. Scholars in the Republic of Letters were building a bridge to the future. For the same reason, they were far more receptive to new knowledge flooding in from other continents than Western scholars ever had been before.

THE MUSEUM

In the sixteenth and seventeenth centuries, a few resourceful eccentrics, most of them wealthy gentleman-amateurs or worldly clerics, began to do something quite new and characteristically early modern: they collected things—passionately, indiscriminately, and with virtuoso flair. In fact they were called *virtuosi,* in honor of their *virtù,* a quality associated more with the appearance of artistic, scientific, or political skill than with their underlying moral character.[23] (Machiavelli, for example, notoriously argued that *virtù* was more important in a prince than what Cicero had called virtue.) Whereas Columbus and Vespucci, Copernicus and Galileo replaced the geocentric universal model that Ptolemy had created at ancient

Alexandria, these *virtuosi* repurposed the very institution in which Ptolemy had worked. The Museum at Alexandria was a place to collect texts indiscriminately, the site of the first library. The museums of the *virtuosi*, like those of today, were places to collect and display all manner of physical objects, natural and manmade.

Swashbuckling merchant-imperialists and overseas missionaries were bringing Europe shipload after shipload of new knowledge about new things in nature and culture while professors were still lecturing from thumbworn copies of Pliny, Ptolemy, and Aristotle. Renaissance people were already taken with fine painting, sculpture, artisanal crafts, and Roman antiques. After Columbus's and other seafaring explorations, Europe was suddenly flooded with spices, silks, and seashells from the world's four corners. *Virtuosi* collections might have upended an entire scholarly culture founded since ancient times on learning from texts. Instead, the Republic of Letters reacted by embracing their wonders, publicizing their achievements, and confronting their implications for the organization of knowledge.

The Wunderkammer

Today's museumgoer is as likely to tire from treading over acres of parquet floors as to experience a sense of wonder at hallowed artworks crammed on plaster walls. But to inspire wonder, by concentrating and containing the rare and the strange, was the original aim of this early modern institution. The typical (albeit not only) form of museum collections was the *Wun-*

derkammer, "cabinet of curiosities." *Wunderkammern* mixed old and new, European and non-European, natural and artificial objects (including fine art) together. The *Wunderkammer* at A. H. Francke's Protestant philanthropic foundations in Halle, Germany, featured conch shells, a Hindu idol, crocodiles (several embalmed and one hanging from the ceiling), and two man-sized solar-system models. Texts counted as collectibles too, as much for their exotic provenance as for their philological value; one shelf held a Chinese scroll placed next to an abacus and just above an Arabic manuscript dominated by an Ottoman sultan's *tughra* (official signature). The *Wunderkammer* was just one of the star attractions at Francke's massive orphanage/school/seminary/mission/pharmacy/print-shop complex (described in the next chapter).[24]

The *Wunderkammer*'s principle of collection was neither encyclopedic—systematically covering everything—nor microcosmic—giving a representative sample of everything from the world of nature, animal, vegetable, and mineral.[25] Collectors chose items specifically for their oddity. Here is a typical list: coral, automatic robots, unicorn horns, South American featherwork, coconut shell goblets, scientific instruments, fossils, antique coins, turned ivory, animal and human monsters, Turkish weaponry, polyhedral crystals, amethysts, a petrified human skull with coral growing out of it, Flemish landscape paintings, Mexican idols, Roman medals, a cyclops, embalmed baby alligators, an operating table, some tortoise shells, and some gold and silver goblets.[26] What could these "marvelous" objects possibly have in common? Collectively, they formed tent posts staking out the furthest boundaries of nature's prolific creation and stretching the spectator's imagination to encompass everything the Creator was capable of. Insofar as any theory or practice of synthesis could be said to undergird the new museum collections, it was that nature's promiscuity revealed more of its truths than manmade ordering schemes. More like the inspired anarchy of Callimachus's paradoxography than Aristotle's careful, systematic taxonomies of natural knowledge, *Wunderkammern* invited spectators to think for themselves about how the world was put together, and quite often to disregard what Aristotle had said about it.

Museums as books

In 1655, the four-volume *Museum Wormianum* of Ole Worm gained posthumous fame for this somewhat remote (Copenhagen-based) collector of, among other things, embryological specimens and Viking-era runic inscriptions. As Worm's title shows, the word "museum" could refer both to a place and to a book. Illustrated books functioned as the prime medium through which *virtuosi* and their *Wunderkammern* entered the Republic of Letters. Besides newfound wondrous objects, they publicized many physical sites where new knowledge of nature was gathered and produced: botanical gardens, anatomical theaters, and astronomical observatories, not to mention seafaring expeditions, the ultimate source of the world maps for which the early modern period is justly famous.[27] Print put the quadrivium on a par for the first time with the trivium: musical notation, astronomical charts, mathematical formulas, and geometric diagrams could now be reproduced just as easily, and just as reliably, as words on a page. Here again the technology of print revolutionized Europe's scholarly world, this time not through the mass production of texts but, via woodcuts and later copperplates, through the mass dissemination of images as well. One could hardly imagine a greater stimulus to the reimagination of nature than the confluence of overseas exploration, astronomical discoveries, and copperplate reproductions in early modern Europe.

But "published museums" raised an acute problem: having found out about them, scholars did not know exactly what to do with the piles of wonders accumulating in museum collections all over Europe. The temptation was to cram them awkwardly into traditional schemes, such as those derived from the Bible, Aristotle, and systems of occult wisdom—hieroglyphics, Pythagorean mysteries—shrouded in hazy antiquity. The German-born polymath Athanasius Kircher (1602–1680) attempted exactly this. Kircher sat like a spider at the center of the world's largest missionary and correspondence network in Rome, that of the Jesuits. There he constructed one of Europe's finest collections in the Roman College Museum. Drawing on its strengths in Egyptian and Chinese texts and artifacts, Kircher publicly claimed to have deciphered hieroglyphics and linked them to the equally challenging Chinese script. In the revealingly titled *China Illustrata*, he traced China's original settlers via Egyptian colonists back to Noah's son Cham and provided pictures to prove it.*[28] Certainly Kircher's mixture of new findings with biblical and Egyptian lore was greeted with skepticism even in its own day, but he was by no means exceptional. Hasty conclusions, credulousness toward marvels and wonders, and a penchant for premature system-building were the besetting vices of the museum collectors, who brought not only new objects but also new interpretive claims to the Republic of Letters.

Coping with the new

Collectors' enthusiasm put new knowledge of objects in conflict with the old authority vested in texts.[29] It was one thing to dissolve the authority of ancient synthesizers like Ptolemy, Pliny, and Aristotle, and quite another to begin offering new explanations of the natural world based on new discoveries. Textual scholars always based their conclusions on claims about texts verifiable by recourse to the manuscripts themselves, sitting in libraries. Observations of nature were prone to error, dependent on subjective sensory data, and given over to the flights of fantasy endemic to the study of wonders.

The many wonders that occurred outside museum walls—reports of an eighteen-year pregnancy or the appearance of mul-

---

*Kircher also got hold of "snakestones" from India, performed experiments on dogs to prove that they could suck venom out of snakebite wounds, and ascribed their wondrous powers to his pet theory that magnetic attractions lie at the heart of all natural phenomena.

tiple suns in the skies over southern France—only heightened these difficulties.[30] And what about wonders confected by human craft and invention, what we today call "experiment"? Early modern people could just as easily label these "magic" as "science." Who was to say that Giambattista della Porta's claims, in *Natural Magick*, to produce counterfeit gems or transmute lead into quicksilver were any less believable than Robert Boyle's famous air-pump experiment, which challenged the old saw that "nature abhors a vacuum" by suffocating a bird under a glass dome emptied of air? Under conditions of uncertainty, the English courtier Francis Bacon offered the only sensible prescriptions: focus on facts, reserve judgment, discipline your imagination, and resist the urge to theorize. The inductive or "scientific" method he developed raised the questions of how new knowledge could be legitimated, how bogus claims could be separated from verifiable ones, and how coarse facts could be smoothed into the general theoretical understandings that any ordered mind craves.

These were the kinds of questions increasingly asked at Europe's learned academies. Amid the flood of marvels, curiosities, and outright deceptions populating the woolly world of the early modern imagination, observers of nature had to cull the genuine breakthroughs and explore their implications.[31] Groups of *virtuosi,* first in Italy and then in France, England, and Germany, began to form themselves into academies, societies, conferences, and other, unnamed but regular groupings. Their published "transactions" and "proceedings," the ancestors of today's scholarly journals, brought their findings to international attention. Academies also included "corresponding members" to supplement those on site, which embedded them in the Republic of Letters. Scholars looked to these institutions to sift fact and truth from error and fraud, a task the Republic of Letters could not perform at a distance. By witnessing scientific experiments like the air pump firsthand, academicians confronted and tested claims to new knowledge through personal encounters. The modern scientific ideal of objectivity was developed in the European academy, not so much as a philosophical doctrine but as a method of dispassionate investigation. Even today, academies function less to promote creative thought than to give new achievements their imprimatur: witness the Royal Swedish Academy of Sciences, founded in 1739, which awards the Nobel Prize.

THE ACADEMY

As we have seen, the letter, the book, and the museum together reformed many practices of the university, the monastery, and the library and opened up new vistas for scholars. The Republic of Letters founded its legitimacy on these new institutions, which complemented yet often radically extended the old ones. But midnight correspondents, isolated and persecuted book authors, and eccentric collectors piling up stuff in curiosity cabinets could make for a very lonely scholarly universe. One other Renaissance institution, the academy, came about to put people in the same room, whether to witness scientific demonstrations, hear a lecture on Petrarch, participate in an experimental work of music, or debate agricultural reform schemes. With traditional intellectual authorities in retreat, laypeople took unprecedented initiative in founding these new communities of learning.

Literati *and* virtuosi

There were many usages of the term "academy" in early modern Europe; for convenience, we can distinguish two. One model hearkened back to ancient Athens: it was designed to teach young gentlemen and featured a humanist curriculum. The academy in this sense was interchangeable with the gymnasium (another Athenian institution) as a character-building alternative to university arts faculties. It is the ancestor of today's elite preparatory schools, still often called academies. The other, more relevant model—the one eventually absorbed by the Republic of Letters—was for *adult* gentlemen. It took its inspiration not so much from Plato's Academy as from the *academia* Cicero founded as a scholarly retreat for himself and other well-born friends at his luxurious country villa.[32] This form of academy provided a meeting ground for what Renaissance Italians called *literati,* men of letters.

Just as Cicero strove to put his rough native Latin on a plane with the Greek learning he respected so much, so the first academicians in Italy, a millennium and a half later, sought to elevate vernacular tongues to the stature of Cicero's own Latin. The Florentine Accademia della Crusca (still active today) produced Europe's first vernacular dictionary by systematically cataloging the words its members found in the great Florentine works of

Dante, Petrarch, and Boccaccio. Early modern academies were in fact the first European institutions to take native languages and vernacular literatures seriously and to place modern creative achievement on a par with that of the ancients. When possible, academicians translated Greco-Latin scholarship and philosophy into languages that sophisticated nonintellectuals could understand, such as Italian, French, and English. Like Cicero, the *literati* were linguistic nationalists and modernizers.

And just as Cicero saw his academy less as an educational center than as a refuge from his contentious life in the Senate and the law courts, so the early modern academicians sought an alternative to the Renaissance princely courts, the sites of pomp and ostentation, hierarchy and intrigue. The sixteenth-century Italian academies adopted names ostentatious only in their absurdity—the Dazed, the Enflamed, the Humid, the Confused, the Infatuated, the Elevated, the Somnolent—as if to highlight their disdain for and detachment from the mundane world. Self-mocking names also deflected suspicions of conspiracy or sedition that watchful rulers, like the Medicis or the Habsburgs, might have conceived toward these private meetings. Not only could learned gentlemen socialize for the first time in them as equals outside court settings, they could collaborate with university professors who were disaffected with scholasticism (or perhaps just the callowness of youths) and with university graduates who were unenthusiastic about embarking on careers as notaries or lawyers. Some academies even included literate artisans and merchants in their midst.[33]

By the 1600s, academies had evolved into a sort of halfway house between the princely court and the Republic of Letters. In them the *virtuoso* shed his reputation as a showman jockeying for favor at court for the image of a serious *literatus*. Courtiers were addicted to marvels and wonders, magic tricks and scored dances, costume dramas and fireworks displays, improvised poetry and parades of dwarves. Academicians brought textual scholarship, craft skill, and a measure of intellectual gravitas to these traditional spectacles and entertainments. Thus Italian opera originated when courtiers, musicians, stage designers, instrument makers, and mathematicians with a knowledge of harmony teamed up in various academic and quasi-academic venues to revive what they thought was the sung drama of the ancient Greeks, extolled by Plato and Pythagoras for its miraculous effects on the soul. French ballet took its inspiration from a similar Neoplatonic academy constituted at the height of the wars of religion, literally to orchestrate the reconciliation of hostile Protestants and Catholics through participation in graceful movements mimicking the harmonies of the cosmic spheres. (After Catholics massacred Protestants in Paris on St. Bartholomew's Day, 1572, one could say that the effort had largely failed.)[34]

Even those academies that became renowned for their scientific rigor—the Lincei ("Lynx-eyed") in Rome, the Cimento ("Experiment") in Florence, and the Parisian Academy of Sciences—descended from venues organized to test recipes for natural magic and other esoteric phenomena. In them, the

Renaissance magus graduated from lone speculation to the collective, disciplined investigation of natural phenomena. The famous London Royal Society counted many occultists, alchemists—Isaac Newton, for example—and freemasons in its number. In an era before science had produced the fantastic results that would later make it self-sustaining, those who scrutinized nature's mysteries needed some other reason to believe that their experiments would yield insight. Early academies gave them this, promising that organized "natural philosophy" would eventually reveal God's truths, perhaps even a "primordial theology" underlying and reconciling Europe's, and the world's, divergent religions. For obvious reasons this was an exciting proposition to men of affairs in the Republic of Letters.[35]

We now call a question "academic" when it bears no relation to the real world. But these examples prove that early modern academicians, even when pedantry got the better of them, always aimed to captivate people of stature and influence, to educate and entertain them at the same time. Academies grounded the Republic of Letters in the social life of European elites. Their growth highlights the increasing role of gentlemen—and, originally at least, gentlewomen—in the production of knowledge.

Ladies and gentlemen

Owing to their origins in European court culture, which always featured mixed company, many early academies in France and Italy welcomed women. Catherine de' Medici was instrumental in establishing the Parisian academy that pioneered ballet, and her relative Eleonora di Toledo counted as the only female member of the Florentine Academy of the "Altered." (The Medicis may rightly be called the Ptolemies of early modern Europe.) The closer they stood to modern science, however, the more women felt themselves pushed aside. Margaret Cavendish was excluded from London Royal Society meetings despite her accomplishments in natural science and close connections to many of its members; her science fiction tellingly included a Female Academy as an imagined alternative to the all-male venues she encountered in real life. Maria Winkelmann, an amateur astronomer who accumulated enough scientific knowledge to discover a comet in 1702, was likewise held at arm's length by the Berlin Academy of Sciences.[36]

A fissure between literary and scholarly pursuits, and in particular between the classical arts of fine expression and the serious business of empirical science, was opening up in the Republic of Letters, and men and women fell on opposite sides of it. By the early eighteenth century, the only academies welcoming women were the branches of the Italian Arcadia movement, which focused on improvisational poetry. Women in France had also begun to gather star intellects in conversational salons in their homes, unnofficial settings that coalesced as alternatives to increasingly stuffy and conservative royal academies.[37] But the very institutions they chafed at—the Académie des Sciences, the Académie Française, and other state academies still active today—were precisely what scholars in the Republic of Letters demanded. It was their stodgy, official quality, whether as royal appendages in France or as redoubts of independent male sobriety in England, that made the scientific academies the guarantors of credibility. Academies acted as the tribunals of the Republic of Letters, in the terminology of this chapter's epigraph. Only in them could academicians manage face-to-face the acrimonious disputes—on the interpretation of the air-pump experiment, for example—that would otherwise threaten to tear the Republic of Letters apart.[38] And only gentlemen enjoyed the social standing to grant an academic imprimatur to new discoveries. Trading on the honor and impartiality of the wellborn, academies functioned increasingly to validate new knowledge before the international community of scholars. No one, it was said, could gainsay the word of a gentleman; his witness testimony was felt to be theoretically beyond reproach.[39] The same simply could not be said of money-grubbing artisans or middle-class social climbers—or gullible women.

Academies vs. shuyuan

Like Cicero and even Plato himself, academicians retreated from the world and devoted themselves to the pursuit of knowledge but never lost the aim of reentering and reshaping social life. But one key difference separates the early modern European academy movement from its ancient inspirations. Read the chapter epigraph again: it sets a clear distance between the world of power and the world of knowledge. Scholars in the Republic of Letters purchased their intellectual freedom at the cost of acquiescing to whatever form of political regime they happened to find themselves living under. Socrates drank hemlock rather than compromise his intellectual integrity before political persecution. Plato envisioned a republic ruled by philosopher-kings, and his Academy placed its alumni in positions of influence throughout the Greek-speaking world.[40] Cicero heroically upheld the centrality of fine speech and Latin learning to political virtue even as his beloved republic died at Caesar's hands. But early modern academies enjoyed a choice that Cicero and the others did not have: they could join a virtual Republic of Letters, thriving on the discussion of new knowledge, rather than do battle in real politics against the encroachments of dictatorship and absolutism. How else could academicians proclaim themselves citizens of an international "republic" and not be taken as an organized political conspiracy?

The notion that the academies might have groomed Platonic philosopher-kings or Ciceronian republicans rather than apolitical *virtuosi* is not all that farfetched. The Italian Jesuit missionary Matteo Ricci (1552–1610) found institutions in contemporary Ming dynasty China that did exactly that. Chinese academies, called *shuyuan*, served mainly to prepare students for the empire's hypercompetitive civil service examinations. Ricci might logically have called these groupings universities, but instead he dubbed one an *accademia di letterati,* after similar literary gatherings in his homeland.[41] And he was right to do so: Chinese academies acted as key nodes in an empire-wide Republic of Letters, attracting local gentlemen to topical lectures, sponsoring traveling scholars from elsewhere in the empire, and using published books, handwritten letters, and personal contacts to circulate moralistic critiques of state policy anchored in rereadings of the Confucian classics.[42]

The most famous Chinese academy, the Donglin Academy (founded in 1604) in the heavily urbanized Yangzi River delta, used the examination system to pack the imperial bureaucracy with its brightest graduates. Alumni in the Donglin faction then took on the famously corrupt eunuch official Wei Zhongxian (1568–1627), and many of its leaders ultimately suffered martyrdom at his hands.[43] But not even a capricious absolutism could stop Chinese *literati* from reforming the state. Later imitators of the Donglin Academy significantly named themselves the Restoration Society (founded in 1629), reflecting their desire to apply ancient Confucian teachings to contemporary policy problems. Constituting themselves as an empire-wide pressure group, they bullied official examiners into accepting the Restoration Society's own publications as the de facto standard for grading candidates' examinations and thus deciding who would enter the civil service. By the mid-1600s, a literary public sphere of a size and power comparable to Europe's was challenging the government for the right to control intellectual standards.[44] After the Manchu invasions toppled the Ming dynasty, many of these scholar-gentlemen mobilized local communities to mount heroic (and ultimately futile) resistance against the foreigners.[45] Neither the Donglin martyrs nor the Ming loyalists had any parallel in early modern Europe: it is inconceivable that a group of learned gentlemen there would have mounted open and organized resistance, to the point of martyrdom, using academic institutions as their base of operations and intellectual critique.*

Ancient China, ancient Greece, and ancient Rome had all but equated the instruction of youth with the need to prepare students for civic responsibilities, emphasizing the importance of moral education over practical skills. In the early modern period, humanists in both Europe and China (where Neo-Confucians staged a similar classical revival) sought to make learning and comportment, not just birth and bloodlines, the measure of a man and the basis for an active life in politics and society. (The Chinese, however hierarchical, even celebrated the few peasants who by dint of miraculous self-application rose up to become mandarins through success in the examination system.) All looked for guidance to their respective ancients as paragons of knowledge and virtue.

Academies of various stripes served this function in both societies, but *literati* developed in radically different relations to political power in the two cultures. In Ming China, scholars reaffirmed the authority of ancient texts as a basis for criticizing an imperial government vested with theoretically absolute power. In early modern Europe, scholars reached for the authority of gentlemen, princes, courts, and kings in order to validate new

---

*An influential strain of interpretation in French Revolution historiography offers one limited counterexample, holding that modern Europe's most famous revolutionary upheaval was prepared by quasi-academic institutions like Masonic lodges and the French *sociétés de pensée*.

knowledge not sanctioned by ancient texts. In neither case could scholars have their cake and eat it too. Chinese gentlemen were as worldly, literate, and curious as their European counterparts, and with the Jesuits bringing European discoveries to them, and to the imperial court, they had ample opportunity to abandon themselves to the pursuit of new science.[46] But they elected to remain faithful to the Confucian classics and thereby retain the political influence this granted them. By contrast, Europeans achieved unprecedented breakthroughs in astronomy, physics, anatomy, and natural history but at the cost of abandoning politics and constructing an imaginary Republic of Letters that thrived in the midst of unprecedented violence and chaos. Europe's *literati* melded with its *virtuosi*, but both left behind the specifically Ciceronian virtue that came from the study of letters. Ever since then, scholarship, humanistic and scientific alike, has aimed at finding "objective" truth and producing new knowledge rather than cultivating character.

5

The Disciplines

1700–1900

EVANGELICAL PROTESTANTS AND SECULAR HUMANISTS
COMBINED TO CREATE THE FIRST NATIONAL SYSTEM OF
MASS PUBLIC EDUCATION, AND WITH IT A NEW MARKET
FOR ACADEMIC SPECIALTIES.

THE ENLIGHTENMENT produced the West's first mass market for knowledge and with it the specialization of intellectual labor we call the disciplines. No less a free marketeer than Adam Smith explained the connection. Writing in *The Wealth of Nations* (1776), Smith argued that the "subdivision of employment in philosophy, as well as in every other business, improves dexterity, and saves time." Knowledge he saw as a commodity, its production a form of industrial labor, its progress additive and cumulative. As "each individual becomes more expert in his own peculiar branch, more work is done upon the whole, and the quantity of science is thereby increased."[1] Disciplines, to Smith, were an artifact of scholars' seeking a niche in the marketplace of ideas. This cheery capitalist vision comported well with the modern, secular, competitive arena the Republic of Letters had become by the eighteenth century.

By Smith's time, some of Europe's most market-savvy intellectuals had taken on the effort to collect, organize, and disseminate knowledge from the Republic of Letters. Despite widespread censorship, publishers catalyzed an eighteenth-century "reading revolution" enveloping all social classes in widening literacy. Enlightenment thinkers therefore put their faith in the written word to bring useful knowledge to a mass readership. Significantly, they wrote in vernaculars, which soon overtook Latin as languages of scholarship. Ephraim Chambers, writing in English, and Pierre Bayle, writing in French, compiled encyclopedias, dictionaries, and newsletters to popularize discoveries from the various branches of learning. The creators of the best-selling French *Encyclopédie* gathered together all the arts, sciences, and even crafts in 71,818 articles. Among its 2,885 copperplate engravings were diagrams showing how to build a mine and assemble a clock. Entries were arranged not by subject but alphabetically, from A to Z, with an elaborate system of cross-references that invited readers to piece together information through leaps of common sense. Of all the books produced between 1500 and 2000, none aimed more sincerely to "assemble all knowledge scattered on the surface of the Earth," in the words of its coeditor, Denis Diderot.[2] Encyclopedias were only the most prominent among many new genres meant to commercialize Enlightenment for the people, including newspapers, journals, intelligencers, almanacs, travelogues, and even novels. Think of Benjamin Franklin, the humble print-shop typesetter, self-educated through voracious reading, who made a famously profitable career publishing his practical wisdom and inventions.

Yet the trumpeters of print capitalism never succeeded in replacing the hierarchy that attends face-to-face learning. Seekers of knowledge today do not simply furnish themselves with a set of quality encyclopedias and venture forth into the world. They must instead submit to years and years of schooling. Top acolytes consecrate their careers to particular fields of research, such as history, chemistry, and psychology. In a surprising rebuke to the bellwethers of laissez-faire in Western Europe, it was underdeveloped, impoverished Germany, at the moment of its defeat by Napoleon, that put the disciplines atop the world's first comprehensive systems of universal, public, compulsory education. The German research university, now imitated from Boston to Beijing, made professors into secular high priests. Its lecture halls capitalized on the simplicity and economy of classroom learning to compete for the best scholars and students. Its seminar rooms cultivated the intense master-disciple relations from which specialized disciplines grew. German states, which funded schools staffed by university graduates, led the Western world in assuming responsibility from religious organizations for reproducing culture in each generation.

Nineteenth-century nationalists congratulated themselves for using public education to forge unified cultures out of societies fragmented by religion, ethnicity, and class. But the conditions that made this possible first arose in a very different quarter, in the pious counterculture of eighteenth-century evangelical Protestantism. Protestants in Germany made intensive scrutiny of scripture, not casual thumbing through encyclopedias, the cornerstone for what became a universal program of methodical discipline. Secular humanists then coopted their methods to build systems of higher and lower education for rising nation-states. In

this way a true mass market for knowledge could finally arise—
one soon peopled, just as Smith predicted, by specialists in every
conceivable field of learning. Still, even today, each of the disciplines
retains a sectarian cast, long after shedding a religious orientation.
Insulated groups driven by their own questions and methods, they
make the production of new research an end in itself, often with
little regard for fitting it into the wider world of learning.

DISCIPLINE AS METHOD: THE SEMINAR

Faust, the quintessential seeker of knowledge, first appears in
Goethe's poetic drama lamenting the uselessness and pedantry of
"Philosophy, Law, Medicine, and—what is worst—Theology,"
the four faculties of the medieval university. Imprisoned in
an "accursed, musty hole of stone" dimmed by stained glass,
"restricted by this great mass of books that worms consume," he
turns to magic, makes a pact with the devil, and beguiles and
betrays a pious girl. Faust ends his life as a developer reclaiming
land from the sea, in what is often seen as an allegory of technological modernity in its triumph over traditional learning.[3]

Europe's universities indeed counted among the last places
most Enlightenment figures looked for the rejuvenation of knowledge. Oxford and Cambridge were best known for polishing the
manners of young gentlemen and sending them on to more serious
pursuits. The Sorbonne in Paris was vastly outshone by France's
royally endowed learned academies and private aristocratic
salons. In the German-dominated Holy Roman Empire, with its
three-hundred-odd independent states and statelets, specialized

vocational institutes vied for careerist up-and-comers, while private finishing schools with equestrian pretensions siphoned off many of its aristocratic scions. Indiscipline and immorality abounded at its traditional universities. Jena (which Goethe helped supervise) attracted the rowdy, alcoholic sort, its students "waving glasses, guzzling, vomiting, kissing maidens, screaming, running off to the villages, and dueling." One group, a self-anointed Faculty of Beer, held mock disputations and awarded the winners a *Doctor cerevisiae et vini.* Unpopular professors might have their windows smashed by crowds of irate students. In one case a teacher was physically assaulted for giving boring lectures.[4]

The story of how Germany led the world into the age of modern scholarship thus counts among the most stunning reversals in the history of knowledge. It begins with two new university foundations, at Halle in 1694 and at Göttingen in 1737. What distinguished each, for our purposes, was a new institution, the seminar: an island of discipline amid the chaos and confusion of university life. Originating at Halle in the need to produce religious teachers for a strict program of universal education, the seminar evolved at Göttingen to train professional researchers in the pagan classics. By the time it migrated back to Halle, the seminar had become a model for other fields of learning, a seedbed for the disciplines.

Piety and profit at Halle

Prussia, Germany's most aggressively expanding state, opened its flagship university at Halle to lure students from rival Protestant institutions in neighboring Saxony, Luther's homeland. Halle's Seminarium praeceptorum was founded just two years later. Best regarded not as a seminar but as a seminary, it offered up to 130 needy theology students room and board—and a chance at upward mobility—in exchange for teaching local schoolchildren to read the Bible and other basics. The Halle seminar was undistinguished in its scholarly production. It nonetheless forged a novel and critical link between higher and lower education, tying Halle's university to the massive missionary complex created by the Pietist social reformer August Hermann Francke (1663–1727). Francke transformed what had been a decaying salt-mining town into a New Jerusalem, its nerve center a walled cluster of over forty buildings dominated by imposing Baroque edifices.

Pietists recoiled from the sterile doctrine and drab style of worship found in the traditional Lutheran church and instead gathered in private circles to pore over the Bible and experience scripture directly and emotionally. They shared with other evangelical Protestants, like Puritans and early Methodists, a severe moral code, a desire to uplift the poor, and a missionary impulse. The drive to discipline informed every aspect of the Pietist educational project. After Francke became a pastor in Glaucha, a village near Halle, he found that there were fully thirty-seven taverns for its two hundred residents. He began by clamping down on vices like drinking and Sunday dancing. He then established a charity school where orphans were taught the four R's: reading, writing, arithmetic, and religion.[5] Among Francke's

pedagogical innovations, all too familiar today, were the class roster, to compel daily attendance, and recess, which left the rest of
the schoolday free for work. Other Pietists invented the practice
of raising hands to ask questions and the arrangement of classroom desks in rows. Their approach became so famous that pros-
perous, respectable burghers and even noblemen from other parts
of central Europe were soon clamoring for their own (separate)
schools, for girls as well as for boys. Latin schools for the elite,
plus grammar schools for the poor and orphaned, soon sprouted
up at Halle and beyond. The Halle Seminarium furnished theology students with good Christian morals to staff them.

"Behold, a *Seed of Piety*, & of Pure Christianity, which is the
Kingdom of God in the true Essence, and Glory of it, Quickened
& Expanding in the Bowels of *Germany*."[6] So wrote the archetypical Harvard Puritan Cotton Mather, envious in then provincial Boston of Francke's rapidly expanding foundations. By the
1720s, the Halle complex included, besides schools for several
thousand students, a library, a *Wunderkammer*, a hospital, a free
dining hall for the poor, and dormitories for indigent women
(whether widowed or fallen). Missionaries from Halle could
soon be found from wintry Siberia to tropical Malabar, in India.
The engine of all this growth was profit. Capitalizing on generous donations from the faithful and on tax breaks from the
Prussian government, Francke erected a pharmaceutical factory
and a printing press to further fund his philanthropic enter-
prises. His agents bought sugar, tea, and coffee for resale in
Venice and at Dutch East India Company auctions in Amster-

dam, shipped ironware and glassware up the Elbe River toward the North Sea port at Hamburg, conducted wholesale trade in Pomeranian livestock and Russian grain, and harnessed orphan labor to manufacture linens, stockings, and especially medicines, such as *essentia dulcis*, a gold tincture marketed as a cure for various nervous ailments. If ever there was a place where the Protestant work ethic yoked pious devotion to capitalist industriousness—a factor overlooked by Adam Smith—the Francke Foundations were it.[7]

Above all, Halle's Bible-printing operations testified to this link. In the course of the 1700s, the bookshop at Halle sold nearly 3 million Bibles in various formats and translations, particularly into the Slavic languages. Cheap editions marketed en masse turned ready profits. Despite their distaste for stifling Lutheran orthodoxy, the Halle Pietists relied on Luther's Bible to spread the word of God. Francke, who held a theology chair at Halle University in addition to his pastoral and entrepreneurial duties, might have been expected to quail at this. Recall that Christian scripture had never been a watertight canon but instead a perennial site of theological contestation. Luther's German translation had its flaws, as did the Latin version of the Greek New Testament, somewhat hastily prepared by Erasmus, on which it rested. In the late 1600s an English scholar had gone back to the original Greek manuscripts and catalogued over 30,000 discrepancies among the various versions of the New Testament. In Catholic France, theologians argued that this simply validated their claim that the one true church, not the fal-

libly transcribed books of the Bible, offered the only sure guidance to the faithful.[8] But—initially, at least—none of this fazed
the Halle Pietists, who cared more for the emotional impact of
scripture than the correctness and precision of its wording.

Of greater concern was the threat from apparently godless
philosophers teaching at the local university. The Pietists' most
celebrated target was Christian Wolff, a professor with close ties
to G. W. Leibniz, the polymath who coinvented calculus and
who discerned in Jesuit reports on the Chinese *I Ching* an ancient
forerunner of the binary arithmetic he had devised. On July 12,
1721, Wolff gave a lecture titled "On Chinese Practical Philosophy," extolling the ethical genius and rational precepts of the
Confucian classics. Francke's interest was piqued by the chance
to make inroads in China against Jesuit missionaries, but he and
the rest of the theological faculty took vehement exception to
Wolff's implication that Chinese heathens might have attained
moral perfection without the benefit of Christ.[9] After more than
two years of machinations, Wolff's enemies procured a royal
edict exiling him from Prussian territory—and giving him only
forty-eight hours to leave.

Wolff landed on his feet at another university, and even
returned to Halle after Frederick the Great, Prussia's new,
enlightened despot, vindicated him in 1740. But his expulsion in
1723 exposed Halle Pietism's prior commitment to an international religious counterculture to the Republic of Letters. Its
university had ruptured, notoriously, with Germany's most
famous Enlightenment philosopher. The intellectual challenge of

reconciling scriptural authority with the Enlightenment's secular rationalism was left unanswered. It fell to individual scholars both at Halle and elsewhere, all of them pious but some of them lapsed Pietists, to take up this problem. Only at Göttingen would the painstaking methods of close reading they developed to solve it come to fruition.

Göttingen: a living encyclopedia

Johann David Michaelis (1717–1791) embodied the connection between Halle and Göttingen and the mixture of new scholarly methods that bridged the two. Teaching at Göttingen from 1745 until his death, Michaelis directed its seminar for only one year, in 1762–1763, as an interim figure between two famous classicists. But his career laid the basis for a rapprochement between Pietism and the Republic of Letters. Their potent institutional fusion in a new seminar made the inculcation of schoolteachers serve the broader progress of secular knowledge.

Michaelis came from a notable family of Halle Pietists. His father graduated from the Seminarium praeceptorum. His uncle directed yet another of Francke's creations, the Collegium Orientale theologicum, whose forte was training in eastern languages. Both the modern tongues spoken by peoples to be missionized in the East, like Polish, Persian, and Chinese, and those from the ancient Near East, like Chaldean, Syriac, and Ethiopian, mainly of scholarly interest, found a place in its brief. The collegium thus signaled an underlying commitment to pure scholarship blossoming in the shadow of the worldly, practical, profitable Francke Foundations. Johann David, for his part, wrote his Halle university dissertation on the eminently pedantic subject of vowel points in ancient Hebrew. (Recall that like Arabic, Hebrew was originally written without separate vowels, leading to many problems in interpreting scripture.)

Michaelis also absorbed the new Pietist theology, which had begun, belatedly, to revisit the Bible with a sustained critical eye. The Pietists bucked a trend toward "extensive" reading inaugurated by the media revolution of the Enlightenment. While country lawyers reclined with encyclopedias and maidservants devoured cheap novels—reading a lot, but superficially—the scholarly devout attended to a precious body of texts ever more *intensively*. The New Testament naturally became the first object of scrutiny. Vexed by the 30,000 discrepancies in the manuscripts, scholars began the exacting task of reconstructing the original Greek text, imitating but also surpassing what the Alexandrians had done to resurrect Homer. Working far from Halle, in Pietist Württemberg, J. A. Bengel pioneered a technique, still de rigueur among scholars, of arranging manuscripts by family, grouping those with common errors to figure out who had (mis)copied what from whom. And to establish which of two alternative readings was older and more authentic, Bengel developed the counterintuitive principle that the more difficult reading was probably the correct one: ancient and medieval scribes were more likely to err deliberately, simplifying the style and improving the flow of a text, than to interpolate changes that made it more complicated.[10]

Michaelis was steeped in these methods, but he longed to escape the text—to bring knowledge from history, archeology, and the exploration of nature to bear on his studies. A trip in his midtwenties to Europe's cosmopolitan Protestant centers, England and Holland, broadened his horizons. A few years after his return, he was therefore eager to leave Halle, take up a position at Göttingen, and get a breath of intellectual fresh air after the dourness and severity of his hometown. Located in north-central Germany at a crossroads of regional trade, Göttingen had ample space and amenities and was otherwise conveniently unprepossessing—a main reason it was selected to become an outpost of academic openness and freedom.[11]

Göttingen was founded as Hanover's state university to compete with Prussia's Halle and to act as a magnet for aristocrats from all over Europe—and for their money. The Hanoverian rulers, better known as the kings of Great Britain by this time, instituted a liberal, cosmopolitan atmosphere to attract cultured young gentlemen. Courses in horseback riding and fencing were part of this marketing strategy, but so too, more substantively, were English-style freedoms of expression and publication unrivaled by those in other German states. English business sense also figured prominently in their calculations. Monarchs everywhere saw universities as investments for monetary returns and international prestige, but Göttingen truly functioned as a "big business firm for scholarship," in the words of a contemporary. It paid high salaries to woo top scholars from other universities, who often had to break oaths of fidelity to their native rulers and vanish in the night. (One Professor Schmauss duped the officials in Halle into thinking he was moving across town and then darted over the border toward Göttingen with all his worldly posssessions.)[12] A policy of "academic mercantilism" required professors to write their own textbooks so the state did not have to hemorrhage hard currency to publishers across the border. The university's lecture catalog was published in the widely disseminated *Göttingen Learned Newspaper*. The intellectual wares listed therein were grouped not by traditional faculty but by modern-sounding subject titles like "applied mathematics," "theory of civil procedure," and "osteology," all with the aim of enticing readers. "Psychological-moral" readings of the New Testament alternated, sportingly, with lectures on "anti-deistic theology," Turkish statistics and mineralogy with canon law and heraldry.[13] Introductory lectures were called "encyclopedias," syntheses of various fields of learning packaged for the convenience and edification of students, who came and went as they pleased.[14] Göttingen was quite literally a living encyclopedia.

Ensconced at the most dynamic university in Europe, a microcosm of the Republic of Letters itself, Michaelis made Bible scholarship equally encyclopedic. What we now call "lower" criticism, the scrutiny and reconstruction of ancient texts, yielded in his hands to "higher" criticism, the systematic exploration of the *contexts* in which such writings were produced.[15] In particular, the Old Testament, longer, richer, more complicated, and more ancient than the New, came into its own. It opened a window onto an entire culture, more alluring to Michaelis's increasingly secular mind than the four maddeningly discrepant gospel accounts. In approaching the Old Testament, Michaelis again drew on his Pietist background. Halle professors had begun to articulate a radical new vision of the Bible as a human cultural product, not as the unerring transcription of God's eternal word. God "accommodated" his utterances, they argued, to the historically limited intellectual and expressive abilities of the people whom he first chose for his revelations. Modern scholars, then, by attending to all the differences separating ancient Hebrews from modern Europeans, could surgically extract the heart of his message—the keys to salvation transcending space and time—from the peculiarities of its linguistic and cultural expression in the recorded scriptures.[16]

The best way to do this, Michaelis concluded, was to send an expedition to the Holy Land, to confront the strangeness and unfamiliarity of the world depicted in the Bible firsthand. Recruiting support from the king of Denmark, he sent a multinational team of researchers to southern Arabia, to what is now Yemen, where he believed ancient Near Eastern nature and culture were best preserved. The group included a Danish philologist, a Swedish botanist, a German engineer, a Danish doctor, and a German illustrator. No detail, however small, escaped their attention. Thus, to test John the Baptist's disconcerting culinary recommendation, in Matthew 3:4, that locusts be eaten with wild honey, they confirmed that modern-day Arabs did in fact roast and dry or boil and salt them, adding that the Arabs were just as put off by Christians' fondness for shellfish. Information on matters botanical (Arabian flora), anthropological (native cooking and farming implements), linguistic (Yemeni dialect), and even herpetological (a desert snake) was collected.[17] For all of its scholarly success, the mission was a personal tragedy: of the five scholars sent forth, only the engineer, Carsten Niebuhr, made it back alive. But the expedition was utterly in keeping with the spirit of the Republic of Letters, and a brilliant companion to the more famous naturalist ocean voyages that sent men like Captain Cook to the South Pacific.

Philology: the first discipline

Finally we come to Göttingen's Seminarium philologicum, the university's most important contribution to the history of the disciplines. Its subject matter was taken neither from the New Testament nor the Old but from the Roman and especially Greek classics. The latter still provided the traditional curriculum for gentlemen in the Republic of Letters.

Founded in 1738 (just after the university that housed it), Göttingen's seminar modeled itself directly on Halle's precedent. Despite the shift from biblical to classical content, it shared with Halle the aim of training schoolteachers. Indoctrination—the molding of character and conscience, the quintessentially Pietist gift to the life of the mind—remained its central pedagogical goal. Göttingen's seminar pedagogy aimed to reshape the inner person, not to fashion cookie-cutter gentlemen by drilling them, as was customary, to ape Cicero or Pericles in their outward manners and speech. Instead the Göttingen classicists instilled in their students a deeply internalized sense of what it meant to think like an ancient pagan.

In keeping with its secular orientation, the Seminarium philologicum resided in the arts, not the theology, faculty. The Latinized Greek word "philology" replaced the function of training "preceptors" in the Halle seminar. Philology denotes the love of words, which at Göttingen became a love disciplined by communal attention to revered texts—the secular version of Pietist Bible study. Previously, students in classical languages had simply memorized a "chaos of words and phrases, rules and exceptions, elegances and barbarisms" to pepper their discourse while the "other intellectual powers slumbered comfortably." Such knowledge could be dispensed in lectures. Now, however, instruction in Greek and Latin aimed to simulate native language acquisition.[18] This could take place only in a seminar setting, where participants gathered to work through a difficult classical writer. A variety of format changes enlivened these lessons and elevated their scholarly tenor. The hierarchy of the medieval disputation, where masters often literally stood on elevated platforms above their students, gave way to the "circular disputation," wherein discussants sat around a table together as equals. Students took turns as "directors for a day," gaining classroom experience by emulating the professor. They were expected to deliver original presentations based on novel research rather than parrot the shopworn arguments of their predecessors. Often they picked their own topics instead of having them assigned by the professor. Peer pressure and competition for professorial approval induced them to take on the most difficult research problems and tackle them assiduously. All this compelled students to prepare their essays beforehand: written scholarship became a new gold standard for disciplined scholarship in the face-to-face settting of the seminar.[19]

Such rigor held a special appeal for middle-class students wanting to become schoolteachers, and perhaps to rise to something more. The philological seminar catered to this upwardly striving clientele, typically recruited from the bookish sons of the pastorate. At a university where they were surrounded by aristocrats, the philological seminar offered aspiring commoners the chance to surpass the grace and comportment of their social superiors. The pedantry that marked seminarists as awkward in the company of noblemen could now be deployed in the service of mastering their own classical models. Nor did they have to compromise their career prospects in the process. The philological seminar satisfied their material and psychological needs at once, by *identifying* classical scholarship with the practical skills needed for the teaching profession. A belief in ascent through talent became its ideology, rooted in a neohumanist (re)reading of the ancient Greek achievement. Thus the Göttingen seminar disbursed its scholarships on the basis of merit, not need, as had been the case at Halle. Statutory mechanisms were put in place to expel lazy and unmotivated students. Discipline in both its senses, scholastic focus and behavioral conditioning, came together for the first time in the Seminarium philologicum.

The birth of classical philology as the first discipline can be dated precisely: to 1776, when Friedrich August Wolf (1759–1824) insisted on enrolling at Göttingen neither in arts nor in theology but as a "student of philology." (This was the same year, incidentally, that Smith published *The Wealth of Nations*.) Göttingen's seminar director, the eminent classicist Christian Gottlob Heyne, perceived this as an act of hubris so Wolf never joined as a formal member. He got along much better with Michaelis, whose use of the Old Testament to tap into Hebrew culture Wolf adapted to the study of classical antiquity. But unlike Michaelis, Wolf determined not to supplement text with context—sending archeologists to the Parthenon, for example—but to submerge himself completely in the minute details of the documents themselves.[20] This harmonized beautifully with the approach then being taught in the Göttingen seminar: it required few monetary resources, no connections to royal patrons, no globetrotting inclinations. Wolf's method could be practiced anywhere. So when Prussia lured him to Halle in 1783, he famously reintroduced seminar education to its place of birth. Active from 1787 to 1806, Wolf's seminar trained a whole generation of classicists. His move to the citadel of Pietism betokened a triumph for the Greek neohumanist revival then sweeping literature, culture, and architecture all over Germany.

At Halle, Wolf took scholarship further back than it had ever been: before Cicero's Latin, before Socrates' Greek even, and all the way back to Homer, who ostensibly represented Hellenic culture in its most primitive genius and truest, most original form. Wolf's 1795 book, the *Prolegomena to Homer*, scandalized the learned establishment by arguing that we will never possess the original epics of the blind bard we call Homer. The texts we know as the *Iliad* and the *Odyssey* were instead the products of centuries of manuscript accretions. At best we can restore the composite edition produced by the philologists of Hellenistic Alexandria. But by peeling back the layers of accumulated manuscript corruptions, Wolf argued, scholars could also do something better: reconstruct the historic culture of archaic Greece from which the epic poems descend.

In its aims, this project owed clear debts to Michaelis, but in his methods, Wolf replaced the ethnographic and naturalistic study of the present with a determination to grapple with the strangeness of the past. Immersion in history depended in turn on another counterintuitive insight: that focusing on errors, inconsistencies, and anachronisms in texts yields something more precious than the "original" manuscript. Such a method produced new insights—better even than restoring an old classic. For example, in 1793, Wolf corresponded with a colleague, the future educational reformer Wilhelm von Humboldt, about whether, in Book XIII, line 257 of the *Iliad*, the word κατεάξαμεν might have been mistranscribed as κατεαξάμην in the documents handed down to us.[21] Two simple changes of accent and vowel would have shifted the meaning from singular to plural and thereby implied that a minor hero named Meriones had fought with a personal retinue instead of alone. A numbingly detailed comparison with similar case endings elsewhere in the poem was needed to pin down just how individualistic the Homeric hero was supposed to have been. Why care about such a pedantic piece of linguistic detective work? Because it reveals details of a lost world revered as the standard for all human values, and, if such work is pursued for every word in the *Iliad*, it produces a mosaic reconstruction of that world.

By pulverizing dry texts in this way, Wolf undertook a voyage in the mind far more profound than any ocean journey. It offered him and his disciples intuitive access to the spoken tongue lurking beneath the written text. Homer and his contemporaries were illiterate rhapsodists, after all. But their very language was the fount of later Greek genius. As Humboldt put it, "A language so rounded as the Homeric must already have long journeyed to and fro on the waves of song, throughout ages of which no record now remains to us." The genius of Greek, in other words, predated even Homer. "Language is an involuntary emanation of the mind, no work of nations, but a gift fallen to them by their inner destiny."[22] From this it followed that methodical, even mechanical training in language imparts to the student the genius inherent in that language. With sufficient diligence, discipline, and practice, any seminar novice could convert himself into a critical thinker. Instead of merely imitating the genius of the ancients, the scholar could now tap the wellsprings of that genius, the ultimate source of what was later called Western civilization.

In fashioning a program of training for the mind, philologists could finally claim to have improved upon the wide-ranging but ultimately superficial self-education peddled by the encyclopedists. Only a vanishingly small number of print consumers—perhaps Benjamin Franklin alone—had the self-discipline to make their own contributions to the Republic of Letters. Pietist pedagogy made intensive reading in classroom settings routine, but at the cost of adopting a provincial and sectarian mindset. The classical philology seminar combined the best of both worlds. Wolf's students imbibed the modern, secular, research-oriented mission of the Republic of Letters precisely through painstaking scholarship in ancient Greek. His critical methods enabled them to join the culture of the people who invented philosophy. Beyond how Cicero spoke, beyond what Jesus said, beyond what Homer sang, philology revealed how cultures think, collectively and creatively. Having acquired critical thinking skills through language study, devotees of philology could then tackle other problems—indeed, any problem, to the minds of the neohumanists. Scholarship had finally replaced scripture as the ultimate source of human knowledge.

SPECIALIZATION: PANDITS VS. PROFESSORS

The philological seminar had been spawned by the interstate competition that drove Halle and Göttingen to outdo each other. By the end of the nineteenth century, academic politicking would make Germany the undisputed world leader in a whole series of specialties hived off from or modeled upon it. But before this could happen, real politics made a very nasty intrusion. On July 14, 1789, two years after Wolf founded his seminar, a Parisian mob stormed the Bastille, starting the French Revolution. In 1792, France became the first nation to export liberty at the barrel of a gun, marching east and southeast to free Germans and Italians from petty dictatorships. The hero of the Italian wars, Napoleon Bonaparte, crowned himself emperor of the French a dozen years after that. By 1806 he had vanquished Germany at the Battle of Jena. The Prussian military machine once battle-tested by Frederick the Great was shattered, as was morale in all the other German states. Fears that rowdy students would erupt into overt political rebellion led Napoleon to shut down Halle University that same year. Wolf found refuge in Berlin, where he enjoyed great renown but never quite recovered from the trauma.

And what of the seminar? Having abandoned their religious roots, Wolf's disciples now occupied an obscure and lonely niche in the Republic of Letters. Greek philologists might well have been swept away by modern conquerors and the "useful knowledge" they prized. Half a world away, this was exactly the threat faced by the pandits of British India, in fact. Devotees of another ancient language, Sanskrit, pandits suffered their own disruptive encounter with imperialists from the West. They nonetheless parlayed their specialized expertise into status, wealth, and influence as leaders of an Indian national revival. Understanding how this happened helps us to account for a miraculous occurrence back in Europe: how Napoleonic conquest triggered the proliferation of university-based research specialties, making Germany the envy of the world.

Sastras *after Serampore*

Since classical times in India, pandits had acted as custodians of Sanskrit knowledge. They adjudicated legal disputes, provided sage counsel to political leaders, composed family histories, advised wealthy patrons on the proper procedures for ritual celebrations, and issued learned findings on the various rules and restrictions associated with Hindu castes. Many pandits had their own schools, essentially seminaries, where they were revered as gurus. As Brahmins (the highest caste), they were loath to take payment for their services, whether from students or from kingly maharajas. Accepting only "voluntary" donations of money or land instead, pandits traded on their learning to make careers as political, legal, and spiritual advisers. By the late 1700s, many had lost their scruples, however, becoming what we still call pundits, only too happy to accept payment for their expert opinion.[23] The agents of their transformation were the British, who while battling Napoleon were simultaneously building an empire in South Asia.

Traditionally, pandits derived their expertise from one or more of the *sastras*, which together comprise the world's oldest system of specialized academic disciplines. These Sanskrit treatises encompassed every conceivable domain of human activity or cognition. Familiar fields of learning such as grammar, logic, astronomy, mathematics, and literature had their analogs. Other *sastras* built on indigenous philosophical concepts, like the sciences of duty (*dharma*, approximating law), wealth (*artha*, akin to political economy), and pleasure (*kama*). There were also canonical works for many subjects with no place in the European tradition. There were *sastras* to lay down rules for rearing elephants, practicing yoga, cooking, or, most famously, making love, whose polymorphous techniques the *Kamasutra* dissects in minute academic detail. The *sastras* were thought to give comprehensive theoretical guidance for every contingency, problem, or question that might arise in human practice. As the *Kamasutra* says of the sexually incompetent, "That some who know the *kamasastra* are not skilled in practice is entirely their own fault, not the fault of the *sastra*."[24]

Sastras originated as commentaries and distillations culled from the Vedas, the Upanishads, and other bodies of sacred ancient scripture. But most of these "scriptures" were for centuries unwritten, and even after they were committed to manuscript form (usually on perishable palm leaves), they were transmitted, taught, discussed, and debated orally. Acolytes had to commit entire tracts to perfect memory. Copious aphorisms (*sutras*) and various mnemonic tricks and recitational drills helped, as did Sanskrit's astoundingly systematic metrical and grammatical rules. Pandits also subscribed to—and benefited from—the pervasive cultural belief that uttered sounds (like mantras and magic spells) harbored the power to reveal the world to understanding and even to control it. They thus exhibited a verbal agility unknown to any other world knowledge tradition, engaging in debates (*sastrarthas*) that often attracted hundreds of spectators. Such an extreme emphasis on orality engendered specialization at a very early date. With no repository of canonical scriptures in fixed written form, like the Quran, the Bible, or the Confucian classics, to fall back on and consult, pandits necessarily gravitated to individual subsets of this textual tradition as parts of a collective effort to transmit Sanskrit learning by word of mouth.[25]

The epic *Mahabharata* describes *sastras* as compositions of Brahma the Creator, millennia old but progressively abridged and broken up as men's lives shortened and their capacities deteriorated.[26] Notionally, the *sastras* continued to partake of divinity. One British writer observed how "the Hindoos have deified their shastrus," worshiping books as idols, anointing them with perfume, and adorning them with garlands.[27] But even then they were not stagnant, passively received, reverentially unmodified texts. Pandits could always "revise" them by claiming divine inspiration to reveal the timeless *spoken* truths inadequately preserved in the hand-copied manuscripts. In order to couch such innovation in the authority of antiquity, clever pandits used their expertise in texts to bridge the distance between past and present, not accentuate it, as European philologists did.[28] In critical areas like law, pandits' considerable room for maneuver allowed regional variations and local customs to coexist within a vast mental universe everywhere governed by the primacy of the Sanskrit language.[29] The panoply of *sastras* was part and parcel of India's diversity.

Two developments conspired to disrupt the pandits' position in the late 1700s. First, the British created a huge new market for their services as consultants, drawing them from the rural areas into Calcutta, Benares, and other centers and weaning them from their traditional aversion to salaried payment. When Bengal's governor, Warren Hastings, decided in 1772 to rule Britain's Hindu subjects according to their own law, the *dharmasastra*, British judges were instructed to hire native pandits, who alone possessed the requisite learning to untangle complex lawsuits on mundane matters like inheritance and property disputes. A later governor, Richard Wellesley (whose brother Arthur would defeat Napoleon at the Battle of Waterloo), felt that British administrators should themselves learn India's languages in order to love—and rule—it. In 1800 he founded Fort William College to steer young clerks disembarking from England out of Calcutta's brothels and hookah dens and into the classroom. Native pandits were paired with European philologists, who brought to Indian texts the same critical-historical methods Wolf was applying to Homer back in Germany.* For their own part, many pandits responded with creative "restorations" of "ancient" texts. In one possibly fabricated treatise on tantric

---

*It was a Calcutta Supreme Court judge, Sir William Jones, who made the mind-blowing discovery that Sanskrit shared its roots with Greek and Latin and, by his lights, surpassed them in perfection and refinement. The Indo-European family of languages, the world's largest, stretches from Iran through much of South Asia and from Europe to its colonies in the Americas and beyond.

spirituality, arguments against widow self-immolation (*sati*) and for cross-caste marriage, a "sweetened" image of the warrior-goddess Kali, and a euphemistic handling of tantric sex all betray the subtle infiltration of Western mores.[30]

In a second development, Baptist missionaries unleashed a media revolution with the founding of a printing press, in 1800. At first British authorities had banned the missionaries, fearing a Hindu and Muslim backlash against their proselytizing, so they set up shop in the Danish colony of Serampore, fifteen miles upriver from Calcutta. Echoing Francke's Pietists, the Baptists established a publishing empire there. Over the next three decades the Serampore Mission Press printed 212,000 books in 40 different languages. Thirty Bible translations, somewhat hastily prepared, spread the gospel in Indian tongues. In a far-sighted, cosmopolitan spirit, the missionaries also translated into local vernaculars many indigenous scholarly and literary works, notably the *Ramayana* and the Bhagavad Gita. Finally, the Baptists opened elementary schools, 103 of them in 1816–1817 alone, together serving nearly 7,000 pupils. Along with printed materials, they thought, mass schooling would upend the pandits' monopoly on hand-copied *sastras* and shatter the sacred guru-disciple relationship that kept education in the clutches of learned Brahmins. In their self-congratulatory judgment, "the common people are almost imperceptibly acquiring that rank and importance in the *republic of letters*, which the founders of their religion and institutes denied them."[31]

Many pandits did react by retreating into sullen obsolescence.

But the most enterprising of them took to new print media with abandon. They published poetry and devotional texts and founded reform-oriented journals targeting the Bengali reading public. Fully twenty-six such periodicals were established between 1820 and 1835. Raja Rammohan Ray (1772–1883), a Calcutta Brahmin later dubbed the "founder of modern India," revisited the Upanishads and other ancient scriptures to condemn *sati*. His "One God Society" (Brahmo Samaj) sought to restore the ancient, unitarian, nonpolytheistic Hinduism he believed the scriptures revealed. A later figure, Isvarcandra Vidyasagar (1820–1891), a professor at Sanskrit College (founded in 1824), campaigned successfully to grant widows the right to remarry. His popular schoolbooks blended precepts from the *nitisastra* (the science of wise conduct) with Victorian morality. This earned him the mockery of Calcutta street pantomimes, who chided him for introducing the word "obscenity" into the Bengali language.[32]

Westernized Indian pandits had come to view English culture as a fount of "useful knowledge." Made upwardly mobile by access to a prestigious nonnative language—much like German classicists in this respect—they sparked a Bengali Renaissance that upturned India's sense of its historical past and textual heritage. What fell by the wayside were ways of dividing and imparting knowledge that were centuries old. Ambitious pandits had moved from specific areas of human practice (law, sex, cooking), aimed at specific clienteles, to general, comprehensive moral, spiritual, social, and (by Gandhi's time) political reform activity, aimed at the literate public at large.

State patronage, missionizing, and print culture: in Bengal they spelled the decline and dissolution of the *sastras* and induced pandits to create a public sphere that laid the basis for Indian nationalism. These same forces gave rise to the philology seminar in Germany. Why, then, would Europe experience a new splintering of knowledge during these years? In a word, Sanskrit was a living language, Greek a dead one. Those in one tradition could simply transpose their activism to new media of influence; those in the other were forced to seek out new frontiers of purely academic study. Unlike the *sastras*, philology and the disciplines derived from it lacked any practical, applied, performative component. Their aims and methods of research claimed no authority over human affairs outside the bully pulpit of the university, no ambition to guide or govern cooking or sex, statecraft or salvation. Professors still eschew the worldly engagement that pandits (and now pundits) claim. They traffic solely in the marketplace of ideas. No ties to the wider world prevent them from specializing in ever more arcane ways to their heart's content. In this way the founders of new disciplines would finally fulfill Adam Smith's prediction that market forces would generate a division of intellectual labor. All that was missing by the early 1800s was a source of demand for their purely educational services—the role soon provided by mass schooling.

Publish or perish: the national market for ideas

Prussia's state-sponsored, tiered, integrated system of universal public education—the world's first—was designed by one of its leading neohumanists, the aristocrat Wilhelm von Humboldt (1767–1835). Educated at Göttingen, mentored by Wolf, a seasoned diplomat, and a founder of linguistics with special expertise in Sanskrit, Humboldt ranked among the very few gentleman-scholars in Germany (along with his brother, Alexander, whom we will meet in the next chapter). Wilhelm was, however, an accidental revolutionary. Stationed in Rome as ambassador to the pope, Humboldt was reluctant to leave the Eternal City when he was summoned to Berlin in 1808. His light ambassadorial duties had left him ample time to cultivate himself through study of the ancient world that surrounded him in ruins. In addition, his wife, Caroline, was pregnant, and she and their daughters would have to stay behind for what was to become a two-year separation. But after Prussia's humiliating defeat at Jena, Humboldt felt the call of patriotism and the stirring of ambition. While Caroline remained in Rome to preside over a lively circle of artists and antiquarians, Wilhelm set off across the Alps to Germany, which eagerly awaited him.[33]

A personal favorite of the royal family, Humboldt was reportedly charged by the king himself with "replacing in spiritual powers what we have lost in material powers" as a consequence of Napoleon's seizure of Prussian territory. Given an open mandate as minister of culture and education, Humboldt determined to make the benefits of his own learning and intellectual well-roundedness widely available to others. Bemused, he wrote to Caroline that "people act as if, without me, no one in

Prussia could learn to read."[34] Embarking on an extensive over-haul of Prussian schooling, he updated Francke's educational project for a more secular age. The 30,000 primary schools opened or refurbished in the first half of the nineteenth century secured universal compulsory education as a public responsibility of the state. And to replace Halle, Humboldt founded what is now recognized as the world's first research university, in Berlin. But elite high schools, the gymnasia, formed the linchpin of his system; only with this intermediate institution in place could a market in higher education develop.

Wolf's philology might have become a footnote in the history of scholarship but for Humboldt's appreciation of its utility in welding together a defeated state. Frederick the Great's famed drillmaster regime had been revealed as brittle and weak by the French invaders. The neohumanists' gymnasia furnished the remedy, inculcating a new Prussian elite in a comprehensive classical education focused on Latin and Greek, plus modern languages and mathematics, some religion, and remarkably little science. Such a curriculum was nowhere more useful than in Germany, the heartland of the Reformation, divided between Protestants and Catholics. Lutheran Prussia in particular, ruled by Calvinists, absorbed millions of new Catholic subjects in Silesia and the Rhineland between Frederick the Great's rise and Napoleon's fall. Neohumanism provided the ideological raw materials to build an integrated national culture. Healing the same religious divide that had called the Republic of Letters into being in the first place, the worship of Western civilization would become the new religion of modernity. Gymnasium teachers were thus in sudden demand as the shock troops of secular knowledge, dispensed now in the classroom rather than in the pulpit. Humboldt's reforms made every one of these schools a junior philology seminar—a nursery for flexible, adaptable, critical thinkers able to serve the state as civil servants or private professionals.

The gymnasium also prescribed an upward path for anyone who wanted to go further. Mastering its curriculum became the main requirement for admission to the University of Berlin, and increasingly for its competitors. With a grounding in classical philology, students could specialize at the university level within the all-encompassing domain of "philosophy." Philosophy picked up where philology left off. The old arts faculty was formally rechristened a philosophy faculty, and a new degree, the Ph.D., came into widespread use at German universities in the 1800s. Today it still counts as the highest professional credential in all the disciplines, and professors of physics, anthropology, and Russian literature are all "doctors of philosophy."

A generation of German thinkers made philosophy into a master methodology adjudicating among empirical findings in every field of knowledge. Not only that—they made philosophy chic. Immanuel Kant, the elegant bachelor, calmly demolished law, medicine, and theology as mere practical pursuits, extolling the very uselessness of philosophy for its untrammeled intellectual freedoms.[35] G.W.F. Hegel, when he lectured, coughed, stuttered, took snuff, paused to shuffle through his notes, closed his eyes for minutes at a time, and waved his hands spasmodically, yet became so popular for being "deep" that his lecture notes could soon be found on Berlin's black market.[36] But among the philosophers it was Johann Gottlieb Fichte, the University of Berlin's first rector, who explicitly linked the provision of mass education to the stirring of Germany's national ambitions.

Fichte had risen to prominence at Jena in the 1790s, mesmerizing its alcoholic, riot-prone student body with abstract ruminations on the difference between the "I" and the "not I." Listeners lined up out the doors, standing on tables and benches and "each other's heads" for his Friday evening lectures on "Morality for Scholars." One observer called him the "Bonaparte of philosophy," as he was short, stocky, and combative; another recounted how he entered the lecture hall fresh from a vigorous horseback ride, with riding whip, boots, spurs, and all.[37] Fichte was not a humble man. He cut his teeth writing books such as *Attempt at a Critique of All Revelation*, *Concerning Human Dignity*, and the modestly entitled *Foundations of the Entire Theory of Knowledge*. But in a replay of the Christian Wolff controversy, accusations of atheism forced him to leave Jena for Berlin in 1800. Biding his time there, he met his destiny after Prussia's defeat, delivering a series of "Addresses to the German Nation" to a wide public audience in 1807 and 1808. In them he argued that Germany, above other nations, had a special mission to redeem humanity. But having proved too pusillanimous to resist the French conquerors, Germans must first be reeducated to develop their own national genius, just as the Greeks had. Fichte sketched a program of national education beginning in childhood. It culminated in an elite academy, which he envisioned as a Platonic military barracks complete with uniforms and consecrated to the task of grooming poor boys on scholarship to become philosopher-kings.[38]

It was too much to hope that Prussia would actually replace its aristocratic elite with Fichte's disciples. University graduates were instead left to the tender mercies of the free market. Many German Ph.D.'s simply became teachers in gymnasia. Those who wanted to become university professors became *Privatdozenten*, "private" lecturers. This meant that a newly minted Ph.D. could apply for a license to teach at the university of his choice, whereupon his courses would be listed in its lecture catalog. Starting with Berlin, many universities provided heated auditoriums for these wandering academics, who had previously given lessons in their own apartments or rented lecture rooms.[39] *Privatdozenten*, however, had to live on lecture fees paid directly by students, without much or any salary from the state. This incentive made them responsive to student demand and encouraged healthy competition to fill seats. A young academic might even show up at a university and schedule his lectures to coincide with those of a rival senior professor, as the hapless philosopher Arthur Schopenhauer attempted but failed to do against Hegel.[40] Only a lucky few, with the right talents, the right politics, and lots of politicking, could acquire first an "extraordinary" and then an "ordinary" university chair. These posts, few and far between, entitled them to state salaries and the godlike social status that the German professor came to enjoy.

The system's many washouts joined a swelling "academic proletariat" likened by contemporaries to starving artists or traveling comedy troupes.[41] The only way up and out was to publish. Unlike the lecturer's reputation as a teacher, which spread off campus only in the most exceptional cases, printed scholarship acted as a calling card for the professional intellectual. Hegel secured his chair at Berlin by writing books with arcane titles like *The Phenomenology of Spirit*, finished at Jena in 1806 and spirited out of town when Napoleon's armies were literally outside the window. Specialized monographs and journals, like Hegel's *Critical Journal of Philosophy*, created a publishing industry by and for academic specialists. In this way a fundamentally artificial market in print became the favored means to gain national exposure outside an academic's home institution and garner a call from a rival university.

Entrepreneurs with a taste for risk could, of course, throw in their lot with profit-driven publishing ventures. This was the career path chosen, ironically enough, by Dr. Karl Marx, the cofounder of communism. Marx began as a typical academic, writing a dissertation on Greek natural philosophy at the University of Berlin. But his politics forced him out of Berlin's conservative establishment—he was a "left" Hegelian instead of a "right" Hegelian—so he submitted the work for the Ph.D. at Jena. He then spent several years in Paris, Brussels, and the Rhineland, gaining notoriety as editor and contributor to a series of radical newspapers. Conflicts with censors and stockholders kept his writings from making money, but Marx soon found a new investor in Friedrich Engels, the son of a wealthy industrialist, who became his intellectual collaborator. Engels subsidized Marx's life of exile in London, where the two men developed their analysis of capitalism and witnessed its human costs first-hand. Marx had always shown an acute sense of Germany's inferiority as a nation next to the industrial powerhouses of England and France. He once wrote that "the Germans have *thought* in politics what other nations have *done*."[42] He was right about the Germans' intellectualism, but not in the way he meant: while real-life Oliver Twists and David Copperfields roamed the streets of Marx's London, children in his homeland were already busily occupied in the very first kindergartens—an institution created in the 1840s by the German pedagogue Friedrich Fröbel.

Spanning every level from the kindergarten to Kant, public education spread all over Germany in the first half of the nineteenth century, breeding healthy competition among the various states of this still disunited nation. Their rivalry led directly to the inception of specialized disciplines. After 1816, Berlin required new Ph.D.'s to indicate which precise subjects among the various branches of "philosophy" they would teach.[43] This date is a convenient marker for the point at which professional academics were required to set aside their generalist inclinations, but the real impetus came from competition among rival universities eager to imitate and surpass Berlin. Operating in a national job market limited only by the geographical extent of the German language, state culture ministers jockeyed to lure the best professors to their respective institutions. Each university had only one chair per discipline. But since there were so many universities already on the ground in Germany, academics could play one off against the other. A star academic willing to turn himself into a commodity could even get a new chair created in his chosen field. The polymath Hermann Helmholtz moved in this way from studying philosophy in Berlin to holding a physiology chair at Königsberg. Helmholtz's mentor had migrated from theology at Berlin to philosophy at Göttingen. His own student, Wilhelm Wundt, leapt from physiology to experimental psychology, a new discipline he carved out within the philosophy faculty at Leipzig.[44]

Acquiring a chair in this way guaranteed a professor's personal success, but guaranteeing the spread of new disciplines required a venue in which to train acolytes. By the 1820s the seminar had become the favored means whereby chaired professors indoctrinated Ph.D.'s in their own methods of scholarship. In this way, one man's personal research agenda could lay the basis for establishing a new field of study. There were, to be sure, a few false starts. Early natural science seminars founded at Bonn and Königsberg either petered out or produced better teachers than original researchers. Lasting success in the natural sciences required, in addition to the seminar, the institution of the laboratory (discussed in the next chapter). And the arts—like the sciences, performative by nature—flourished in academies and museums, not universities. As disciplines, they developed around seminar-based textual interpretation: instead of art, art history; instead of music, musicology; instead of poetry or fiction, literary criticism. The most rapid success came in fields whose methods grew directly out of the philological culture of close reading inculcated in the gymnasia, whether philology proper, history, philosophy, law, theology, or even mathematics.[45] The brothers Grimm, for example, as philologists at Göttingen, found in German folktales a native equivalent to Homer's genius, thus inaugurating folklore.

A new masculine sociability crystallized in the seminar, where the impulse to conquer was displaced from other men onto the object of inquiry. Leopold von Ranke (1795–1886), regarded as the founder of the discipline of history, is an excellent illustration. Ranke acquired public and professional fame at Berlin by making a fetish of detailed documentary analysis. His preferred sources were the *relazioni* produced by early modern Venetian ambassadors, eyewitness reports of wars and diplomacy that cut through the self-serving pabulum of official accounts.[46] As Ranke wrote of one archival find, "Yesterday, I had a sweet, magnificent fling with the object of my love, a beautiful Italian"—no *signorina*, but a cache of musty papers—"and I hope that we produce a beautiful Roman-German prodigy" (a work of scholarship!). Following one late-night bout at the writing desk, Ranke wrote, "I rose at noon, completely exhausted."[47]

Likewise in Ranke's seminar, the ritualized combat of the Abelardian disputation yielded to an atmosphere of cooperation, camaraderie, fraternity, and male bonding. Reliance on verbal spontaneity to spark new insights, in real time, took the modern disciplines back to the symposia of the Athenian philosophers. Ranke's seminar had no formal statutes and enjoyed no state financing; lessons were held in his own apartment in Berlin. What mattered was the intimacy of the master-disciple relationship, the scholar's reverence for the *Doktorvater*, or "doctor-father." This relationship helped create the "disciplined" academic personality, each disciple making a piece of the family inheritance his own. Such constellations of acolytes mark a crucial shift from Humboldtian well-roundedness to modern specialization as the end point of the academic's vocation; the one prizes moral-intellectual cultivation, while the other emphasizes systematic rigor. The scholars produced by the disciplines gained distinction through depth rather than breadth. Unlike the encyclopedic intellects of the Republic of Letters, they were willing to pour their energies into ever narrower fields of knowledge—and were rewarded handsomely for doing so, with higher incomes and the acclaim of their fellow men.

Nearly 10,000 Americans studied in Germany during the 1800s, proof of the neohumanist appeal in yet another developing nation. On their return they seeded the renewal and spread of education in the United States. Among them were the founders of Johns Hopkins, the first graduate school in the United States, and the reformers who transformed Harvard from a regional college into what is now the world's richest university. Even as Germany's musical chairs began to fill up, droves of land-grant universities were being opened in the American Midwest and elsewhere. Walter Prescott Webb, a devoted Rankean, took his archival passions to Texas, investigating the "historical significance of the six-shooter." He likened the seminar leader to an expedition leader, its members to "axe-men, observers, hunters, and scouts," the library to a "high mountain," the seminar table to "the campfire where the party gathers and each member reports."[48]

However faint its echo in today's dry academic writing, the frontier spirit lives on in the institution of the academic discipline. To add to the encyclopedia of knowledge requires more than the industry and calculation of Adam Smith's earnest businessman. It requires the passion born of a missionary impulse and transferred to the calling of specialized research. Secular humanists were the first to steal the fire of Protestant evangelism in this way, and it was they who first made the production of research a cardinal task of the modern university. But they would not have prospered if not for their utility to another quasi-religious movement: nineteenth-century nationalism. National culture still defines the mission of the research university, and in every country professors act as its agents.[49] They speak the national vernacular—German, English, or French, for example, and not the international Latin of the Republic of Letters—and give it scholarly substance. Driven by the search for work in niche markets for their various specialties, they move from place to place and collectively trace the boundaries of national cultural regions. Professors carry high culture to the provinces, raising those with merely local horizons to a sense of belonging and participation in larger national networks that scholars know firsthand through their travels. In bringing the panoply of knowledge to publics eager for education, the disciplines thus fulfilled what had been the dream of the Enlightenment all along: to reach the masses.

6
_____

The Laboratory

1770–1970
_____

PRECEDING PAGE:
Women and men working together in a laboratory at the Massachusetts Institute of Technology. From Frank Leslie's Illustrated Newspaper *of Dec. 18, 1869.*

THE LABORATORY PHYSICALLY ENCLOSED A DOMAIN OF
OBJECTIVE FACT, AND THE EXTENSION OF ITS METHODS
TO EVER WIDER PUBLIC AND PRIVATE SPACES ENLARGED
THE REALMS OF SCIENTIFIC EXPERTS.

A FASCINATING entanglement of love and science adorns the history of the laboratory in the heady years for nuclear physics around 1900. In 1894, Marie Skłodowska (1867–1934) met Pierre Curie at a tea party in Paris. Nine years later, by then a married couple, Pierre and Marie Curie shared a Nobel Prize in physics with Henri Becquerel. (After Pierre's tragic death, in 1906, Marie won a second Nobel, in 1911.) Marie spent her married life shuttling between scientific and domestic duties, at one moment changing diapers, at another bombarding nuclei. She referred to radium as her third child, after daughters Irène and Eve. Only by fusing home and work life, sacrificing household tidiness to the demands of dual careers, could Marie and Pierre find time to probe the mysteries of radioactivity.[1] But what the Curie family lacked in bourgeois comforts, it made up for as a breeding ground for pathbreaking scientists. Irène Curie met her husband, Frédéric Joliot, when he joined Marie's Radium Institute in 1925, and the two claimed their own Nobel Prize a decade later. Similarly, their daughter Hélène met and married her husband, Michel Langevin, at the Curie-Joliots' nuclear physics laboratory. (Michel was the grandson of Paul Langevin, a onetime lover of Marie's and later Joliot's professional mentor.)

Scientific dynasties and academic intermarriage are not unheard of in European history. What made the Curies novel was that women now stood as near equals beside their husbands. We often think of hard science as a quintessentially masculine domain, yet after women were admitted to universities in the late nineteenth century they achieved their first notable academic success in fields like physics and chemistry, not literature, history, or philosophy. The Curies were no anomaly; other female figures, such as Lise Meitner (a pioneer in nuclear fission) and Mileva Marić (Einstein's wife), gained access to the citadels of male academia through the portals of laboratory science. In laboratory settings, a woman might graduate from helpmeet to test-tube cleaner to principal investigator through a combination of ambition and talent, work and dedication. Irène Curie-Joliot did exactly that (if with considerable indulgence from the boss) as a young assistant in her mother's laboratory.[2]

Famous women of science, however few, illustrate the profound challenge that scientific technique put to the traditional humanities. The success of laboratory science is an objective fact. Even "unqualified" women, having mastered experimental apparatus, could produce tangible results in manipulating the natural world. Scholars rooted in the all-male culture of the philological seminar might object to the incursion of "mere technicians" but eventually had to concede the stunning success of laboratory methods. In a way, the possibility of women's ascent was programmed into an institution that originated in the early modern period in the private quarters of well-to-do families and the craft workshops of middle-class artisans.[3] Home, work, and school all overlapped in the premodern household, as they could in the modern laboratory.

As a physical space, then, the laboratory smuggled artisanal techniques, a species of informal knowledge, into formal academic disciplines. Laboratory scientists, after learning to control nature within the four walls of their experimental domains, capitalized on their methods to change the way people lived in homes, neighborhoods, even whole countries. Social scientists were likewise eager to treat the world at large as a laboratory. Whereas laboratory science perpetuated aspects of the preindustrial household, the social sciences coalesced to study the new spaces of industrial modernity. The era of steam and steel remade the physical and human landscape, throwing people together in huge urban and industrial agglomerations that themselves became sites of deliberate experimentation. Because the social sciences involved people, these disciplines had special obstacles to confront in their quest for scientific "fact." Yet their pervasive influence in modern workplaces, schools, and homes strikingly illustrates how protocols of objectivity originating in the confinement of the laboratory went on to conquer the outside world.

THE SPACES OF LABORATORY SCIENCE

Several familiar characteristics of laboratory science distinguish it as a fundamentally new kind of scholarship. First, laboratory science yields results that are reproducible at will, in a controlled, contained, predictable environment; they're not wonders, or miracles, or magic. Second, the laws it derives are universally applicable across space and time. The universal gas law, $PV=nRT$, is true wherever you are, and it is as true today as it will be millennia hence.* Third, while the humanities thrive on dispute and dialectic, science privileges academic consensus. Achievements deemed "true" are rapidly accepted as "fact" by the entire community of scientists. This helps to explain, fourth, why laboratory science came to enjoy public acclaim and widespread acceptance even after it ceased to be practiced in the relative openness of the gentlemanly academy and retreated behind closed doors. "Objectivity" is a label we might give to this bundle of characteristics, and the laboratory localized it in hallowed spaces where scientific craftsmen tricked nature into doing the unusual—not once, but replicably and reliably.

The laboratory as the world: Humboldt

At the dawn of the 1800s, natural science and the humanities coexisted in remarkable harmony, as exemplified by the careers

---

*Roughly speaking, this law predicts that increasing the temperature (T) of a given quantity (n) of gas will expand either its volume (V) or, if it is confined in a rigid space, its pressure (P). R denotes the universal gas constant.

of the two Humboldt brothers, Wilhelm, the architect of the research university, and his younger brother, Alexander (1769–1859), who became one of the most famous scientists of the century. Wilhelm spent his life at a writing desk, drawing up the blueprints for Prussia's educational system, penning treatises on comparative linguistics, and conducting diplomatic correspondence as the Prussian ambassador in, successively, Rome, Vienna, and London. Alexander became a world traveler. His epic voyage to South and Central America from 1799 to 1804 garnered him worldwide fame and generated thirty volumes of research findings in the decades after his return. Years later, at the peak of his influence, Alexander returned to the roving naturalist's life with an expedition through Russian central Asia. Today the Humboldt Current, the Humboldt penguin, three Humboldt counties in the United States, and the Mare Humboldtianum moon crater all attest to the sheer physical sweep of his impact on the study of nature. (Alexander even dabbled in philological research to establish for the first time how Martin Waldseemüller had come to name the Americas after Vespucci.)

Alexander's nomadic lifestyle was one that Wilhelm and his wife, Caroline, though they periodically separated to pursue their respective intellectual interests, could never have imagined for themselves. A confirmed bachelor, to use a quaint term, Alexander formed close attachments with male traveling companions; his sexuality remains an enigma. In any case, Alexander's kind of science was incompatible with a stable household life. His vocation, after all, was fieldwork. Alexander worked as far away from the enclosed spaces of the laboratory bench or the seminar room as one could get. The world as a whole was his laboratory, the totality of nature the object of a singleminded celibate pursuit. Lord Byron, in *Don Juan*, satirized "Humboldt, 'the first of travelers,'" for taking readouts on the color of the sky rather than indulging in baser pleasures. Instead of "measuring the intensity of blue," Don Juan says to a lover, "Oh Lady Daphne, let me measure you!"[4]

Indeed, wherever Humboldt found himself, whether in the Amazon jungles or the snowy Urals, he pulled out his barometer and his sextant and scooped up handfuls of dirt and rocks. He took numerical measurements of every conceivable climatic and geographic phenomenon. He penned journal entries on rock and cloud formations, flora and fauna, and human populations and customs. Understated allusions to his own emotional reactions, whether to sublime mountaintops or to the cruelties of slavery, gave his works a light literary quality. Imperturbable in the midst of an earthquake (like "awakening from a dream; but a painful awakening"), undaunted by treks across an endless steppe (like the "naked stony crust of some desolate planet"), compassionate in his tale of a Guahiba Indian woman on a futile search for her kidnapped children ("a touching story of maternal love in an often vilified race"), Alexander was no bloodless collector of desiccated natural specimens.[5]

Undergirding Alexander's multifarious observations was a Romantic belief in the unity of all nature, "a totality moved and enlivened by inner energies," as he called it.[6] "Humboldtian science" came to refer to the disciplined, obsessive collection of particular facts, reams of them, assembled with the aim of linking them all together. Standardized instruments would be strewn over the world at measuring stations: thermometers and barometers, of course, but also eudiometers, to measure atmospheric oxygen, and the cyanometers mentioned by Lord Byron, to calculate the blueness of the sky. Scientists would coordinate this information to map zones of similar vegetation, climate, altitude, and the like, at one glance visually conveying both the diversity and the patterned uniformity of the globe. "Isotherms" depicting ribbons of similar temperature across continents, found today on the weather page of every newspaper, were just one species of the isomaps, cross-sectional diagrams, and other graphic techniques Humboldt invented.[7]

To sustain this enterprise Humboldt cultivated an international network of correspondents. Between 1789 and 1859 he wrote 50,000 letters and received 100,000, sometimes as many as 80 a week. He particularly cultivated contacts with German émigrés in Australia and North America; one such correspondent in St. Louis, Missouri, collected thermometer, barometer, and hydrometer readings three times a day for forty-seven years.[8] But Alexander was as international as the scholarly community itself. He wrote in cosmopolitan French, not his native German, and could converse in English with Thomas Jefferson and in Spanish with missionaries to the Amazon. He used his network to patronize other scientists and jumpstart their careers and to win patronage for his own science.

Humboldt presided over a supercharged Republic of Letters grafted onto the global networks of European colonialism, putting remote scientists in contact with one another. His world-girding enterprise depended on the ability of dispersed nonexpert practitioners of natural observation to share data via post. Operating in the openness of the Republic of Letters, Humboldtian science could, in principle, be taken up by anyone who came into possession of his writings. Thus Charles Darwin, despite a desultory university education, set off on his own adventure in the Galápagos Islands after reading Humboldt.

Humboldt's science aspired to universal applicability but otherwise lacked the characteristics of objectivity found in the laboratory. He did not aim to manipulate nature reliably and reproducibly, only to observe it. His theories on natural phenomena—the causes of volcanoes, for example—aimed to provoke debate and discussion, not establish consensus. His methods commanded enthusiastic public support, but only because they invited public participation; none of them required expert or private knowledge. The qualities of openness and spontaneity found in Humboldtian science did not apply to all subfields of the scientific endeavor, however. The chemical revolution, inaugurated half a century earlier, depended on a much more private science conducted behind closed doors, with instruments and vocabulary that were intelligible only to insiders. Its pioneering practitioner, Antoine Lavoisier, demonstrated in a way Humboldt never did the opportunity—and also the threat—that craft technique brought to the gentlemanly public.

The laboratory as workshop: Lavoisier

The French chemist Antoine Lavoisier (1743–1794) lived and died in the years surrounding the French Revolution. He built his laboratory in Paris in a gunpowder arsenal on the right bank of the Seine River, where for a time he also took a private apartment. His much younger wife assisted him at every turn and, as an especially accomplished draftswoman, furnished us with many vivid and precise depictions of his scientific equipment and laboratory life. If Lavoisier thus practiced his science in conditions of ideal privacy, his business entanglements made him an all-too-public figure. To finance his researches he had bought a share in the notorious General Farm, which subcontracted France's tax collection and which fell under suspicions of malfeasance soon after the revolution broke out. As a result, Lavoisier lost his head to the guillotine in 1794; Mme. Lavoisier survived, impoverished, to publish his remaining works. (In yet another overlap of love and science, her sometime paramour, Pierre-Samuel DuPont, himself a chemist and one of Lavoisier's collaborators, also ran afoul of revolutionary politics and fled to Delaware, where his son founded the now-famous chemical conglomerate.)[9]

Antoine Lavoisier is credited with overturning the theory of phlogiston, which postulated that a colorless, odorless, nearly weightless "fixed fire" is released whenever an object burns. He showed instead that the real element we call oxygen is the crucial element in combustion. To prove this, the Lavoisiers had to weigh their reactants exactly, demonstrating that some substances actually *absorb* a tiny mass, as oxygen, in burning. Precise measurement and especially quantification became the hallmarks of their approach. Not only did Lavoisier produce a balance accurate to less than one one-thousandth of a gram; he coinvented the calorimeter (with Pierre-Simon Laplace, who proved that the solar system runs stably) to measure small temperature changes in chemical reactions. During the revolution, he even helped to design the metric system to standardize weights and measures. Before Lavoisier, chemists reported subjectively on the smells, tastes, and colors of their reagents—even their sounds. Shockingly, his mentor Gabriel-François Rouelle poured alkaline solutions on animals and used their screams to document the solutions' "caustic nature."[10] After Lavoisier, however, chemists concentrated on the physical properties of substances measured by a proliferating array of newer, ever more precise devices with quantified readouts. Standardized and transportable, such instruments helped secure widespread acceptance for scientific findings and made possible Humboldt's later aspiration to discern regularities in nature over space and across time.

But chemistry was not Humboldtian science. It relied not on passive observation to quantify impressions already available to the senses but on active intervention to manipulate what seemed to be occult, unseen forces. Joseph Priestley, the chief defender of phlogiston theory, objected in principle to the kind of science this entailed. The equipment, for one, was too complex and costly. Eighteenth-century laboratories were still funded mostly by gentleman experimenters and more rarely by royal academies and other forms of patronage. The Lavoisiers' instruments also required delicate and dextrous maneuvers, an artisan's skill, to make them work. Finally, they forced chemists to interact with nature only through the mediation of technology and even allowed them to blame experimental failures on bad instruments. Replacing sensory description with mathematical analysis, Lavoisier could do inexact experiments and average out the errors to achieve a precise result. This procedure, now standard practice in laboratory science, challenged the idea that scientific facts ought to be clear-cut and indisputable as witnessed by the naked eye. Thus Priestley objected that Lavoisier's revolution impaired the powers of independent judgment and ocular testimony central to the role and identity of the gentleman-scientist.[11]

A related problem lay in the innovations Lavoisier introduced to chemical nomenclature, which he basically reinvented. Coinages like "carbonate," "nitrate," and "sulfate" struck many contemporaries as "harsh and barbaric words that shock the ear and are not at all in the spirit of the French language."[12] But Lavoisier believed that a properly designed language was much more than an arbitrary set of names and signs; clear language and clear signs enabled greater analytical creativity, while unclear language hindered it. Just as roman numerals yielded to arabic ones, so too must vague, qualitative description yield to precise chemical terminology. So, for example, when Lavoisier proved that water, one of the four putatively indivisible ancient elements, was actually produced by the combustion of "dephlogisticated air" and "flammable air," he gave these reactants new names. "Hydrogen" and "oxygen" replaced vague but evocative terms with artificial but precise descriptors.

Science had become a craft, the gentleman's laboratory a workshop for specialists. Lavoisier finally realized the French *encyclopédistes'* dream of a collaboration between academic scholars and craftsmen of the traditional arts and crafts, but at the expense of their ambition to teach the public. Laboratory science, with its arcane formulas and complex apparatus, could no longer appeal to a universal culture of fact, a common public discourse. It lacked the consensus of scholars in the Republic of Letters and even forced a breach with some of them. So how did the laboratory manage to become the nineteenth century's dominant scientific institution?

The laboratory as seminar: Liebig

One answer to this question was provided by Justus Liebig (1803–1873). He proved that chemistry works—that it's profitable—and should therefore be supported by universities, states, and private industry. Liebig developed organic chemistry as a field and with his followers proved that it could have tremendous practical value in producing agricultural fertilizer, chemical dyes, and medicines (like Bayer aspirin, invented in Germany in 1897). These chemicals, the products of collaboration between university laboratories and big business, helped fuel imperial

Germany's rise to economic superpower status. Liebig himself parlayed his chemical knowledge into the development of commercial products such as bouillon cubes and baby formula.[13]

Liebig also gave a deeper, more institutional answer to the question of the laboratory's rise: natural science would henceforth capitalize on the success of the disciplines. He established the world's first and most influential research school in chemistry at the University of Giessen, a sleepy Hessian town where a post opened up in 1824 and the twenty-one-year-old Liebig, with Alexander von Humboldt's intervention, set up shop after returning from Paris, then the world capital of chemistry. Liebig tirelessly lobbied university deans and state administrators for the funds to set up a laboratory and after lots of backroom politicking put tiny Giessen on track to become an international center of chemistry by the end of the 1830s. His institute began modestly, as a center of vocational training, before ascending to the empyrean heights of pure research. Pharmacists seeking local licensing in Hesse outnumbered scholarly chemists for a full decade after Liebig's arrival at Giessen.[14] Mounting fame, however, attracted a better cadre of students. Over his career, Liebig fathered 24 "children," Ph.D.'s who went on to research careers at other universities. Another 150 chemists went into private industry.[15] A seven-generation family tree at the Liebig Museum in Giessen enumerates scores of Nobel Prize winners, including the codiscoverers of Vitamin C and plutonium.[16] Fawning disciples likened their master (who was bisexual) to a conquering general, identifying themselves as "young companions in arms" ready "to make any attack at his bidding."[17] His new institution transposed the culture of the university seminar to the science laboratory, complete with the masculine swagger.

With Liebig, the old Anglo-French scientific republic, with its gentlemanly private laboratories and public academy demonstrations, yielded to the German-dominated research university, where natural-science disciplines finally came into their own. The intrusion on the traditional humanities was hardly welcome, however. Liebig had first to convince the powers that be that science was a worthwhile endeavor alongside philosophy, classics, and history. In an impolitic but widely influential publication directed at the Prussian government, he viciously criticized the veneration of dead languages and mocked classical philologists for their idolatry of the ancients, labeling them "strangers to all true humanity." He further charged that traditional academics denied not only the practical value of laboratory science but its true status as a discipline reaching the highest philosophical standards. They "consider chemistry as an experimental craft . . . useful for making soda and soap, or for manufacturing better iron and steel, but they are unacquainted with chemistry as a field of scientific research." University professors replied, with good Humboldtian reasoning, that "the university must represent primarily theoretical instruction in chemistry, in which students of all disciplines can take part without any practical-chemical orientation" to laboratory apparatus and hands-on techniques. Lectures and seminars should suffice, they argued.[18] To secure a lasting place for his science in the university, Liebig therefore had to demonstrate that laboratory technique was essential not only to applied chemistry, the work of technicians, but to the progress of research itself.

Organic analysis—the identification of unknown organic substances—offered the critical test case. Liebig's generation was the first to discover that organic compounds (like urea) and inorganic substances (like salt) obey the same chemical laws; the former should be described not in terms of mystical life energy but as combinations of (among other elements) carbon (C), hydrogen (H), and oxygen (O). The trick was to measure precisely the relative proportions of these basic elements in order to identify a given organic compound. Chemists knew from Lavoisier that burning a substance causes it to react with oxygen (O_2):

$$C + O_2 \rightarrow CO_2 \text{ (gas)}$$
$$H + O_2 \rightarrow H_2O \text{ (water)}$$
$$O + O_2 \rightarrow O_2 \text{ (more gas)}$$

Weighing water is straightforward; oxygen could be estimated (by Lavoisier's method, subtracting the weight of the products from that of the reactants); but CO_2, carbon dioxide, particularly in large amounts, was hard to measure, especially if intermixed with oxygen. Liebig's "Kali apparatus" (after the Latin *kalium*, for potassium) exposed the CO_2 to potassium hydroxide (KOH), which caused it to condense and enabled researchers to weigh it as a liquid. An ingenious glass triangle arrayed with five condenser bulbs to catch the chemical product, the Kali apparatus had to be constructed by a glassblower. It was simple enough to be mastered quickly, which ensured its rapid adoption by others, but sufficiently complicated that it caught on mainly through hands-on demonstration, which gave Liebig and his allies a critical advantage over rivals.[19] The Kali apparatus exemplified what management gurus call a "best practice," a breakthrough that competitors quickly adopt to keep up with a fast-moving research front.[20]

More deeply, Liebig's breakthroughs in organic chemistry demonstrated how crucial collective, practical pedagogy was to scientific advance. His training methods had made a skill tradition industrially replicable: witness the Erlenmeyer flask (invented by one of Liebig's students), usually placed on top of the Bunsen burner (perfected by another German chemist-pedagogue), both of them stock, mass-produced elements of the chemistry laboratory today. In Liebig's school, as in its rivals and imitators and just as in seminars, training in craft technique built scholarly lineages. But unlike textual interpretation, which thrives on debate and even requires disagreement to keep the research front moving, craft technique builds a culture of consensus. The scientist must commit himself or herself to the authority of the master to learn precious skills that cannot be imparted in any other way. Only by accepting that craft wisdom, those secrets, does an individual become initiated into the fraternity. One does not argue with a Bunsen burner (not successfully, at least); one learns how to make it perform.

Consensus among active practitioners became in this way a

key basis for the establishment of scientific trust and scientific truth. Ensconced within the hierarchical, disciplining culture of the research seminar, researchers possessing arcane knowledge could present a unified front to the outside world—even if neither the public nor their fellow university professors any longer understood their activities. This still left the question of how to persuade the public to accept what scientists claim is true about the natural world. With Pasteur we turn to the achievement of reproducibility and reliability in the mastery of nature through laboratory techniques.

The world as laboratory: Pasteur

Louis Pasteur (1822–1895) began as a chemist, proving in an early set of experiments that alcoholic fermentation depends on yeast and not, as Liebig and Lavoisier believed, on reactions with oxygen. Microbes—microscopic organisms like yeast and fungi, and particularly bacteria and viruses—became his research specialty. Pasteur elucidated their role as a primary cause of disease and applied his findings to the prevention of rabies, anthrax, cholera, and spoiled milk. Today the simple technique of pasteurization, flash-heating milk to kill bacteria and delay their return at cooler temperatures, applies Pasteurian microbiology to every household refrigerator. In reshaping our domestic environment, Pasteur's science literally made the world into a laboratory.

A potent illustration of this came with the development of a vaccine against anthrax, a costly epidemic among French livestock. Pasteur began by locating anthrax-ridden bacterial samples on unkempt rural farms. After he removed them to his laboratory in Paris, he and his associates could grow and manipulate various cultures at will, under sterile and controlled conditions, and develop a vaccine against anthrax. The Ottoman Turks had long known that a different ailment, smallpox, could be prevented by injecting people with a small dose of the disease; Edward Jenner later proved that inoculation with a related bovine disease, cowpox, conferred cross-immunity to smallpox. Pasteur, however, was the first to create an *artificial* (laboratory-manufactured) vaccine from a virulent strain of the original disease by cultivating a specially attenuated bacillus over generations and generations of cultures. Once he had this strain, he could produce as much serum as he wanted, then ship it out to France's farms for dispensing to cattle. Staging a dramatic demonstration in 1881 at a farm in the rural village of Pouilly-le-Fort, he accurately predicted that every diseased animal there would die but that no vaccinated creature would.

What were the lessons of the anthrax demonstration? The historian of science Bruno Latour summarizes them so well that he is worth paraphrasing.[21] First, training and domesticating microbes is a difficult craft, like printing, electronics, cooking, or building furniture, and the laboratory was the workshop where this craft was practiced. Second, by growing cultures visible to the naked eye, Pasteur made an invisible killer suddenly visible and controllable; he reduced the large scale of an epidemic raging through the countryside to a phenomenon containable within the laboratory's four walls. Most important, Pasteur showed how the world outside could be made similarly controllable. For his demonstration at Pouilly-le-Fort, and for any farm that wished to adopt his remedy, the sanitation of the site and the administration of the vaccine had to be handled according to strict procedures that he had personally established. Without disinfection, cleanliness, inoculation, timing, recording, and statistical analysis, the vaccine would not work and could not be *proven* to work. Farms were not generally clean, farmhands were not generally trained to administer shots, and farm owners were not generally disposed to collect statistics on their cattle. Yet Pasteur's success depended on convincing them to change their ways and in so doing to change the way the world works. He had extended the exacting procedures of the scientific laboratory out from private rooms in university buildings and into wider public spaces.

Only ten short years after Pouilly-le-Fort, Pasteurian science had begun its conquest of the rest of the world, as large swaths of non-European territory came under the purview of laboratory-based microbe-fighters. Starting in 1891, Pasteur Institutes began to be established throughout France's overseas colonies (in Tunis, Tangiers, Casablanca, Saigon, and Dakar) and beyond (in São Paulo, Shanghai, Tehran, and Bangkok). These laboratories made imperial France's medical science a key component of its "civilizing mission" abroad. Tunis, an important site of French colonial and commercial interests in North Africa, offers a revealing illustration. Like European cities, Tunis suffered a series of cholera, typhus, and plague epidemics during the nineteenth century. Muslim doctors had ample experience with quarantine measures; pilgrims returning from Mecca were a known disease vector, for example. Muslim rulers duly solicited learned opinions from the local *ulama* to ensure that such quarantines were consistent with Quranic precepts, the *hadith*, and other components of Islamic law. Over the course of the 1800s, however, even before formal French rule, Islamic medicine all but collapsed in the face of the more effective methods of European science introduced by expatriate physicians. By midcentury, Tunisian doctors were asking their European counterparts to issue them *ijazas* to practice medicine, reversing the flow of medieval knowledge transmission while maintaining a centuries-old practice of written certification. By 1881, with the establishment of an official French protectorate, European doctors had asserted full control over the colony's public health policies and medical practitioners.[22]

Tunis' Pasteur Institute, founded twelve years later, made life safer and more profitable for European colonists and indigenous North Africans alike. It produced vaccines for rabies and smallpox, performed drinking-water analysis, and carried out fermentation studies for vintners fleeing the phylloxera epidemic that almost destroyed the French wine industry. It also transplanted the research mission onto foreign soil. It was in Tunis in 1909 that the Pasteurian Nobelist Charles Nicolle discovered that typhus is transmitted by lice. As a consequence, the colony was divided into sanitary districts, with "doctors of colonization" sent out to teach the "most intelligent" locals to boil their clothing to prevent the spread of the disease. This simple technique—a change of household behavior replicated in a whole population—spread by word of mouth, and typhus was ultimately eradicated from the colony. Nicolle and his collaborators eventually developed a vaccine against the disease, plus others targeting gonorrhea and cholera, and manufactured and shipped serum worldwide from Tunis, in what was no longer a provincial outpost of Parisian laboratory science. "The extension of civilization—that is to say, the work of colonization," Nicolle (no rank imperialist) concluded, "—includes a medical component."[23]

It is useful to contrast Pasteurian with Humboldtian science, for both made the world their laboratory and won public acclaim for their achievements. Humboldt emphasized the universal scope of science, by gathering data all over the world. Pasteur's method emphasized controllable replicability, by carefully establishing laboratory conditions and only then extending them to outside spaces. Why did Pasteur prevail? As Latour writes, his approach meshed with networks of social, economic, and political power—the farm interests, the government statisticians, the overseas colonists. To these powerful interests he added that of the laboratory scientist, who through microtechniques developed in a small room engineers macro-level changes that extend throughout the physical world. What Pasteur accomplished was in many ways a well-crafted illusion—his private notebooks reveal many cut corners and some outright public deceptions[24]—

but Pasteur's public relations know-how meant that he could mobilize economic, political, and social resources on his behalf, to get people to buy expensive sterilization equipment, to get governments to pass laws requiring certain treatments, to get people to change their most intimate habits of food consumption and cleanliness. Science gains its public authority by making amazing predictions, but only by turning the world into a laboratory can scientists establish conditions that enable them to say reliably, "This will happen."

The Humboldt brothers mark the beginning of a split between what are often called the "two cultures" of science and the humanities, albeit one still bridged by the bonds of brotherhood. Pasteur marks its consummation. Beyond Lavoisier's private retreat from the gentlemanly science of the learned academy, and beyond Liebig's antihumanistic crusade to secure "technicians" a place in the sun at the German research university, Pasteur signaled the decisive rift between those who work with texts and those who work with objects. Setting a new standard of objectivity, Pasteurian science proved once and for all the social utility of the laboratory, the very real ways in which it could improve human life. No amount of neohumanist recourse to the values of the Greeks could deny the value of this.

SOCIAL SCIENCE: EXPERIMENTING WITH PEOPLE

The ability of modern science to manipulate and master nature, to command public esteem, and to change public behavior arose from the synergy of a craft workshop fused with a disciplinary seminar. This occurred during the same epoch that the craft workshop itself succumbed to the industrial factory and its rural equivalent, the family farm, lost millions of emigrants to the big city. These changes, and the social problems that ensued, became the province of nineteenth-century social science. Industrialization and urbanization divorced work from home and home from school. New physical spaces, most notably the public school, the factory floor, and the immigrant slum, formed from the dissolution of the premodern household. Novelty made each an open field for experimentation. The values governing each domain— democracy or hierarchy, solidarity or productivity, diversity or assimilation—were still in flux and under negotiation.

Social scientists rose to influence by applying laboratory techniques to places where people now learned, worked, and lived. Disciplines such as economics, sociology, and anthropology were already developing around traditional philological methods. Writers like Adam Smith, Max Weber, and Emile Durkheim provided a body of canonical texts for endless analysis, and written sources like government statistics and travel reports gave their acolytes the means to produce new scholarship. Increasingly, however, the spaces of industrial modernity furnished these disciplines with laboratories of their own. Social scientists became intelligence testers, efficiency experts, scientific philanthropists, and much else besides. Humanists transformed into scientists, they took their white-coated counterparts as a model. They measured and quantified; they indoctrinated cadres of experts in experimental methods; and they crossed into the public domain bearing "objective," impartial findings meant to effect widespread social change.

Intelligence testing in the public schools

Craniometry, the science of measuring heads, enjoyed a golden age in the 1800s. In one of the first sustained applications of laboratory techniques to human beings, scientists—some of them crackpots, but many of them quite respectable—used calipers and other precision instruments to calculate skull volumes in human subjects, both living and dead. The aim was to test hypotheses correlating cranial capacity with racial superiority or the propensity to commit crimes. Despite extensive reliance on exact measurement and quantification, the experiments were inconclusive. The very idea that small (or large) head size might explain, say, the academic underperformance of Africans seems like the worst kind of nineteenth-century pseudoscience. But this is only because scientists have since convinced us that it is possible to quantify what is inside, not outside, the brain, objectively and without bias. Every human being, whatever his or her particular constellation of intellectual faults and fortes, carries a two- or three-digit "intelligence quotient" (IQ), largely invariant over a lifetime, that denotes his or her inherent mental capacity. Intelligence testing is an enduring victory for modern psychology, whose centrality to the development of social science is analogous to that of chemistry in the natural sciences. As a signal technology in the scientific study and assessment of human beings, the IQ test acquired its power when it migrated from Europe's laboratories into America's public schools.

The pioneer of intelligence testing was the Frenchman Alfred Binet (1857–1911). After joining the Sorbonne's physiological-psychological laboratory as an unpaid (and uncredentialed) volunteer in 1891, he rapidly rose to its directorship in 1894—a by now familiar pattern of ascent through craft skill. Binet knew and used craniometric methods, but his experiments straddled the full range of techniques available to the early science of psychology. Hypnosis and handwriting analysis, personal interviews and precision calipers, and a panoply of human subjects, from blindfolded chess wizards to the mentally enfeebled to everyday schoolchildren, all had a place in his investigative arsenal. Binet criticized the overreliance on "sterile experimental conditions" then ascendant in Europe thanks to Wilhelm Wundt (1832–1920) and his students at the University of Leipzig. Wundt, the Liebig of psychology, was the doyen of "brass instrument" methods. Subjecting the study of humans to the artificial controls of the laboratory, he aimed to distill universal truths from particular cases. Binet preferred the diagnostic challenges of the medical clinic, with its attention to individual complexity and variation. He in fact made his own daughters the subject of thirteen years of clinical investigations: Madeleine he found to be the "observer," Alice "the imaginative one."[25]

As a father, Binet refused to rank or compare the incommensurable—his children—but as a scientist he did exactly that. He devised a test including thirty mental tasks sequenced in order of increasing difficulty, such as identifying a window in a picture (#7) or thinking up rhymes for the word *grenouille* ("frog," #24). The point at which a child stalled in completing these tasks indicated his mental age. By 1908, Binet and his collaborator, Théodore Simon, had standardized the test on a sample of 300 normal children so that 80 to 90 percent of them would succeed at each age-appropriate task. The Binet-Simon test collapsed the various qualities that make up "intelligence" into a single quantifiable aggregate linked to the test subject's age. It was replicable by any trained psychologist and ostensibly objective in its content.

The next steps were to gain scientific and then public acceptance. Unlike Wundt, Binet lacked a seminar and therefore failed to create a school to propagate his methods. His intelligence test might have sunk into obscurity if not for Henry Herbert Goddard (1866–1957), an American who chanced on Binet's findings during a scholarly tour of Europe. Trained by G. Stanley Hall, Wundt's first American student, Goddard brought the Binet-Simon test into the psychology discipline's mainstream. Forsaking a traditional professorial career, he worked instead at the Training School for Feeble-Minded Boys and Girls in Vineland, New Jersey. There he obtained far more direct access to experimental subjects. In the moving words of a colleague, "Vineland is . . . a human laboratory and a garden where unfortunate children are to be cared for, protected, and loved while they unconsciously whisper to us syllable by syllable the secrets of the soul's growth."[26] Work with the feebleminded offered a compelling, laboratory-like alternative to the unsystematic methods then prevailing for studying the mainstream youth population. The Child Study movement, for example, converted thousands of schoolteachers into Humboldtian naturalists by sending them surveys asking them to answer all kinds of questions about their students. This procedure yielded an abundance of dubious findings on girls' preferences in dolls (paper edged out china) and 3,000 essays on children's rights. University academics mocked Child Study surveys for their "untrained and untechnical gathering of cheap and vulgar materials."[27]

Goddard was himself an alumnus of the Child Study movement. He gravitated to the Binet-Simon test because it offered a more objective (because experimentally derived), means of studying child development. At Vineland, he could confirm Binet's findings by matching them to a preselected population already stratified by mental ability into idiots, imbeciles, and what, to replace the vague and derogatory epithet "feeble-minded," he nobly termed "morons," after the Greek work for "stupid."*[28] The same method could be applied, he realized, to another, much larger institutionalized group: schoolchildren segregated by grade level. The American school-age population had grown by over 50 percent between 1880 and 1900. During these decades, millions of new immigrants and native-born farmers flocked to the cities and their children flooded their classrooms.

---

*In Goddard's revised definitions, morons have a mental age of eight to twelve, imbeciles three to seven, and idiots below three.

At the same time states enacted new compulsory schooling laws and enforced existing ones. This situation presented a goldmine for psychological research, and Goddard duly introduced the Binet-Simon test to New Jersey's public school population in 1910. Soon teachers from Altoona to Spokane, often far ahead of their school boards, were using it in their classrooms.[29]

School administrators and educational reformers, though, were calling for psychologists not so much to *study* as to *assess* intelligence, and as rapidly and efficiently as possible: to sort students by grade and ability level, to shunt the subnormal into special education, and above all to implement America's democratic promise to give each talented child a chance to rise.[30] It was not Goddard but Stanford professor Lewis M. Terman (1877–1956) who responded most forcefully to schools' crying need for large-scale intelligence testing. Terman earned his spurs when the United States went to war in 1917, working with Goddard and others at Vineland to design protocols for the mass testing of more than a million recruits. (Shockingly, this revealed that the average American soldier had a mental age of thirteen.) He had already developed his now-famous Stanford-Binet test in 1916, and on returning to civilian duties used it to design intelligence testing and tracking programs for the burgeoning school districts of the San Francisco Bay area. Clinching its utility for a growing and very heterogeneous population, Terman adapted the IQ test to mass populations and recalibrated it to measure normal American schoolchildren and even adults.[31] He also popularized (though did not invent) the term "intelligence quotient." Dividing mental age by chronological age yielded what in any normal child, growing in intelligence a typical quantum each year, remains a fixed number. IQ thus became a feature of human individuality itself.

More talented as a statistician than as a Binet-style experimentalist, and bolder than Goddard in deploying his political skill and ambition to step outside the laboratory and engage the world, Terman exemplified psychologists' graduation from laboratory scientists to purveyors of objective expertise whose methods and recommendations informed public policy. Terman's Stanford-Binet test is now in its fifth version, having recently been restandardized using data from the 2000 U.S. Census. Similarly conceived metrics, such as the Scholastic Aptitude Test (SAT), subject teenagers—whether aspiring artists, mathematicians, political leaders, or surfers—to quantitative, one-dimensional asssessments of their mental abilities and scholastic prognosis.

Efficiency experts on the factory floor

Big factories, big bureaucracies, and big machines were all novel features of the landscape of late nineteenth-century capitalism, another domain ripe for the incursions of social scientists. In the United States, industrial robber barons amassed fortunes unmatched before or since in their proportion of the nation's total wealth. A discontented and dislocated working class flirted with European-style socialism more seriously than at any time in history. Self-styled efficiency experts faced with this volatile situation stepped forward with stopwatches and clipboards in hand, ready to make the industrial system run like a well-oiled machine.

Frederick Winslow Taylor (1856–1915) became the guru of what his followers called "scientific management." "In the past," Taylor wrote in 1911, "the man has been first; in the future the system must be first." The first system he put in place was that of the Midvale Steel Company in the dilapidated, malarial, inaptly named "Nicetown" district of Philadelphia.[32] Taylor had worked there as a machinist and later a foreman. Using a method eventually applied to firms across the country, he broke every factory operation into its constituent tasks, tinkered with each one to minimize waste and maximize output, established an exact timetable for its completion, and used crude monetary incentives to get workers to adopt the changes. Taylor won the plaudits not only of business leaders but of progressive reformers like Louis Brandeis, the future Supreme Court justice, who saw in scientific management an opportunity to cut waste in the railroad industry. Taylor's disciples formed themselves into a Taylor Society to spread the gospel of the master from coast to coast and beyond. Even Vladimir I. Lenin, who was dazzled by Taylorism, imported American engineers steeped in its methods to fast-forward Soviet industrialization.[33]

Taylor was not an academic but an engineer. He developed his methods on the job and independently of the European science of work practiced in France, Italy, and Germany. Wundt's students in particular emphasized precise "physio-psychological" measurements of fatigue and laboratory testing of muscle action.[34] Among the first Taylorites to build a bridge to academic psychology were Frank and Lillian Gilbreth, who applied industrial management techniques to their twelve children, two of whom immortalized their parents in *Cheaper by the Dozen*. In a telling reversal of gender roles, it was Lillian, not Frank, who brought academic credentials to the partnership. Frank (1868–1924) was a building contractor by trade, which no doubt provided the inspiration for having his children submit sealed bids to win contracts to remove tree stumps from the front lawn. Lillian (1878–1972) earned a Ph.D. in psychology from Brown University. It was she who humanized the Taylor system by combining insights from academic research with traditionally feminine diplomacy and human-relations skills.[35] Among the Gilbreths' contributions to the American workplace are the suggestion box and the employee lunchroom.[36]

The Gilbreths added scientific cachet to Taylor's methods by combining photography with the stopwatch, thereby creating the time-and-motion study. Scrutinizing workers' movements rather than just timing their productivity, as Taylor had done, brought greater scientific appreciation of the human factor in industrial work. The Gilbreths devised a set of sixteen "therbligs" (their surname spelled backward) to account for every physical action and mental decision involved in factory labor, like "search," "grasp," "inspect," "plan," and "rest." To record these precisely they relied on motion-picture cameras, long-exposure still photography, strobe lighting, and especially stereoscopes (wildly popular at the time, and still ubiquitous in antique stores) to add depth perception. Notionally, photography captured objective "truth" in this world, but the Gilbreths' photographic techniques critically influenced the conditions of experimentation. Rather than eliminating the inaccuracy and subjectivity of the orthodox Taylorite stopwatch method, their bulky apparatus often interfered with natural human movements. But photography also served, positively, as an icebreaker in eliciting workers' cooperation. It gave experimental subjects a break from everyday routine, made them stars on a makeshift movie set, and allowed even the most illiterate and uneducated of them to "put his finger on the materials or the tools in the picture" and offer opinions on developing a new best practice.[37] Lucrative contracts flowed to the Gilbreths' management consultancy on account of their ability to win over workers and managers alike through the mediation of technology. More out of psychological shrewdness than from disciplined psychology, they had discovered and then exploited the social equivalent to Heisenberg's uncertainty principle: that observing human beings changes their behavior.[38]

When this principle was independently discovered by genuine academic psychologists using controlled experiments to test hypotheses, it changed the way social science was done in America. Starting in 1924, the Western Electric Company (the telephone equipment manufacturing subsidiary of what became AT&T) commissioned a group of efficiency experts to carry out a series of studies at its Hawthorne Works plant in Chicago. The experimenters began with a test correlating lighting conditions with worker productivity. They found, not surprisingly, that better illumination induced people to work harder. But they also found that productivity similarly increased when the lights were dimmed, and even that a control group subject to no lighting changes at all boosted its output. From this they concluded that the mere fact of being investigated—knowing themselves to be participants in an experiment—enhanced workers' morale and productivity. The objective for scientific management then became to use this insight to redesign the factory floor to maximize worker contentedness. By 1933, when the Depression finally shut down the Hawthorne experiments, the academic discipline of human relations had been born.

The crucial figure in this development was Elton Mayo (1880–1949), an Australian psychologist who first came to the attention of his American colleagues on an industrial fact-finding mission from Down Under. Mayo soon landed a post at Harvard Business School and also supervised the experiments in Chicago. Among the most intransigent problems he confronted was "soldiering," foot-dragging by workers to diminish output. Mayo's psychology pedigree led him to put great emphasis on workers' emotional maladjustment in explaining the causes of soldiering. Deploying the methods of Freud and Piaget, he instituted an extensive counseling program to get to the bottom of their unhappiness. An elaborate "analyzation" department carried out both quantitative analysis and qualitative interpretation of the results of these interviews, 13,000 of them in 1930 alone. Some managers and experimenters were content to take aggregate statistical data to address the obvious fixable complaints.

Others, though, saw the opportunity to convert the shop supervisor into a lay psychiatrist, insinuating academic techniques into the operation of the factory floor.

Eventually Mayo brought the anthropologist and fellow Australian W. Lloyd Warner on board, and it was he who explained soldiering not as an individual psychological deficit but as an artifact of shop-floor culture, of the group spirit and solidarity that caused workers collectively, if only tacitly, to adjust their work routine to combat management intrusiveness. Warner even likened shop-floor cliques to Chicago gangs or the Australian "totemic clans" he had studied on a Rockefeller Foundation grant.[39]

If America's public schoolchildren were virgin ground for the deployment of scientific IQ testing, its factory workers put up subtle resistance to the techniques of scientific management. Efficiency experts had waltzed into the sites of America's bitterest class conflicts. Their claims to expert status had little to do with scientific objectivity and instead piggybacked on the power of management over labor. However, when efficiency experts actually instituted laboratory conditions, their science forced them to confront the worker not as a recalcitrant test subject but as a participant in factory-floor experiments. In Chicago, the study of individuals matured into the study of groups, and with it a truly *social* science emerged.

Scientific philanthropy and immigrant slums

In these same decades, and in this same city, yet another transformation was pushing social work and charitable activity into the mold of objective, empirical social science. Between the 1890s and the 1920s, two rival forms of private philanthropy carried out experiments involving people. Both addressed the problems of uprootedness and the challenges of assimilation in Chicago's immigrant slums. Both relied on fieldwork to generate research findings and effect public reform. Both targeted their generosity where scholarship, not sentiment, dictated. One, the settlement house, took the neighborhood as its field of experimentation, seeking local knowledge and local improvement as immediate goals on the way to broader social change. The other, associated with the giant philanthropic foundations of capitalist multimillionaires, took the city itself as a laboratory and aimed to produce general policy recommendations applicable on a national, even global scale. The settlement house was preeminently a creation of female social scientists, while the "scientific philanthropy" that ultimately displaced it originated in the highly masculine domain of frock-coated businessmen.

Of the more than 400 American settlement houses that had emerged by the early 1900s, Jane Addams's Hull-House was easily the most consequential. Taking as its model the Oxford University men of Toynbee Hall, who repaired to London's East End to effect moral uplift among the dispossessed and downtrodden, Hull-House combined Christian charity and noblesse oblige with a rare opportunity for elite women (many of them unmarried) to live intimately with the poor. Addams (1860–1935) financed Hull-House from her personal inheritance and a network of fundraisers dominated by college-educated women. Growing from a Victorian mansion to a thirteen-building complex, the institution strikingly resembled Halle's Francke Foundations in its reformist impulses and comprehensive community impact. Hull-House included a kindergarten and child-care facilities for factory laborers, a communal kitchen, clubs catering to different interests and age groups, a gymnasium and a swimming pool, and three stories of living quarters. Many settlement workers lived in unconventional household relationships and sexual partnerships. An art gallery and concerts, a library and a bookshop, a night school for adults and public lectures given by the likes of John Dewey (the famous pragmatist philosopher from the nearby University of Chicago), made cultural and educational outreach an integral, not just incidental, aspect of its mission.

More than a community center, Hull-House also functioned as a prolific site of knowledge production. Its members authored twenty-seven books and contributed over fifty articles to the recently established *American Journal of Sociology*. The pathbreaking, collaboratively written social survey *Hull-House Maps and Papers* documented a quintessential Chicago melting-pot neighborhood bounded by Twelfth, Polk, Halsted, and Jefferson streets. It devoted separate chapters to Jewish, Czech, and Italian populations, exposed child labor and sweatshop conditions, and pioneered the use of color-coded maps (taken for granted today) to depict patterns of income inequality and ethnic settlement in one of the country's most diverse metropolises.[40] The volume won a place on the syllabi of academic sociologists at the University of Chicago, where researchers even sought to annex

Hull-House to the university as a "social laboratory." Addams, however, disavowed this term, because, as she wrote, "Settlements should be something much more human and spontaneous than such a phrase connotes."[41]

Reformers did see settlements as human experiments, but less as contained sites to generate objective data about slum-dwellers than as places to practice encounters crossing lines of class, gender, ethnicity, and ideology. The broader conception of knowledge ascendant at Hull-House was particularly salient in the Working People's Social Science Club (WPSSC), formed in the aftermath of the class warfare surrounding the 1886 Haymarket Riot. The WPSSC did not serve, as the name might suggest, to empower workers with findings from academia, nor to inculcate them with investigatory techniques to document their own disadvantaged condition. It aimed instead to bring rival political viewpoints, even extreme ones, into democratic interchange. Julia Lathrop (1858–1932) called Hull-House a "free platform" offering "hospitality to every man's honest thought," with the WPSSC acting as a venue where "men who differed widely in their social theories might meet."[42] Worker-members harbored not "grievances" or "opinions" but "thought" and even "theory" in the view of this future child welfare activist. Knowledge was local, participatory, contested, subjective, even partisan; "social" science was what people taught each other.

By contrast with settlement houses, the larger philanthropic foundations sought answers to, not questions about, social ills. The tycoons who established them, like John D. Rockefeller, Sr., and Andrew Carnegie, had little patience for open-ended debate, least of all with workers and socialists. By the early twentieth century, they had also realized that giving away a fortune was actually a monumentally difficult task for anyone who cared, as they did, how the money was spent. They therefore targeted their giving scientifically. Carnegie Corporation leaders had for some time felt beleaguered by aid petitions from settlement houses and other charities. They thus determined to put an end to "benevolent receptivity" and "passive sorting" in favor of more active "initiative in seeking out those forces in the social order that promise to be significant and fruitful."[43] At the Laura Spelman Rockefeller Memorial (LSRM), a new, bureaucratic model of scientific philanthropy displaced the personalized giving of wealthy women like Laura Spelman Rockefeller herself. In its early years, the LSRM supported traditionally feminine causes like the Girl Scouts and the Salvation Army. (It also raised $100,000 to buy Marie Curie a single gram of radium.) But by 1929, foundations like the LSRM had made the unreconstructed male domain of capitalist financiers and corporate boardrooms a key determinant of social-scientific research agendas. Ironically, this was the very time that women gained a toehold in academia—witness Edith Abbott and Sophonisba Breckenridge, two Hull-House alumnae who became University of Chicago professors.

Three characteristics of foundation-funded social science marked a profound departure from the intellectual freedom of the Humboldtian research university and also influenced the later twentieth-century "big science" described below. First, foundation officers used grants and contracts to direct monies to specific projects they deemed important and to set out criteria by which their recipients' efforts could be measured.[44] Second, interdisciplinary teams of scholars working on coordinated tasks were favored over the seminar leader and the spontaneous researches of Ph.D. students. Finally, practical results were expected from even the purest science. The Hawthorne experiments embodied this ideology—not surprisingly, since they were in fact funded by Rockefeller philanthropy.

The sociological study of race relations at the University of Chicago (itself a creation of Rockefeller largesse) offers a still more relevant illustration. After the southern and eastern European immigrants around Hull-House, the next great wave of arrivals in Chicago came with the Great Migration of southern blacks. After World War I, Jim Crow and boll weevils sent them north. Robert E. Park (1864–1944), a white man, followed this movement and then studied it as a leader of the so-called Chicago School of sociology. Park had worked under Booker T. Washington at the Tuskegee Institute in Alabama, which taught southern blacks self-reliance and practical skills, before joining the University of Chicago in 1913. After the 1919 race riots, he was commissioned to write *The Negro in Chicago* (1922) with his black student Charles S. Johnson (1893–1956). As was typical of the new empirical sociology, this volume adopted a much more detached, objective, nonpartisan method than the practical experiment of melting-pot assimilation found at Hull-House.

Black female fieldworkers gathered data on 274 families, not in one neighborhood but instead distributed representatively over 238 city blocks.[45] Park explicitly distanced himself from the "explorations" of "social politicians." He particularly disdained what he regarded as the unscientific tenor of female social work. True sociologists, he thought, forsook the local and the personal in order to frame and test broad-gauged hypotheses about ethnic newcomers. Thus Park's fivefold race-cycle theory postulated a progression through contact, conflict, competition, accommodation, and assimilation, styling itself as a model applicable to all types of multiracial encounters.[46]

Midwifed by foundation grants, experimental fieldwork to test hypotheses about the social world finally replaced the interpretive, library-based, philological methods and inconclusive "dialectics" marking the early social-science disciplines.[47] With national horizons, vast wealth, and a nimble, entrepreneurial approach to capital investment unavailable to universities and charitable do-gooders alike, philanthropic foundations committed tremendous resources to a certain kind of social knowledge, one that was statistical and capable of being generalized, free of subjective partisan bias and therefore equally free to dictate public policy. So confident was the Rockefeller Foundation of its objectivity that it even helped the Bolshevik regime in Russia to fight famine and disease and build laboratories and hospitals in the 1920s.[48] Without the support of foundation philanthropy, new forms of social-scientific fieldwork would not have emerged when they did. Rockefeller funding supported scholarship as far-flung as anthropological expeditions to sub-Saharan Africa and the South Pacific, producing studies that served both the progress of knowledge and the needs of colonial adminis-trators.[49] Rockefeller money financed the Kinsey Reports on American sexual behavior, unearthing sensational findings of homosexuality and masturbation in postwar America. With projects such as these, the laboratory had truly graduated into an institution able to unite the public world of science with the most private lives of individuals scattered across the globe. The whole space of human encounters, from the bedroom outward, had now entered the purview of social-scientific experts.

CODA: SPACE AGE MANAGEMENT

In 1969, at the height of the cold war, NASA director James Webb published *Space Age Management*, heralding the applica-tion of social-scientific techniques to the one space still uncon-quered by the laboratory: the cosmos itself. "No nation that aspires to greatness," he argued, "can continue to rely on the methods of the past. Unless a nation purposefully and systemat-ically stimulates and regulates its technological advances . . . it will surely drop behind." The challenges of space travel were as much managerial as technical. In five years under Webb, NASA's workforce had grown from 75,000 to 420,000 people, dispersed in scores of laboratories, universities, government agencies, and industrial contractors. The craftsman's workshop had given way to "adaptive, problem-solving, temporary systems of diverse specialists, linked together by coordinating executives in organic flux." Webb's challenge was to ensure that they could be made to perform new miracles, on budget and on schedule.[50]

Three decades of war, hot and cold, inspired Webb's analysis. Historians have christened this the era of "big science," in contrast to the smaller scale of the pre–World War II laboratory. Beginning with the Manhattan Project, which created the atomic bomb, scientists had brought new, unseen spaces under their purview. They tapped hidden potentials, splitting the atom and revealing the structure of DNA. They mobilized against invisible threats, from polio lurking in swimming holes to Sputniks beeping menacingly from the night sky. Their achievements required vast resources, drew together multiple subprojects running concurrently, and enlisted huge teams of dedicated scientists, engineers, adminstrators, and workers collaborating in worldwide interdisciplinary systems. Laboratory scientists had been charged with scaling up their production of knowledge to benefit American democracy in life-or-death struggles against totalitarian rivals. Under intense pressure, their leaders naturally reached for practices pioneered in the prewar social sciences to guarantee a steady stream of innovations.

Entrepreneurial grant-makers, management experts, and the "best brains" all found central and interlocking roles in the big science projects of the cold war. National science policy czar Vannevar Bush (1890–1974), a veteran of the Hawthorne illumination experiments and a former Carnegie Institute president, led the federal government to adopt foundation philanthropy's best practice in constructing a vast empire of research grants for basic science.[51] However commonplace today, free and open competition for grants was unthinkable in America's Soviet rival, where big science was dominated by central planners and bureaucratic cutthroats.[52] "Think tanks" were another uniquely American creature of federal munificence, trading on the cult of pure intelligence to take on projects undreamed of by the military (and later civilian) officials who wrote their checks. Their archetype, RAND ("Research and Development"), exhibited a promiscuous interdisciplinarity possible only in a climate where sheer IQ could trump specialized expertise. Graduating from a maiden project on the design of an "experimental world-circling spaceship," RAND also produced mathematical simulations of nuclear warfare, studies of Arab class systems, and a mockup of the Soviet Ministry of Economics at its Santa Monica headquarters.[53] RAND's "systems analysts" helped Robert McNamara bring cost-benefit and kill-ratio calculations into the Vietnam-era Pentagon, and helped New York City design urban renewal programs during the Great Society reforms.[54] Systems analysis itself descended from British "operations research," invented to coordinate men, weapons, and materiel during World War II. Along with systems engineering and project management, these social-engineering toolkits were all late offshoots of Taylor's scientific management.[55]

Cold war America was gripped by the belief that raw brainpower, steeled by objective analysis and nourished by farsighted patrons, could meet all of America's military, scientific, and social challenges. Webb's Apollo space program was its clearest expression: a philanthropic mission for all humanity ("one small step for [a] man, one giant leap for mankind"), the biggest of big science management systems, created by rocket scientists who were the best of the best brains. It is easy in retrospect to identify cases where such visions went right (the moon landing), went wrong (Vietnam), or produced ambiguous results (the Great Society, nuclear energy). In every instance, though, Americans view their accomplishments and failures alike as the unique experiences of a cold war superpower, without parallel in Western Europe or before the war. And so they were. Still, the institutional building blocks of big science were already in place by the early decades of the twentieth century. They were simply the twin guises of the laboratory, physical and social, fused together. Uninterrupted wars, for all the dazzling new technologies they inspired, left little time for fundamental institutional innovation. Even today, nearly two decades after the cold war ended, this is the world we inhabit.

Conclusion

By THE mid-twentieth century, the laboratory had ascended to an almost impossibly dominant status as an institution of knowledge. In the summer of 1945, Vannevar Bush,* the leader of America's wartime scientific efforts, prophesied an "endless frontier" of scientific progress at war's end. But the Manhattan Project, which he helped direct, also threatened a darker fate for humanity. The atomic bombs detonated over Hiroshima and Nagasaki gave scientists a transcendent responsibility traditionally reserved for established religions. "I am become death, the destroyer of worlds": thus spoke J. Robert Oppenheimer, father of the bomb, quoting from the Bhagavad Gita (which he read in Sanskrit) after witnessing the first mushroom cloud explode over a site named, aptly enough, Trinity.

Fourteen years later, Walter M. Miller, Jr., published one of

---

*Vannevar is pronounced Vuh-*nee*-ver.

the most famous works of cold war–era science fiction, *A Canticle for Leibowitz*. An army air force gunner who took part in the bombing raids that leveled the ancient monastery at Montecassino in 1944, Miller was deeply affected by its destruction. His novel opens in a postapocalyptic landscape devastated by nuclear war, with the monastery as the sole surviving institution of knowledge. A twenty-sixth-century monk discovers a cache of texts left behind by a certain Leibowitz. An engineer, converted Jew, and modern-day Cassiodorus, Leibowitz had established an abbey in the desert Southwest to preserve knowledge from the twentieth-century "flame deluge." Comically, the uncomprehending monks treat his circuit diagrams and his grocery list ("pound pastrami, can kraut, six bagels") with equal reverence.[1] But these texts ultimately enable people to rebuild civilization, before a new global conflagration sends monks off to the stars in the 3700s. However farfetched this fantasy scenario, Miller's real world was one in which serious intellectuals confronted the threat of imminent apocalypse for the first time since Bede and Abbo of Fleury. Atomic scientists like Oppenheimer had arrogated from monks the guardianship of time. In 1947 they invented the famous "Doomsday Clock," its hands positioned a few minutes before midnight and continually adjusted backward and forward to reflect the likelihood of nuclear holocaust.[2]

Over sixty years have passed since the destructive potential of the laboratory first awed the world. That epoch has witnessed not only a cold war fought and won but also a parade of marvels, gadgets, and discoveries demonstrating the laboratory's ongoing capacity to inspire the human imagination and improve human lives, from immunizations to information technologies, from a man on the moon to the mapping of the human genome. Today we live in an age when the dilemma between Armageddon and Bush's "endless frontier" has (it seems) been resolved in favor of the latter. The threat of nuclear holocaust has drastically diminished since the fall of Soviet communism in 1989, and the same cold warriors who designed computer networks to anticipate and withstand nuclear attack are now celebrated as the pavers of the information superhighway.*[3] Epochal historical events have determined that the laboratory, not the monastery, will continue to dominate the life of learning. Other late-twentieth-century trends, like the democratization and commercialization of knowledge, are now pressuring existing institutions to meet the demands of a "knowledge society." Above all, the ascendancy of the laboratory is reshaping the basic missions of other institutions, pushing some toward obsolescence, giving others a new lease on life.

THE LIFE OF INSTITUTIONS

This book has argued that knowledge has been fundamentally reinvented fully six times in the history of the West. Each chapter has shown how a new institution has replaced the last, react-

---

*It was at RAND, the cold war think tank, that Paul Baran began to develop packet-switching as a means to route messages through networks devastated by nuclear attack; later, this flexible, scalable technology unexpectedly allowed the Internet to expand exponentially.

ing to sweeping transformations unanticipated and unaccommodated by its predecessor. Each such institution has in fact superseded all its forerunners in generating entirely new rationales and practices for pursuing knowledge. This does not mean that of the institutions described in this book, all but the laboratory are now defunct. The monastery is marginalized, but libraries, universities and their disciplines, and the auxiliary institutions of the Republic of Letters—books, museums, and even academies—remain as familiar as the sun in all parts of the Western world and most places beyond. What explains their survival, and in what forms do they endure under the laboratory's aegis? In this book we have focused exclusively on moments of institutional transition and coalescence. In order to understand the current organization of knowledge, however, we need briefly to examine the ongoing life of old institutions once new ones come to predominate.

We have seen that whenever a new institution of knowledge coalesces, it may either absorb its predecessor and give it a new purpose or adopt a wholly different mission and leave it behind. The earliest pair of institutions bear witness to the first pattern. Libraries spread as agents of empire in ancient times, transplanting Greek culture throughout the Mediterranean world. Monasteries later formed amid the collapse of the Roman Empire in the West. But Christians like Augustine had long since adopted the scholarly traditions of the Greco-Roman library and remade them to serve the illumination and analysis of scripture.[4] Every monastery in fact enclosed its own small library, which contained scripture, the Rule, liturgical books and customaries, and calendars and computus manuscripts. Stripped of its previous rationale as an instrument of political power, refashioned as a handmaiden to devotional reading and patient waiting, the library devolved into a mere storehouse of written texts—which it remains today, an empty vessel ready to hold whatever is demanded of it. Monks were the first to reshape its contents and uses, setting a precedent for all later scholars. The library persists, then, as a critical auxiliary to the pursuit of knowledge, but no longer as an institution actively shaping and applying it.

When the university coalesced in the twelfth century, by contrast, it left the monastery in its wake, intact but irrelevant. A rural institution in a newly urbanizing world, one predicated on stability in an increasingly mobile society, the monastery could not be remade to fit new times. Men and women continued to be drawn to it as a spiritual refuge, as some still are today. Even Abelard, that harbinger of Europe's intellectual revival, retreated into one after his showdown with the monk Bernard. But only a few generations later, the university had overtaken the monastery in the preservation of religious learning. Universities indeed vocally propagated Christian teachings through their theology graduates, and added entirely new functions, such as the training of lawyers and physicians. Monasteries, in their capacity as organizers of knowledge, simply never recovered. As Miller foresaw, only a cataclysmic upheaval again rendering civilization a wilderness could restore the monastery to relevance as an institution of learning.

And so each institution has superseded the last, variously eliminating or redefining older practices of knowledge in submitting them to an all-encompassing new rationale. Humanists in the Republic of Letters spectacularly circumvented the university, made intellectually bankrupt by religious conflict, by using long-distance correspondence and reviving ancient rhetorical models to validate new discoveries. Yet the republic was upended in turn by scholars in the disciplines, who renovated and completely redesigned moribund universities, recognizing their continuities with the medieval *universitas* in name only. Indeed some, like Fichte, advocated abandoning the term, so thoroughly did the new "research university" depart from the practices of the past. In particular, the humane letter so beloved of the republic had no use in a world that reconcentrated scholars in face-to-face seminars; academics in the disciplines used correspondence, as we use e-mail and telephones today, merely for convenience. So too books, museums, and academies, which once performed indispensable functions in legitimating knowledge not found in canonical texts, continued (and continue) to thrive in various public and scholarly roles, for education, entertainment, and outreach. But their contributions to knowledge are now governed in every case by disciplinary protocols from art history to zoology; in essence, they have met the fate of the library before them.

The history of knowledge bifurcated in the nineteenth century, the disciplines and the laboratory both emerging from what had still been a unified scholarly republic in the time of the Humboldts. The natural and social sciences of course won secure places among the academic disciplines at the research university. But Pasteur and the institutes named after him demonstrated that stand-alone laboratories could also produce life-altering medical and social benefits, tangibly improving humanity in ways that humanities scholars could only talk about. Social scientists likewise found homes both inside and outside the ivory tower, transforming industries, schools, neighborhoods, and other spaces with their expertise, most notably with the help of large philanthropic grants. Today the laboratory and the research university still stand as partly overlapping, intermeshed institutions of knowledge. Although the laboratory is increasingly the dominant one, the disciplines are in no danger of fading like the monastery. Academic specialties remain a vital means of coping institutionally with the ongoing proliferation of knowledge. But since the central dynamic in the history of knowledge has been for a single institution to supersede its predecessor, the laboratory stands poised to reform and possibly reinvent the disciplines in turn.

ORIGINS OF THE "KNOWLEDGE SOCIETY"

Since 1945, powerful trends in the production, application, and dissemination of knowledge have decisively favored the laboratory's continued hegemony and at the same time undermined the authority of the disciplines, particularly in the traditional humanities. The postwar democratization of American higher learning relied on social-scientific practices to engineer a radical expansion of the university, leaving its disciplinary core an embattled remnant. In the natural sciences, life-enhancing discoveries and profit-making inventions have multiplied the laboratory's links to the business world, driving the commercialization and privatization of knowledge and distancing many scientists from the disciplinary values of pure and public-minded research. Finally, the Internet, hatched in secretive cold war computer laboratories, has revived the ancient dream of a universal library to serve the dictates of democracy and commerce, empowering the public to share information—and possibly knowledge—wholly outside the disciplines. Back in the 1970s, social analysts still spoke of the research university as the institutional anchor of the post-industrial economy.[5] A generation further on, the balance has shifted, with laboratories both inside and outside the university driving the growth of our vaunted "knowledge society."

Democratization

By the 1960s, the universal aspiration to higher education had become a permanent fixture of the American dream. Student enrollments surged in the postwar period, thanks to the combined effects of the GI Bill, the baby boom, the dramatic increase in federal education and science funding after Sputnik, and the scramble for draft deferments during the Vietnam War. Clark Kerr, president of the University of California system, with close to 100,000 students on several campuses by the early 1960s, spoke glowingly of the new American "multiversity" as the world's first truly democratic institution of higher learning. A labor-relations expert, Kerr saw the multiversity as a giant management system with many centers, serving a variety of needs and constituencies—"a mechanism held together by administrative rules and powered by money," as he called it.[6] But no sooner had Kerr issued his paean to the "knowledge industry" in 1963 than students at California's flagship campus in Berkeley presented him with a crippling human relations crisis. What began in 1964 as a protest against racial segregation in the American South cascaded into a full-fledged riot directed against Kerr for his alleged mishandling of students' intellectual freedoms. Activists in the Free Speech Movement, a harbinger of later campus radicalism, also targeted the dehumanizing technology mediating their interactions with university bureaucracy. One donned an IBM punch card with the slogan "Please don't bend, fold, spindle, or mutilate me," venting his rage against the huge computers helping to manage the multiversity.[7]

The student counterculture erupted at a moment of tectonic shift in the cold war university, as the values and practices of the laboratory rolled over an increasingly antiquated institution with the liberal arts disciplines at its core. In the same year Kerr was fired, 1967, the University of California system reached again for the social sciences, using intelligence testing to help implement Kerr's "Master Plan" to sort California high school graduates mechanically into the state's three tiers of universities and junior colleges.[8] A direct outgrowth of the early-twentieth-century IQ-testing movement, the now ubiquitous Scholastic Aptitude Test was designed explicitly to measure not academic achievement but mental aptitude, a quality seen as much closer to basic intelligence. In the 1940s, Harvard president James Conant, a renowned chemist and Vannevar Bush's wartime deputy, had helped secure the use of the SAT as an architect of American meritocracy. And while Conant had also lobbied for a Great Books program at Harvard in an influential 1945 report, "General Education in a Free Society," postwar demographics ensured that the SAT, not the liberal arts and sciences core, would remain his more lasting legacy. The year 1968 was (and is likely to remain) the last time that liberal arts and science majors predominated over those seeking vocational, practical, or preprofessional training in fields like business and education. The 1970s saw a surge of new (sometimes pseudo) disciplines, from mortuary science and recreation services to social work and, notably, computer science.[9] In a pattern reminiscent of the thirteenth century, rioting students had reverted to the search for credentials, with the university reprising its medieval role as the servant of a knowledge economy.

Meanwhile, sixties veterans who held fast to their countercultural principles staged a "long march through the institutions," in the words of one critic. Upon maturing as tenured professors in the 1980s, they led a campaign against classical humanism from within the universities.[10] Gains made in the interim by women, African-Americans, and others cast the traditional curriculum as an anachronism. Students lent their voices to the cause, in 1988 chanting "Hey hey, ho ho, Western Culture's gotta go" in a fleeting revival of sixties-era protest at Stanford. (The chant referred to a required course, not to an entire intellectual tradition.) A program of liberal learning once seen as furnishing the very architecture of the mind was now recast, two centuries after classical philologists created it, as an indefensible glorification of the dead white European male. Even as the democratic demand for more relevance and currency in course offerings licensed the proliferation of ever more specialties, the research university unmoored itself from humanism, neohumanism, and textual canons in any form. Combined, the attack on the canon of Western civilization, the rise of vocational fields of learning, and the substitution of quantitative metrics such as SATs and grade point averages (GPAs) for the subjective, humanistic evaluation of intelligence eroded the very foundation on which the disciplines were first erected.

Above all, the disciplines have ceased to act as lodestars for mass systems of primary and secondary education, as they did when mastery of language and culture formed the chief prerequisite for university admission. Instead, social scientists in schools of education, abetted by large grants from federal philanthropy, have assumed from scholars elsewhere in the research university the task of designing curricula and instructional standards at the precollegiate level.[11] For all the hue and cry surrounding "political correctness," the disciplines' quiet abdication of their former commanding influence over pedagogy represents their most consequential departure from the comprehensive, integrated, tiered system of teaching and research established by Wilhelm von Humboldt.

Commercialization

Even with the humanities disciplines in turmoil in the 1980s, the natural-science and engineering fields thrived as engines of economic growth both inside and outside the research university. Here too the laboratory's institutional expansion built on ample postwar precedent. In his seminal *Science: The Endless Frontier* of 1945, Vannevar Bush had signaled that postwar federal funding for basic science would respect and even reinforce the autonomy of the disciplines. Battling populists in Congress who clamored for practical, applied scientific results from the investment of taxpayer dollars, the former MIT engineer ensured that universities would continue to pursue basic research, leaving the development and marketing of its products to other entities.[12] Federal philanthropy, however, transformed many scientists into grant-seeking entrepreneurs, even if only the highest standards of academic peer review governed the awarding of grants through agencies like the National Science Foundation and the National Institutes for Health. The interface Bush established between university laboratories and their patrons outside the disciplines in fact opened what has now become a revolving door for people, ideas, and organizational practices, eroding former boundaries between the two.

The lures of the laboratory have drawn some of the brightest scientific minds out of the university entirely, many trading research autonomy for more lucrative and influential positions, sometimes in government agencies but above all in the corporate world. Under Bush's student Frederick Terman, son of the famous IQ tester Lewis Terman, Stanford University became, already in the 1950s, the center of what later grew into the world's mightiest concentration of high-technology research and development.[13] Dubbed "the father of Silicon Valley," Terman made partnerships with local industrial laboratories (many at defense contractors) a dominant and still rapidly expanding feature of the postwar research university. He provided critical support to his own students David Hewlett and William Packard, cofounders of one of today's largest information technology companies, and to William Shockley, an inventor of the transistor, a precursor to the silicon-based integrated circuits (ICs) now found in every computer. Just beyond Stanford's campus, Silicon Valley's entrepreneurs, hobbyists, and hackers made the personal computer into one of the laboratory's most profitable and empowering inventions. Illustrating a surprising continuity with the craft workshops of the nineteenth-century laboratory, computing became perhaps the last major engineering field open to uncredentialed tinkerers. Witness Steve Wozniak, a university dropout, and Steve Jobs, who cobbled together the first Apple computer out of commercially available ICs in a San Jose garage.

Silicon Valley today ranks as the most prominent of a number of regional "cities of knowledge" anchored by universities (Stanford and Berkeley, MIT and Harvard, Duke and Chapel Hill), surrounded by business spinoffs in computing, electronics, pharmaceuticals, and biotechnology.[14] The amphibious capability of the laboratory, able to thrive both inside and outside campus walls, has enlarged many such fields to a status dwarfing the research universities where they are now only partially housed. Many of the world's greatest universities all but cower in the shadows of their health centers; even at Harvard, nearly 11,000 of 13,000 total faculty members worked in the medical school in 2007.[15] Thousands more cluster in greater Boston's burgeoning genetics and life-sciences empires. Computing, above all, has generated concentrations of intellect in unlikely locales and without the assistance of nearby feeder universities. Bill Gates, another university dropout, made Seattle the world's software capital after relocating Microsoft, which he cofounded, from Albuquerque. Gates got his break when IBM, of punch-card fame, was in a scramble to match Apple with its own PC and contracted Microsoft to produce what unexpectedly became an astonishingly lucrative operating system. Having become the richest man in history as a result, Gates then used his wealth, as other tycoons did before him, to create the world's largest philanthropic foundation.

The new knowledge economy entices many university scholars out of their professional disciplinary networks and into a host of connections to corporate entrepreneurs, managers, and in-house scientists. The phenomenon of "academic capitalism" now sustains steady channels of two-way contact and mutual influence between research universities and the business world.[16] On many university campuses, technology transfer offices take an active role in patenting and licensing profitable scientific innovations. Faculty members often choose to capitalize on proprietary discoveries rather than publish their findings for the benefit of the wider scientific community. Corporations and universities are in some ways trading places. While university administrators are again turning to corporate management techniques to induce departments to generate more student credit hours and assess professors' scholarly performance, high-technology companies like Microsoft compete for scarce talent by offering generous sabbatical leaves and verdant corporate campuses, even by supporting open-ended academic research.[17] In similar fashion, management consultancies such as McKinsey & Co. recruit talented minds from academia and make them into experimental social scientists. Redesigning hospitals, factories, and other institutions to "mobilize minds" for economic gain, management consultants apply academic methodologies to reap profits and command influence, free from the strictures of disciplinary and professional credentialing.[18] For many "knowledge workers," intellectual excitement is best found not in the traditional havens of academic freedom but where the experimentalism of the laboratory meets and meshes with the entrepreneurship of the corporation.

The Internet

At the center of the knowledge society stands the networked computer, an information appliance born in the laboratory and democratized by commerce. In yet another 1945 essay, "As We May Think," Vannevar Bush envisioned a personal desktop machine that would take the place of an entire library.[19] A keyboard and a viewing screen would allow its user to call up the collected knowledge of all humanity. The machine's memory would record the individual's inspired leaps through masses of texts, enabling the searcher to cope with the overload of learning produced by a civilization more advanced than any that had come before it. Bush's dream for what he called the Memex had been gestating since the 1930s, but computers in his day offered little chance for its realization. The term "computer" originally referred to women enlisted during World War II to perform tedious ballistics calculations by hand, then set to work maintaining behemoths like the ENIAC, the first digital computer, which ran calculations for the H-bomb. True to the artisanal traditions of the laboratory, Captain Grace Hopper and Lois Haibt graduated from the scut work of replacing vacuum tubes to the design of advanced programming languages like FORTRAN and COBOL.[20] It was not until the 1960s that computer scientists could begin to "implement [new] ways in which man produces, stores, and consults the records of the [human] race," as Bush had predicted. Among those inspired by his essay were Douglas Engelbart, inventor of the computer mouse, and J.C.R. Licklider, whose *Libraries of the Future* (1965) described a digitized library networked for access by multiple users and able to learn from and continuously adapt to their queries and feedback.[21]

Bush had never anticipated the networks, both human and electronic, that would call his vision into being by accelerating the act of communication and eliminating the constraints of space and time. The virtual domain we call cyberspace originated in the cold war laboratory's bid to create a "closed world" visualized on computer screens and instantaneously responsive to human direction.[22] Its intellectual forefather, the MIT mathematician Norbert Wiener, developed a comprehensive theory for control of and interaction with machines after Bush assigned him to work on automating antiaircraft gunnery during the war. Reverting to his pacifist instincts after the conflict ended, he cast "cybernetics," after the ancient Greek word for "steersman," as a bridge between the physical and social sciences guiding the "human use of human beings."[23] Licklider, an MIT cognitive psychologist active in Wiener's cybernetics circles, became perhaps the most enthusiastic proponent of this new "man-computer symbiosis."[24] A veteran of the U.S. military's computerized SAGE early-warning system, designed to detect Soviet bombers coming over the North Pole, Licklider helped to convert computer networks from a technological dream into an engineering reality at the Advanced Research Projects Agency (ARPA), the Defense Department think tank that later created the ARPANET, the precursor to the Internet.

Born in a climate overshadowed by war and the use of science for weapons development, computers and computer networks spread in short order to research universities, corporate installations, and ultimately the wider consumer market. The "cyberculture" of the early Internet pioneers bears remarkable similarities to the early modern Republic of Letters as it broke free from medieval universities politicized by religion. Between the late 1960s and the early 1980s, long-haired renegades working within the bowels of a modern-day knowledge-power complex transformed the computer from a symbol of corporate regimentation into a technology facilitating personal expression and open collaboration. Stewart Brand stood at the center of their (human) networks, brokering surprising encounters between the San Francisco Bay area counterculture and research laboratories at Silicon Valley defense contractors. Brand celebrated Norbert Wiener in the pages of his *Whole Earth Catalog* for alternative living; filmed Douglas Engelbart's now legendary demonstration of the mouse, hypertext, and online networking in 1968; convened a 1984 hacker conference attended by Steve Wozniak and other PC pioneers; and recently proposed the 10,000-Year Library described in our introduction. Mediators like Brand instilled the practice of computer networking with the same utopian values of togetherness associated with hippie communes, acid trips, and Grateful Dead concerts.[25] Today's information utopianism, born of a homegrown countercultural humanism to replace the discredited classical humanism of the Republic of Letters, is one of the most enduring legacies of the sixties, and one with deep roots in American history.[26]

The decision to open the Internet to commercial Internet Service Providers in the 1990s was merely the result of a recognition that many thousands of users in computer laboratories across the country and the world had already effectively democratized the network.[27] PCs colonized homes, schools, and workplaces and in short order enlisted users of all ages, interests, and skill levels in the practice of networking. Not long after the defeat of communism in 1989, a new consumer-driven internationalism blossomed with the development of the World Wide Web. A belief in citizen empowerment through access to and consumption of information now acts as one of its chief ideological supports. Users of the Internet themselves reshape the information it makes available. Wikipedia, for example, is an increasingly reliable online encyclopedia created and continually updated by its own users.[28] Google, the Internet's most successful search engine, "relies on the uniquely democratic nature of the web" to rank pages by their popularity, with "a link from page A to page B" interpreted "as a vote, by page A, for page B."[29] Such algorithms apply the "wisdom of crowds," the genius of the modern consumer economy, to the problem of information overload that the Memex was designed to solve.[30]

But the democratized, commercialized Internet in fact serves far more needs than the automated library envisioned by Bush and Licklider. The laboratory has put so much information at our fingertips that many now identify information with knowledge itself. So successful has the "man-computer symbiosis" become, adapting to and simultaneously reshaping human uses of the computer, that craft skill is no longer necessary to secure effortless and instantaneous access to texts, images, music, games, and a cornucopia of useful products and information found online. It merely remains to be seen whether the Internet will continue to embody the laboratory's most powerful technological contribution to the knowledge society or enable online communities to become the germ of an entirely new institution of knowledge.

KNOWLEDGE TODAY

Today the laboratory and the disciplines stand as the dominant remaining knowledge institutions, not only in America but across the globe. Only in the Islamic world do traditional *madrasas* thrive alongside Western-style universities. But those now functioning as training camps for terrorists have catastrophically undercut the ability of what remains a remarkably diverse institution to speak for the humane values of most Muslims.[31] The West's two other historical rivals have long since conceded the university's supremacy. China abolished its Confucian examination system early in the twentieth century, following Meiji Japan in adopting the German research university as a model. Its Confucian traditions of scholarly political activism (and even martyrdom) abided, however, right down through the Tiananmen Square protests led by Beijing University students in 1989.[32] India, as we have seen, has had English-speaking colleges since the nineteenth century, a tradition today facilitating its high-tech takeoff. Gurus, pandits, and *sastras* do still survive in a few fields unrepresented in the Western curriculum, like yoga and Ayurvedic medicine. Already in the early 1900s, however, laboratory researchers in India were hooking up yogis to electrocardiogram machines and respiratory monitors to evaluate *yogasastra's* claims.[33]

Laboratory science and its accomplishments now act as the chief means by which Western knowledge systems manifest their superiority to the rest of the world. The laboratory is, after all, the only Western institution without a non-Western analog. It is also the only one whose benefits to all societies are tangibly demonstrable, and the only one able to travel across international borders largely unencumbered by culturally and linguistically specific canons of knowing. In recent decades, both China and India have sent many thousands of students to North American universities, where they traditionally enter science and engineering fields. Research universities like Stanford and MIT still funnel the best of these foreign scientists into America's knowledge economy. By the late 1990s, Chinese and Indian immigrants were running an astonishing 29 percent of Silicon Valley high-technology startups.[34] But the very portability of the laboratory may soon join with the forces of globalization to draw such firms outside the United States entirely, as has already happened in centers like Taiwan and Bangalore and will no doubt continue to occur in cities of knowledge across the globe.

Amid the worldwide ascendancy of the laboratory, we now face the task of discerning what is enduring from what is ephemeral in a climate of relentless technological hype and brittle American triumphalism. Promoters of the vaunted "information age" often forget that knowledge has always been about connecting people, not collecting information. Computers and the Internet, for all their democratic potential, merely allow us to live out dreams of high-tech wizardry conceived decades ago in an epoch of can-do American ingenuity. New electronic communities such as wikis and blogs, at the moment collectively dubbed Web 2.0, if anything make the pursuit of reliable, authentic knowledge more, not less, difficult online, by drowning out traditionally credentialed cultural gatekeepers.[36] Relatively few networked forums provide a truly democratic alternative to the focused, substantive, reasoned—and elitist—debate that still governs the disciplines. The widespread conflation of knowledge and information reflects what we no longer value about the ways that disciplines interpret texts and ideas, art and music, and other products of culture. Yet the Internet has done nothing to call into question the experiential, technological know-how that has always been the strength of the laboratory. Public fascination with its achievements confounds our attempts to resolve lingering issues raised by the laboratory's hegemony. Conflicts between the scientific manipulation of nature and core human values fuel some of today's most heated political debates. In the health-care industry, the laboratory's most unimpeachable postwar successes—in the cure of disease—are threatened by skyrocketing costs and inequitable delivery, outstripping our best social-scientific policymaking and corporate management systems. And ongoing environmental degradation, arguably civilization's greatest future challenge, looms as a technologically induced catastrophe from which only better technology, it seems, can save us.

Despite such challenges, unbounded faith in science continues to paint humanistic discussions of values as outmoded and sentimental. The very definition of a human being has been unsettled. The analytical tools of information theory have guided the decipherment of the genetic code, leading the Harvard geneticist Walter Gilbert to proclaim, "One will be able to pull a CD out of one's pocket and say 'Here's a human being; it's me!' "[37] The power of computerization has transformed economics into a rigorously quantitative discipline, enabling its practitioners to manipulate large data sets on human behavior and emboldening them to redefine the quintessentially human attributes of rationality and choice.[38] Interdisciplinarity reigns supreme in fields such as cognitive neuroscience and evolutionary biology, breeding excitement but also the hubris that comes from transgressing disciplinary boundaries. Confronting humanities scholars on their own turf, their practitioners offer explanations for why we believe in God or love our children, hate our enemies and help our friends—questions we used to answer by reading Homer or Shakespeare. Even philosophy, that most ancient of humanistic traditions, has become in many quarters almost a subfield of abstract mathematics.

As the knowledge society goes global, the values of the laboratory are likely to continue reshaping the practices and redefining the mission of the disciplines, even as Western-style universities proliferate. This may yet produce more positive change. People in the future may still teach, learn, and carry out research in places called universities. But the laboratory may transform them into spaces of active institutional experimentation and pedagogical innovation. Universal access to codified knowledge online might enable universities to focus on the uncodifiable experiential learning—always a feature of laboratory life—that can be imparted only in person, whether by chemists or by English professors. Producers of disciplinary knowledge might take their cues from the laboratory's engagement with public needs instead of tailoring their ideas, inventions, publications, and pedagogy to enclosed, self-sustaining communities of subspecialists. Increased contact with spaces outside the ivory tower—businesses, governments, hospitals, neighborhoods, social-service organizations, primary and secondary schools—might give scholars the chance to apply and refine their learning in experimental settings. Sixty years of transformations in knowledge have seen movement, however uneven, halting, and contested, in all these directions. Future developments are naturally unpredictable. They may take decades or even centuries; they may occur outside the United States; and they may take the form of subtle rather than revolutionary change. The task for coming generations is to ensure that the laboratory's values of ceaseless experimentation, democratic equality, and social betterment are institutionalized only in their broadest, most empowering, and most humane senses.

Acknowledgments

THE IDEA for this book was born at the Harvard Society of Fellows, whose three years of unrestricted intellectual freedom gave us a critical perspective on the academic institutions to which we have devoted our careers. Its scheme was then tested on undergraduates at the University of Oregon, who gamely submitted to staging disputations, writing mock grant proposals, and copying manuscripts by hand as part of a course called "The Organization of Knowledge." Our gratitude goes first to them. We would also like to thank the librarians at Oregon, who, while pursuing the latest digitized information technologies, have safeguarded access to physical books in a wonderfully appointed library building. This book would not have been possible without the synergy that the modern research library, like its ancient forerunner, produces.

Many colleagues in departments from coast to coast were generous with their insights, bibliographies, and works in progress: Karl Appuhn, John Carson, Michael Gordin, Ellen Herman, Jack Maddex, David Mengel, Itay Neeman, Daniel Pope, Helmut Puff, and F. Jamil Ragep. Maya Jasanoff and Glenn May pointed us to Steve Forman, our incomparable editor at W. W. Norton & Company. Steve is a cybernetician in its ancient, best sense: the steersman of the project, without whose subtle guidance it would neither have set sail nor come home.

This book has been a truly collaborative project from the start. Ian F. McNeely conceived, researched, and wrote most of it, while Lisa Wolverton drafted Chapter 2, shaped the rest, and kept the book true to its conceptual vision throughout. It is lovingly dedicated to our children, Margot and Jing.

Notes

INTRODUCTION

1. See http://www.longnow.org/projects/conferences/10klibrary and Stewart Brand, *The Clock of the Long Now: Time and Responsibility* (New York: Basic Books, 1999), 93–104.

1. THE LIBRARY

1. Peter Green, *Alexander to Actium: The Historical Evolution of the Hellenistic Age* (Berkeley: University of California Press, 1990), 44–48, 72–73, 85–89.
2. Eva C. Keuls, *The Reign of the Phallus: Sexual Politics in Ancient Athens* (New York: Harper & Row, 1985).
3. Henri Irénée Marrou, *A History of Education in Antiquity* (Madison: University of Wisconsin Press, 1982), 26–35.
4. Rudolf Pfeiffer, *History of Classical Scholarship from the Beginnings to the End of the Hellenistic Age* (Oxford: Clarendon, 1968), 16–56.
5. Randall Collins, *The Sociology of Philosophies: A Global Theory of Intellectual Change* (Cambridge, Mass.: Harvard University Press, 1998), 87–88.
6. Ibid., 101–102.
7. Luciano Canfora, *The Vanished Library* (Berkeley: University of California Press, 1989), 49.
8. L. D. Reynolds and Nigel Guy Wilson, *Scribes and Scholars: A Guide to the Transmission of Greek and Latin Literature* (Oxford: Oxford

University Press, 1991), 5 ff. and esp. p. 12 on this anecdote, concerning Zenodotus' rereading of the *Iliad*, Book III, lines 423–26.

9. Alain Le Boulluec, "Alien Wisdom," in *Alexandria, Third Century BC: The Knowledge of the World in a Single City*, eds. Christian Jacob and François Polignac (Alexandria: Harpocrates, 2000), 56–69, elaborating on Arnaldo Momigliano's terminology and writings.

10. "Letter of Aristeas to Philocrates," in *Alexandria, Third Century BC*, 70–71.

11. P. M. Fraser, *Ptolemaic Alexandria* (Oxford: Oxford University Press, 1972), vol. I, 770–75; Nita Krevans, "Callimachus and the Pedestrian Muse," in *Callimachus II*, eds. Annette Harder, Gerry C. Wakker, and Remco F. Regtuit (Groningen: Peeters, 2002), 173–84, quotations on 175.

12. Philip of Thessalonica, quoted in Mary Margolies DeForest, *Apollonius' Argonautica: A Callimachean Epic* (Leiden: E. J. Brill, 1994), 33.

13. Christian Jacob and François Polignac, "The Alexandrian Mirage," in *Alexandria, Third Century BC*, 17.

14. Adapted from Derk Bodde, *China's First Unifier: A Study of the Ch'in Dynasty As Seen in the Life of Li Ssu, 280?–208 B.C.* (Leiden: E. J. Brill, 1938), 82–83, and Tsuen-hsuin Tsien, *Written on Bamboo and Silk: The Beginnings of Chinese Books and Inscriptions* (Chicago: University of Chicago Press, 1962), 12.

15. Oliver Moore, *Chinese* (Berkeley: University of California Press, 2001), 54–72; Bodde, *China's First Unifier*, 147–61.

16. Mark Edward Lewis, *Writing and Authority in Early China* (Albany: State University of New York Press, 1999), 325–31. The most extreme form of this argument was that of the early-twentieth-century Chinese scholar Kang Youwei, who argued that the Han librarians simply forged an enormous number of "classic" texts to lend legitimacy to Wang Mang's bid to usurp the Han throne. See Liang Qichao, *Intellectual Trends in the Ch'ing Period*, trans. Immanuel C. Y. Hsü (Cambridge, Mass.: Harvard University Press, 1959), 92.

17. Lewis, *Writing and Authority*, 4, 337–62.

18. Tsien, *Written on Bamboo and Silk*, 74–76.

19. Canfora, *Vanished Library*, 78–80.

20. Steve Fuller and David Gorman, "Burning Libraries: Cultural Creation and the Problem of Historical Consciousness," *Annals of Scholarship* 4 (1987): 105–19.

21. Canfora, *Vanished Library*, 66–70.

22. Scott L. Montgomery, *Science in Translation: Movements of Knowl-

edge through Cultures and Time (Chicago: University of Chicago Press, 2000), 89–137.

23. Garth Fowden, *The Egyptian Hermes: A Historical Approach to the Late Pagan Mind*, 2d ed. (Princeton, N.J.: Princeton University Press, 1993), 177–86.
24. Maria Dzielska, *Hypatia of Alexandria* (Cambridge, Mass.: Harvard University Press, 1995), 83–94.
25. Peter Brown, *Power and Persuasion in Late Antiquity: Towards a Christian Empire* (Madison: University of Wisconsin Press, 1992).

2. THE MONASTERY

1. Gregory the Great, *The Dialogues of Saint Gregory* (London: P. L. Warner, 1911), 68; R. A. Markus, *Gregory the Great and His World* (Cambridge: Cambridge University Press, 1997), 52.
2. Gregory's authorship of Benedict's life story is today hotly disputed; see Francis Clark, *The "Gregorian" Dialogues and the Origins of Benedictine Monasticism* (Leiden: E. J. Brill, 2003).
3. Saint Augustine, *Confessions*, trans. Henry Chadwick (Oxford: Oxford University Press, 1991), 21.
4. On early Christians' use of books, see Harry Y. Gamble, *Books and Readers in the Early Church: A History of Early Christian Texts* (New Haven, Conn.: Yale University Press, 1995), 203–41.
5. Elaine Pagels and Karen L. King, *Reading Judas: The Gospel of Judas and the Shaping of Christianity* (New York: Viking, 2007).
6. Gamble, *Books and Readers*, 98–100.
7. Ibid., 205, 216.
8. Bart Ehrman, *The Orthodox Corruption of Scripture: The Effect of Early Christological Controversies on the Text of the New Testament* (Oxford: Oxford University Press, 1993).
9. Kim Haines-Eitzen, *Guardians of Letters: Literacy, Power, and the Transmitters of Early Christian Literature* (Oxford: Oxford University Press, 2000).
10. Colin H. Roberts, *Manuscript, Society, and Belief in Early Christian Egypt* (Oxford: Oxford University Press, 1979), 15, 20; T. C. Skeat, "Early Christian Book Production: Papyri and Manuscripts," in *The Cambridge History of the Bible*, ed. G.W.H. Lampe (Cambridge: Cambridge University Press, 1969), vol. 2, 54–79; Gamble, *Books and Readers*, 63–66.
11. Augustine, *Confessions*, 15.
12. Peter Brown, *Late Antiquity* (Cambridge, Mass.: Harvard University

Press, 1987), 12–15; Robert Kirshner, "The Vocation of Holiness in Late Antiquity," *Vigiliae Christianae* 38, 2 (June 1984): 105–24, building on Brown's arguments about philosophers and holy men.

13. James W. McKinnon, "Desert Monasticism and the Later Fourth-Century Psalmodic Movement," *Music & Letters* 75, 4 (Nov. 1994): 505–6.

14. Douglas Burton-Christie, "Listening, Reading, Praying: Orality, Literacy, and Early Christian Monastic Spirituality," *Anglican Theological Review* 83, 2 (Spring 2001): 197–221; idem, *The Word in the Desert: Scripture and the Quest for Holiness in Early Christian Monasticism* (Oxford: Oxford University Press, 1993).

15. Marcia L. Colish, *Medieval Foundations of the Western Intellectual Tradition* (New Haven, Conn.: Yale University Press, 1997), 49. For Cassian's influence on Cassiodorus, see James J. O'Donnell, *Cassiodorus* (Berkeley: University of California Press, 1979), 199–204 and 189–93 on Vivarium.

16. Cassiodorus Senator, *An Introduction to Divine and Human Readings*, trans. Leslie Webber Jones (New York: Columbia University Press, 1946), 67, 70, 110–11.

17. L. D. Reynolds, ed. *Texts and Transmission* (Oxford: Oxford University Press, 1983), xv, 434, xvi.

18. L. D. Reynolds and N. G. Wilson, *Scribes and Scholars: A Guide to the Transmission of Greek and Latin Literature* (Oxford: Oxford University Press, 1991), 86; Reynolds, *Texts and Transmission*, 132.

19. *The Rule of Saint Benedict*, trans. Anthony C. Meisel and M. L. del Mastro (New York: Doubleday, 1975), 63.

20. Debates rage over whether the Benedictine Rule drew from the Rule of the Master or vice versa; see Joseph Dyer, "Observations on the Divine Office in the Rule of the Master," in *The Divine Office in the Latin Middle Ages: Methodology and Source Studies, Regional Developments, Hagiography*, ed. Margot E. Fassler and Rebecca A. Baltzer (Oxford: Oxford University Press, 2000), 73–98, esp. 77 ff. for a summary and a recent contribution emphasizing the Master's priority.

21. Jean Leclercq, *The Love of Learning and the Desire for God: A Study of Monastic Culture*, trans. Catharine Misrahi, 3rd ed. (New York: Fordham University Press, 1982), 11–17, 21.

22. Adapted from Dom Cuthbert Butler, *Benedictine Monachism: Studies in Benedictine Life and Rule* (Cambridge: Speculum Historiale, 1924), 281; see also 42.

23. *Rule of Saint Benedict*, ch. 22, 70.

24. Eviatar Zerubavel, *Hidden Rhythms: Schedules and Calendars in*

NOTES TO PAGES 61–71

Social Life (Berkeley: University of California Press, 1981), 32, mentioning Frère Jacques and Reinhard Bendix's insight about monks as professionals.

25. James W. McKinnon, "The Book of Psalms, Monasticism, and the Western Liturgy," in *The Place of the Psalms in the Intellectual Culture of the Middle Ages*, ed. Nancy Van Deusen (Albany: State University of New York Press, 1999), 49–50.

26. Joseph Dyer, "The Psalms in Monastic Prayer," in *Place of the Psalms*, 59–65.

27. Leclercq, *Love of Learning*, 73.

28. Paul Saenger, "Silent Reading: Its Impact on Late Medieval Script and Society," *Viator* 13 (1982): 383; idem, *Space Between Words: The Origins of Silent Reading* (Stanford, Calif.: Stanford University Press, 1997).

29. Scott G. Bruce, "Monastic Sign Language in the Cluniac Customaries," in *From Dead of Night to End of Day*, eds. Susan Boynton and Isabelle Cochelin (Turnhout: Brepols, 2005), 273–86.

30. *Rule of Saint Benedict*, 79.

31. Margot Fassler, "The Office of the Cantor in Early Western Monastic Rules and Customaries: A Preliminary Investigation," *Early Music History* 5 (1985): 29–51.

32. Rosamond McKitterick, *History and Memory in the Carolingian World* (Cambridge: Cambridge University Press, 2004), 156–73.

33. Boynton and Cochelin, *From Dead of Night*.

34. Mayke de Jong, *In Samuel's Image: Child Oblation in the Early Medieval West* (Leiden: E. J. Brill, 1996); John Boswell, "*Expositio* and *Oblatio*: The Abandonment of Children and the Ancient and Medieval Family," *American Historical Review* 89 (1984): 10–33.

35. David Hiley, *Western Plainchant* (Oxford: Clarendon, 1993), 10–13.

36. Faith Wallis, *Bede: The Reckoning of Time* (Liverpool: Liverpool University Press, 1999), xx.

37. J. L. Heilbron, *The Sun in the Church: Cathedrals as Solar Observatories* (Cambridge, Mass.: Harvard University Press, 1999).

38. Wallis, *Bede*, xxi–xxii, xxvi–xxviii; Charles W. Jones, "Bede's Place in Medieval Schools," in idem, *Bede, the Schools, and the Computus*, ed. Wesley M. Stevens (Ashgate: Variorum, 1994), chap. 5, 261–85.

39. Richard Landes, "Lest the Millennium Be Fulfilled: Apocalyptic Expectations and the Pattern of Western Chronography 100–800 C.E.," in *The Use and Abuse of Eschatology in the Middle Ages*, ed. Werner Verbeke, Daniel Verhelst, and Andries Welkenhuysen (Leuven: Leuven University Press, 1988), 137–211.

40. Wallis, *Bede*, 157 ff., 195.

41. *Historia ecclesiastica gentis Anglorum* 5.24, Colgrave and Mynors translation, cited in Wallis, *Bede*, xv.
42. Richard Landes, "The Fear of an Apocalyptic Year 1000: Augustinian Historiography, Medieval and Modern," *Speculum* 75, 1 (2000): 123–27. On the introduction of A.D. dating on the Continent, see ibid., 114–16; McKitterick, *History and Memory*, 86–97.
43. David Pingree, "Astronomy and Astrology in India and Iran," *Isis* 54, 2 (June 1963): 229–46; Edward C. Sachau, ed., *Alberuni's India* (Delhi: Low Price, 1989 [1910]), chs. 32–62, esp. vol. 2, 10–11.
44. Sheldon Pollock, "The Cosmopolitan Vernacular," *Journal of Asian Studies* 57, 1 (Feb. 1998): 6–37. For comparisons of Latin and Sanskrit, idem, "Cosmopolitan and Vernacular in History," *Public Culture* 12, 3 (2000): 591–625, and "The Sanskrit Cosmopolis, 300–1300 C.E.: Transculturation, Vernacularization, and the Question of Ideology," in *Ideology and Status of Sanskrit: Contributions to the History of the Sanskrit Language*, ed. Jan E. M. Houben (Leiden: E. J. Brill, 1996), 197–248.
45. Sheldon Pollock, "Mimamsa and the Problem of History in Traditional India," *Journal of the American Oriental Society* 109, 4 (Oct.–Dec. 1989): 603–610; Jan E. M. Houben, "The Brahmin Intellectual: History, Ritual, and 'Time Out of Time,'" *Journal of Indian Philosophy* 30 (2002): 463–79.
46. Quoted in Sally Hovey Wriggins, *Xuanzang: A Buddhist Pilgrim on the Silk Road* (Boulder, Colo.: Westview, 1996), 126. See also Sukumar Dutt, *Buddhist Monks and Monasteries of India: Their History and Their Contribution to Indian Culture* (Delhi: Motilal Banarsidass, 2000 [1962]), 319–48.

3. THE UNIVERSITY

1. Antony Black, *Guilds and Civil Society in European Political Thought from the Twelfth Century to the Present* (Ithaca: Cornell University Press, 1984), 19–23.
2. Abelard, "Historia Calamitatum," in *The Letters of Abelard and Heloise*, trans. Betty Radice and M. T. Clanchy (London: Penguin, 2003), 3.
3. Constant J. Mews, ed., *The Lost Love Letters of Heloise and Abelard* (New York: St. Martin's, 1999), 207; Abelard, *Letters*, 86. See also Constant J. Mews, *Abelard and Heloise* (Oxford: Oxford University Press, 2005), 62–79. Some controversy surrounds Mews's attribution of these anonymous letters to Heloise and Abelard.

4. John W. Baldwin, *The Scholastic Culture of the Middle Ages 1000–1300* (Lexington, Mass.: D. C. Heath, 1971), 38; M. T. Clanchy, *Abelard: A Medieval Life* (Oxford: Blackwell, 1997), 169. *Stultilogia* was the word Bernard used.

5. Bernard McGinn, "The Changing Shape of Late Medieval Mysticism," *Church History* 65, 2 (June 1996): 197–219; Barbara Newman, "'Sybil of the Rhine': Hildegard's Life and Times," in *Voice of the Living Light: Hildegard of Bingen and Her World*, ed. Barbara Newman (Berkeley: University of California Press, 1998), 11.

6. Stephen C. Ferruolo, "*Parisius-Paradisus:* The City, Its Schools, and the Origins of the University of Paris," in *The University and the City: From Medieval Origins to the Present*, ed. Thomas Bender (Oxford: Oxford University Press, 1988), 22–46; Baldwin, *Scholastic Culture*, 47–50.

7. Adapted from M. Michèle Mulchahey, *"First the Bow Is Bent in Study": Dominican Education before 1350* (Toronto: Pontifical Institute of Medieval Studies, 1998), 518–19.

8. See Richard H. Rouse and Mary A. Rouse, "*Statim invenire*: Schools, Preachers, and New Attitudes to the Page," in *Renaissance and Renewal in the Twelfth Century*, ed. Robert L. Benson and Giles Constable (Cambridge, Mass.: Harvard University Press, 1982), 201–25.

9. Mulchahey, *"First the Bow Is Bent in Study,"* 413.

10. Gaines Post, "Alexander III, the *Licentia Docendi*, and the Rise of the Universities," in *Anniversary Essays in Mediaeval History, by Students of Charles Homer Haskins*, ed. Charles H. Taylor (Boston: Houghton Mifflin, 1929), 255–77; Olaf Pedersen, *The First Universities*: Studium generale *and the Origins of University Education in Europe* (Cambridge: Cambridge University Press, 1997), 269–70.

11. Paris ca. 1250 had a population of about 80,000, Bologna 40,000. See Baldwin, *Scholastic Culture*, 25–29.

12. H. Koeppler, "Frederick Barbarossa and the Schools of Bologna," *English Historical Review* 54, 216 (Oct. 1939): 577–607, esp. 590–93; J. K. Hyde, "Commune, University, and Society in Early Medieval Bologna," in *Universities in Politics: Case Studies from the Late Middle Ages and Early Modern Period*, ed. John W. Baldwin and Richard A. Goldthwaite (Baltimore: Johns Hopkins University Press, 1972), 17–46, quotation on 32.

13. Lauro Martines, *Power and Imagination: City-States in Renaissance Italy* (Baltimore: Johns Hopkins University Press, 1979), 7–71.

14. J. K. Hyde, "Universities and Cities in Medieval Italy," in Bender, *The University and the City*, 18. On the forms and origins of the *universitas*, see Black, *Guilds and Civil Society*, 44, 49–65.

15. Alan B. Cobban, "Medieval Student Power," *Past and Present* 53 (Nov. 1971): 28–66. On the death threat, see Hastings Rashdall, *The Universities of Europe in the Middle Ages*, ed. F. M. Powicke and A. B. Emden (Oxford: Clarendon, 1936), vol. 1, 171.

16. Hyde, "Universities and Cities," 19–20; Hyde, "Commune, University, and Society."

17. Lester K. Little, *Religious Poverty and the Profit Economy in Medieval Europe* (Ithaca: Cornell University Press, 1978), 180; John T. Noonan, Jr., *The Scholastic Analysis of Usury* (Cambridge, Mass.: Harvard University Press, 1957), 105–7; on Dante and penalties, James A. Brundage, *Medieval Canon Law* (London: Longman, 1995), 77–78.

18. Brian Lawn, *The Salernitan Questions: An Introduction to the History of Medieval and Renaissance Problem Literature* (Oxford: Clarendon, 1963), 171, 163, 173. See also pp. 40–46.

19. Monica Green, *The* Trotula: *A Medieval Compendium of Women's Medicine* (Philadelphia: University of Pennsylvania Press, 2001), 1–61, esp. 49–50. Green argues that only one of the three *Trotula* texts was actually written by a woman. Glasgow and Wrocław already held some of the best-preserved *Trotula* manuscripts in medieval times.

20. Benjamin of Tudela, *The World of Benjamin of Tudela: A Medieval Mediterranean Travelogue*, ed. Sandra Benjamin (Madison, N.J.: Fairleigh Dickinson University Press, 1995), 97.

21. Quoted in Michael R. McVaugh, "The Nature and Limits of Medical Certitude at Fourteenth-Century Montpellier," *Osiris* 6 (1990): 65.

22. Luis García-Ballester, Lola Ferre, and Eduard Feliu, "Jewish Appreciation of Fourteenth-Century Scholastic Medicine," *Osiris* 6 (1990): 85–117.

23. Michael R. McVaugh, *Medicine before the Plague: Practitioners and Their Patients in the Crown of Aragon, 1285–1345* (Cambridge: Cambridge University Press, 1993).

24. Jürgen Miethke, "Die mittelalterlichen Universitäten und das gesprochene Wort," *Historische Zeitschrift* 251 (Aug.–Dec. 1990): 35–36. See also Brian Stock, *The Implications of Literacy: Written Language and Models of Interpretation in the Eleventh and Twelfth Centuries* (Princeton, N.J.: Princeton University Press, 1983).

25. Nancy Siraisi, *Taddeo Alderotti and His Pupils: Two Generations of Italian Medical Learning* (Princeton, N.J.: Princeton University Press, 1981), 244–45; see also 237–46.

26. Bohumil Ryba, ed., *Magistri Iohannis Hus Quodlibet . . . Anni 1411 Habitae Enchiridion* (Prague: Orbis, 1948), 218–27.

27. See Howard Kaminsky, "The University of Prague in the Hussite Revolution: The Role of the Masters," in Baldwin and Goldthwaite, *Universities in Politics*, 79–106, esp. 90–99.

28. R. N. Swanson, *Universities, Academics, and the Great Schism* (Cambridge: Cambridge University Press, 1979), 2, 18.

29. First flourishing under Caliph al-Mamun (r. 813–833), the House of Wisdom (Bait al-Hikmah) may actually have been founded by his predecessor, al-Rashid (r. 786–809).

30. A. I. Sabra, "Situating Arabic Science: Locality Versus Essence," *Isis* 87, 4 (Dec. 1996): 654–70.

31. Scott L. Montgomery, *Science in Translation: Movements of Knowledge through Cultures and Time* (Chicago: University of Chicago Press, 2000), 60–88, 89–137.

32. See F. Jamil Ragep, "Tusi and Copernicus: The Earth's Motion in Context," *Science in Context* 14, 1–2 (2001): 145–63; idem, "Copernicus and His Islamic Predecessors: Some Historical Remarks," *Filozofski vestnik* 25, 2 (2004): 125–42.

33. Richard W. Bulliet, *Islam: The View from the Edge* (New York: Columbia University Press, 1994), 81–86, 105–11, 180–83; Jonathan Berkey, *The Formation of Islam* (Cambridge: Cambridge University Press, 2003), 144–45.

34. Geraldine Brooks, *Nine Parts of Desire: The Hidden World of Islamic Women* (New York: Anchor, 1995), 41–42.

35. Brinkley Messick, *The Calligraphic State: Textual Domination and History in a Muslim Society* (Berkeley: University of California Press, 1993), 21–36.

36. Jonathan Berkey, *The Transmission of Knowledge in Medieval Cairo: A Social History of Islamic Education* (Princeton, N.J.: Princeton University Press, 1992), 161–81.

37. Francis Robinson, "Technology and Religious Change: Islam and the Impact of Print," *Modern Asian Studies* 27, 1 (Feb. 1993): 229–51; see also Johannes Pedersen, *The Arabic Book* (Princeton, N.J.: Princeton University Press, 1984); William A. Graham, "Traditionalism in Islam: An Essay in Interpretation," *Journal of Interdisciplinary History* 23, 3 (Winter 1993): 495–522.

38. Bulliet, *Islam*, 130–31, 141, 146–51, 166–67.

39. George Makdisi, *The Rise of Colleges: Institutions of Learning in Islam and the West* (Edinburgh: Edinburgh University Press, 1981); idem, *The Rise of Humanism in Classical Islam and the Christian West: With Special Reference to Scholasticism* (Edinburgh: Edinburgh University Press, 1990).

40. Berkey, *The Formation of Islam*, 226–27, 241.

41. See Graham, "Traditionalism," 501–14; Berkey, *Transmission of Knowledge*, 21–43.

4. THE REPUBLIC OF LETTERS

1. Quoted from the *Histoire de la République des Lettres en France* in Lorraine Daston, "The Ideal and Reality of the Republic of Letters in the Enlightenment," *Science in Context* 4, 2 (1991): 367.
2. See Hilde de Ridder-Symoens, "Mobility," in *Universities in Early Modern Europe, 1500–1800*, ed. Hilde de Ridder-Symoens (Cambridge: Cambridge University Press, 1996), 416–48.
3. Translated in Andrea Nye, *The Princess and the Philosopher: Letters of Elisabeth of the Palatine to René Descartes* (Lanham, Md.: Rowman & Littlefield, 1999), 21.
4. Maarten Ultee, "The Republic of Letters: Learned Correspondence, 1680–1720," *Seventeenth Century* 2, 1 (1987): 100.
5. Walter Rüegg, "Themes," in *Universities in Early Modern Europe*, 27.
6. M. de Vigneul-Marville in 1699, cited by Paul Dibon, "Communication in the Respublica Literaria of the 17th Century," *Res Publica Litterarum* 1 (1978): 42.
7. From the peroration to Descartes' *Discourse on Method* (1637), quoted by Marc Fumaroli, "The Republic of Letters," *Diogenes* 143 (1988): 135–36.
8. As reported by Pliny the Elder, cited in Jonathan D. Spence, *The Memory Palace of Matteo Ricci* (New York: Viking Penguin, 1984), 157.
9. See Giles Constable, "Petrarch and Monasticism," in *Francesco Petrarca: Citizen of the World*, ed. Aldo S. Bernardo (Albany: State University of New York Press, 1980), 53–100.
10. Francis Petrarch, *Letters of Old Age*, trans. Aldo S. Bernardo, Saul Levin, and Reta A. Bernardo (Baltimore: Johns Hopkins University Press, 1992), vol. 2, 672. See also Morris Bishop, *Petrarch and His World* (Bloomington: Indiana University Press, 1963), 229–31.
11. Lisa Jardine, *Erasmus, Man of Letters: The Construction of Charisma in Print* (Princeton, N.J.: Princeton University Press, 1993), 150.
12. See Dibon, "Communication in the Respublica Literaria," 46–53, and, for an early example, Ernest Wilkins, "On the Carriage of Petrarch's Letters," *Speculum* 35, 2 (Apr. 1960): 214–23.
13. Daston, "Ideal and Reality," 378.
14. Letter from Henri Justel in Henry Oldenbourg, *Correspondence*, ed.

and trans. A. Rupert Hall and Marie Boas Hall (Madison: University of Wisconsin Press, 1965), vol. 4, 173–75 (letter #778). For this analysis, see David S. Lux and Harold J. Cook, "Closed Circles or Open Networks? Communicating at a Distance During the Scientific Revolution," *History of Science* 36, 2 (1998): 179–211.

15. Peter Burke, "Erasmus and the Republic of Letters," *European Review* 7, 1 (1999): 5–17.

16. Geoffrey Symcox and Blair Sullivan, *Christopher Columbus and the Enterprise of the Indies: A Brief History with Documents* (New York: Bedford/St. Martin, 2005), 24–25.

17. Anthony Grafton, April Shelford, and Nancy G. Siraisi, *New Worlds, Ancient Texts: The Power of Tradition and the Shock of Discovery* (Cambridge, Mass.: Harvard University Press, 1992), 36, 83–85; *Letters from a New World: Amerigo Vespucci's Discovery of America*, ed. Luciano Formiasano (New York: Marsilio, 1992), 30; David Marsh, book review, *Renaissance Quarterly* 47, 2 (Summer 1994): 399.

18. Grafton et al., *New Worlds, Ancient Texts*, 18–20, 36.

19. Robert S. Westman, "Proof, Poetics, and Patronage: Copernicus's Preface to *De Revolutionibus*," in *Reappraisals of the Scientific Revolution*, ed. David C. Lindberg and Robert S. Westman (Cambridge: Cambridge University Press, 1990), 167–206.

20. Nicholas Copernicus, *On the Revolutions*, trans. Edward Rosen (Baltimore: Johns Hopkins University Press, 1992 [1543]), xvi, 3–4.

21. Jane T. Tolbert, "Peiresc and Censorship: The Inquisition and the New Science, 1610–1637," *Catholic Historical Review* 89, 1 (2003): 34–35; see also Peter N. Miller, *Peiresc's Europe: Learning and Virtue in the Seventeenth Century* (New Haven, Conn.: Yale University Press, 2000).

22. Letter of May 12, 1635, translated by Stillman Drake, at http://shl .stanford.edu/Eyes/kircher/galileopeiresc.html, accessed Nov. 30, 2005.

23. Walter E. Houghton, "The English Virtuoso in the Seventeenth Century," *Journal of the History of Ideas* 3, 1 (Jan. 1942): 51–73, and 3, 2 (Apr. 1942): 190–219. See also William Eamon, "Court, Academy, and Printing House: Patronage and Scientific Careers in Late Renaissance Italy," in *Patronage and Institutions: Science, Technology, and Medicine at the European Court, 1500–1750*, ed. Bruce T. Moran (Rochester, N.Y.: Boydell, 1991), 25–50; H. G. Koenigsberger, *Politicians and Virtuosi: Essays in Early Modern History* (London: Hambledon, 1986).

24. Thomas J. Müller-Bahlke and Klaus E. Goltz, *Die Wunderkammer: Die Kunst- Und Naturalienkammer Der Franckeschen Stiftungen Zu Halle (Saale)* (Halle: Verlag der Franckeschen Stiftungen, 1998).

25. Lorraine Daston and Katharine Park, *Wonders and the Order of Nature, 1150–1750* (New York: Zone Books, 1998), 272–73.
26. Adapted from Daston and Park, *Wonders,* 266, and, more generally, 255–301. See also O. R. Impey and Arthur MacGregor, *The Origins of Museums: The Cabinet of Curiosities in Sixteenth and Seventeenth-Century Europe* (Oxford: Oxford University Press, 1985).
27. Paula Findlen, "Building the House of Knowledge: The Structures of Thought in Late Renaissance Europe," in *The Structure of Knowledge: Classifications of Science and Learning since the Renaissance,* ed. Tore Frängsmyr (Berkeley: University of California Press, 2001).
28. Paula Findlen, "Scientific Spectacle in Baroque Rome: Athanasius Kircher and the Roman College Museum," in *Jesuit Science and the Republic of Letters,* ed. Mordechai Feingold (Cambridge, Mass.: MIT Press, 2003), 256. On snakestones, see Martha Baldwin, "The Snakestone Experiments: An Early Modern Medical Debate," *Isis* 86, 3 (1995): 394–418.
29. Grafton et al., *New Worlds, Ancient Texts.*
30. Daston and Park, *Wonders,* 231, and 215–54 more generally.
31. Lorraine Daston, "Baconian Facts, Academic Civility, and the Prehistory of Objectivity," *Annals of Scholarship* 8 (1991): 337–63.
32. James Hankins, "The Myth of the Platonic Academy of Florence," *Renaissance Quarterly* 44, 3 (1991): 434–35, n18; Elaine Fantham, *Roman Literary Culture: From Cicero to Apuleius* (Baltimore: Johns Hopkins University Press, 1996), 48–51.
33. Frances Yates, "The Italian Academies," in *Renaissance and Reform: The Italian Contribution* (London: Routledge & Kegan Paul, 1983 [1949]), 6–29; Richard S. Samuels, "Benedetto Varchi, the Accademia Degli Infiammati, and the Origins of the Italian Academic Movement," *Renaissance Quarterly* 29, 4 (1976): 599–634.
34. Ian F. McNeely, "The Renaissance Academies between Science and the Humanities," http://hdl.handle.net/1794/2960; Frances Yates, *The French Academies of the Sixteenth Century* (London: Warburg Institute/University of London, 1947).
35. Frances Yates, *Giordano Bruno and the Hermetic Tradition* (Chicago: University of Chicago Press, 1964); idem, *The Rosicrucian Enlightenment* (London: Routledge & Kegan Paul, 1972).
36. Londa Schiebinger, *The Mind Has No Sex? Woman and the Origins of Modern Science* (Cambridge, Mass.: Harvard University Press, 1989), 17–35, 47–58, 82 ff.
37. Dena Goodman, *The Republic of Letters: A Cultural History of the French Enlightenment* (Ithaca: Cornell University Press, 1995), 90–135.

38. Mario Biagioli, "Etiquette, Interdependence, and Sociability in Seventeenth-Century Science," *Critical Inquiry* 22 (1996): 193–238.

39. Steven Shapin, *A Social History of Truth: Civility and Science in Seventeenth-Century England* (Chicago: University of Chicago Press, 1994), 65–125.

40. Henri Irénée Marrou, *A History of Education in Antiquity* (Madison: University of Wisconsin Press, 1982), 64.

41. John Meskill, *Academies in Ming China: A Historical Essay* (Tucson: University of Arizona Press, 1982), x–xii. Both of Ricci's labels, "academy" (for *shuyuan*) and "*literati*" (for *shi*), have been adopted by modern historians.

42. John Meskill, "Academies and Politics in the Ming Dynasty," in *Chinese Government in Ming Times: Seven Studies*, ed. Charles O. Hucker (New York: Columbia University Press, 1969), 149–74; Linda A. Walton, *Academies and Society in Southern Sung China* (Honolulu: University of Hawaii Press, 1999).

43. John W. Dardess, *Blood and History in China: The Donglin Faction and Its Repression, 1620–1627* (Honolulu: University of Hawaii Press, 2002); Charles O. Hucker, "The Tung-Lin Movement of the Late Ming Period," in *Chinese Thought and Institutions*, ed. John King Fairbank (Chicago: University of Chicago Press, 1957), 132–62; Benjamin A. Elman, "Imperial Politics and Confucian Societies in Late Imperial China," *Modern China* 15, 4 (Oct. 1989): 379–418.

44. Kai-wing Chow, *Publishing, Culture, and Power in Early Modern China* (Stanford, Calif.: Stanford University Press, 2004), 233–40.

45. Jerry Dennerline, *The Chia-Ting Loyalists: Confucian Leadership and Social Change in Seventeenth-Century China* (New Haven, Conn.: Yale University Press, 1981); William S. Atwell, "From Education to Politics: The Fu She," in *The Unfolding of Neo-Confucianism*, ed. William T. De Bary (New York: Columbia University Press, 1975), 333–68; Chow, *Publishing, Culture, and Power*. Many Ming loyalists did retreat into isolation, cultivating poetry, painting, and calligraphy and often subsisting as hermits.

46. Benjamin A. Elman, *On Their Own Terms: Science in China, 1550–1900* (Cambridge, Mass.: Harvard University Press, 2005).

5. THE DISCIPLINES

1. Adam Smith, *An Inquiry into the Nature and Causes of the Wealth of Nations*, ed. Lawrence Dickey (Indianapolis: Hackett, 1993 [1776]),

8. For his reservations about compulsory public education, which he did advocate, albeit in a limited sense, at a basic level, see 181–92.

2. Denis Diderot, *Political Writings*, trans. and ed. John Hope Mason and Robert Wokler (Cambridge: Cambridge University Press, 1992), 21. See also Robert Darnton, *The Business of Enlightenment: A Publishing History of the* Encyclopédi, *1775–1800* (Cambridge, Mass.: Harvard University Press, 1979).

3. Johann Wolfgang von Goethe, *Faust*, trans. Stuart Atkins (Princeton, N.J.: Princeton University Press, 1994), 13–14.

4. Theodore Ziolkowski, *German Romanticism and Its Institutions* (Princeton, N.J.: Princeton University Press, 1990), 228–37, quotation on 229.

5. James van Horn Melton, *Absolutism and the Eighteenth-Century Origins of Compulsory Schooling in Prussia and Austria* (Cambridge: Cambridge University Press, 1988), 23, 41, 52–53.

6. Kuno Francke, *Further Documents Concerning Cotton Mather and August Hermann Francke* (New York: n.p., 1897), 64.

7. Wolf Oschlies, *Die Arbeits- und Berufspädagogik August Hermann Franckes (1663–1727)* (Witten: Luther-Verlag, 1969), 25–45; Franz Hofmann, ed., *August Hermann Francke: Das Humanistische Erbe des Grossen Erziehers* (Halle: Francke Komitee, 1965), 33, 36–43, 60–64; Renate Wilson, *Pious Traders in Medicine: A German Pharmaceutical Network in Eighteenth-Century North America* (University Park: Pennsylvania State University Press, 2000).

8. Bart Ehrman, *Misquoting Jesus: The Story Behind Who Changed the Bible and Why* (New York: HarperCollins, 2005), 78–88, 102–5.

9. Donald F. Lach, "The Sinophilism of Christian Wolff," *Journal of the History of Ideas* 14, 4 (Oct. 1953): 562–65.

10. Jonathan Sheehan, *The Enlightenment Bible: Translation, Scholarship, Culture* (Princeton, N.J.: Princeton University Press, 2005), 98–101.

11. Emil Rössler, *Die Gründung der Universität Göttingen* (Göttingen: Vandenhoeck & Ruprecht, 1855), 8.

12. William Clark, *Academic Charisma and the Origins of the Research University* (Chicago: University of Chicago Press, 2006), 380; R. Steven Turner, "University Reformers and Professional Scholarship in Germany 1760–1806," in *The University in Society*, ed. Lawrence Stone (Princeton, N.J.: Princeton University Press, 1974), vol. 2, 509.

13. *Göttingische Anzeigen von gelehrten Sachen*, 2 Sep. 1775, 897–912; 24 Mar. 1785, 449–64.

14. Clark, *Academic Charisma*, 53–63; Luigi Marino, *Praeceptores Germaniae: Göttingen 1770–1820* (Göttingen: Vandenhoeck & Ruprecht,

1995 [1975]), 259–62. False advertising, whereby professors touted courses that were never given, became a serious problem for lecture catalogs.

15. Sheehan, *Enlightenment Bible*, 184–85.
16. David Sorkin, "Reclaiming Theology for the Enlightenment: The Case of Siegmund Jacob Baumgarten (1706–1757)," *Central European History* 36, 4 (Dec. 2003): 503–30, 511–13; Marino, *Praeceptores Germaniae*, 283–88, 292–93. The Halle theologians S. J. Baumgarten and J. S. Semler developed the "accommodation" theory.
17. Sheehan, *Enlightenment Bible*, 186–211, quotation on 205.
18. Anthony J. La Vopa, *Grace, Talent, and Merit: Poor Students, Clerical Careers, and Professional Ideology in Eighteenth-Century Germany* (Cambridge: Cambridge University Press, 1988), 209–15, 239, 307–24. These innovations are associated with the seminar's first director (1737–1762), J. M. Gesner.
19. Clark, *Academic Charisma*, 159, 166–77; idem, "On the Dialectical Origins of the Research Seminar," *History of Science* 27 (1989): 111–54, esp. 132–33. These innovations are associated with the seminar's third director (1763–1812), C. G. Heyne.
20. Anthony Grafton, "Polyhistor into *Philolog*: Notes on the Transformation of German Classical Scholarship, 1780–1850," *History of Universities* 3 (1983): 159–92, esp. 179–83. J. G. Eichhorn, another Michaelis disciple and a Göttingen seminarist under Heyne, developed the methods Wolf applied to Homer. See Anthony Grafton, "*Prolegomena* to Friedrich August Wolf," *Journal of the Warburg and Courtauld Institutes* 44 (1981): 101–29, esp. 121–24, showing how in Eichhorn's *Introduction to the Old Testament*, the Masoretic editors of the Hebrew Old Testament functioned as an analog to the Alexandrian editors of Homer.
21. Wilhelm von Humboldt, *Briefe an Friedrich August Wolf* (Berlin: W. de Gruyter, 1990), 52–53.
22. Wilhelm von Humboldt, *On Language* (Cambridge: Cambridge University Press, 1999), 24.
23. Brian Hatcher, "Indigent Brahmans, Industrious Pandits: Bourgeois Ideology and Sanskrit Pandits in Colonial Calcutta," *Comparative Studies of South Asia, Africa, and the Middle East* 16, 1 (1996): 15–26, esp. 18–20.
24. Sheldon Pollock, "The Theory of Practice and the Practice of Theory in Indian Intellectual History," *Journal of the American Oriental Society* 105, 3 (July–Sept. 1985): 499–519, esp. 502, 506–7, 514–16.
25. A. Berriedale Keith, *A History of Sanskrit Literature* (Oxford: Oxford University Press, 1920), 403–11; A. S. Altekar, *Education in Ancient*

India, 6th ed. (Varanasi: Nand Kishore & Bros., 1965), 17–18, 147–53, 162–64; Axel Michaels, ed., *The Pandit: Traditional Scholarship in India* (New Delhi: Manohar, 2001); Jonathan Parry, "The Brahmanical Tradition and the Technology of the Intellect," in *Reason and Morality*, ed. Joanna Overing (London: Tavistock, 1985), 200–25.

26. *Mahabharata* 12.59, discussed in Pollock, "Theory of Practice," 512.

27. William Ward, *A View of the History, Literature, and Religion of the Hindoos: Including a Minute Description of Their Manners and Customs* (London: Black, Parbury, and Allen, 1817), vol. 1, 282.

28. Pierre-Sylvain Filliozat, *The Sanskrit Language: An Overview* (Varanasi: Indica Books, 2000), 98–99.

29. Richard Lariviere, "Justices and *Panditas*: Some Ironies in Contemporary Readings of the Hindu Legal Past," *Journal of Asian Studies* 48, 4 (Nov. 1989): 757–69, esp. 759–62.

30. J. Duncan M. Derrett, "The British as Patrons of the Sastra," in *Religion, Law, and the State in India* (New York: Free Press, 1968), 225–73, esp. 228, 247, 265–67 on the apparently fabricated *Mahanirvana-Tantra*. On this see also Hugh B. Urban, *Tantra: Sex, Secrecy, Politics, and Power in the Study of Religion* (Berkeley: University of California Press, 2003), 63–69. For context, see David Kopf, *British Orientalism and the Bengal Renaissance* (Berkeley: University of California Press, 1969).

31. *Friend of India* no. 1 (1820, emphasis added), cited in M. A. Laird, "The Contribution of the Serampore Missionaries to Education in Bengal," *Bulletin of the School of Oriental and African Studies* 31, 1 (1968): 107; also see pp. 93–94, 98.

32. Hatcher, "Indigent Brahmans," 18–22, referring to Sumanta Banerjee, *The Parlour and the Streets: Elite and Popular Culture in Nineteenth-Century Calcutta* (Calcutta: Seagull Books, 1989), 189; Brian Hatcher, *Idioms of Improvement: Vidyasagar and Cultural Encounter in Bengal* (Calcutta: Oxford University Press, 1966), 49–52, 117–37; Samita Sinha, *Pandits in a Changing Environment: Centres of Sanskrit Learning in Nineteenth Century Bengal* (Calcutta: Sarat Book House, 1993).

33. See Ian F. McNeely, "The Humboldts' Marriage and the Gendering of Intellectual Space," http://hdl.handle.net/1794/1439, accessed July 26, 2007.

34. Anna von Sydow, ed., *Wilhelm und Caroline von Humboldt in ihren Briefen* (Berlin, 1909), vol. 3, 64.

35. This is a key argument of *The Conflict of the Faculties*, trans. Mary J. Gregor (Lincoln: University of Nebraska Press, 1992).

36. Much of this is paraphrased from Terry P. Pinkard, *Hegel: A Biography* (Cambridge: Cambridge University Press, 2000), 371, 456, 611-12.

37. Daniel Breazeale, ed., *Fichte: Early Philosophical Writings* (Ithaca: Cornell University Press, 1988), 19-20, 147; Ziolkowski, *German Romanticism*, 232-36, 240-46.

38. J. G. Fichte, "Deduced Scheme for an Academy to Be Established in Berlin," in *The Educational Theory of J. G. Fichte*, ed. G. H. Turnbull (London: University Press of Liverpool, 1926), 170-259; see esp. 191, 199, 208-11, 227-29.

39. Göttingen's lecture catalog listed *Privatdozenten* starting in 1756, but Berlin was the first to provide public lecture halls. Berlin also pioneered the requirement that lecturers present a second dissertation *(Habilitationsschrift)* for their teaching license. See Alexander Busch, *Die Geschichte des Privatdozenten: Eine soziologische Studie zur großbetrieblichen Entwicklung der deutschen Universitäten* (Stuttgart: Ferdinand Enke Verlag, 1959), 1, 17n45, 29.

40. Rüdiger Safranski, *Schopenhauer and the Wild Years of Philosophy* (Cambridge, Mass.: Harvard University Press, 1990), 252.

41. Busch, *Geschichte des Privatdozenten*, 42.

42. Karl Marx, "A Contribution to the Critique of Hegel's *Philosophy of Right*," in *Early Writings*, trans. Rodney Livingstone and Gregor Benton (New York: Vintage, 1975), 250.

43. Busch, *Geschichte des Privatdozenten*, 21n60.

44. Joseph Ben-David and Randall Collins, "Social Factors in the Origins of a New Science: The Case of Psychology," *American Sociological Review* 31 (1966): 451-65.

45. Gert Schubring, "Kabinett—Seminar—Institut: Raum und Rahmen des forschenden Lernens," *Berichte zur Wissenschaftsgeschichte* 23 (2000): 269-85; idem, "The Rise and Decline of the Bonn Natural Sciences Seminar," *Osiris* 5, 2d ser. (1989): 57-93.

46. Gino Benzoni, "Ranke's Favorite Source: The Venetian *Relazioni*," in *Leopold von Ranke and the Shaping of the Historical Discipline*, ed. Georg Iggers and James Powell (Syracuse, N.Y.: Syracuse University Press, 1990), 45-58.

47. Quoted in Bonnie G. Smith, *The Gender of History: Men, Women, and Historical Practice* (Cambridge, Mass.: Harvard University Press, 1998), 119; see also 103-29.

48. Walter Prescott Webb, "The Historical Seminar: Its Outer Shell and Its Inner Spirit," *Mississippi Valley Historical Review* 42, 1 (June 1955): 9-10, 20. See also Carl Diehl, *Americans and German Scholarship 1770-1870* (New Haven, Conn.: Yale University Press,

1978); Caroline Winterer, *The Culture of Classicism: Ancient Greece and Rome in American Intellectual Life, 1780–1910* (Baltimore: Johns Hopkins University Press, 2002).

49. Ernest Gellner, *Nations and Nationalism* (Ithaca, N.Y.: Cornell University Press, 1983), 34–38; Bill Readings, *The University in Ruins* (Cambridge, Mass.: Harvard University Press, 1996), 12, 54–69.

6. THE LABORATORY

1. Helena M. Pycior, "Pierre Curie and 'His Eminent Collaborator Mme. Curie': Complementary Partners," in *Creative Couples in the Sciences*, ed. Helena M. Pycior, Nancy G. Slack, and Pnina G. Abir-Am (New Brunswick, N.J.: Rutgers University Press, 1995), 48. See also Helena M. Pycior, "Marie Curie's 'Anti-Natural Path': Time Only for Science and Family," in *Uneasy Careers and Intimate Lives: Women in Science, 1789–1979*, ed. Pnima Abir-Am and Dorinda Outram (New Brunswick, N.J.: Rutgers University Press, 1987), 191–214.

2. Bernadette Bensaude Vincent, "Star Scientists in a Nobelist Family: Irène and Frédéric Joliot-Curie," in *Creative Couples*, 57–71, esp. 59, 61, 64.

3. Londa Schiebinger, *The Mind Has No Sex? Women in the Origins of Modern Science* (Cambridge, Mass.: Harvard University Press, 1991), 66–101.

4. Quoted in Malcolm Nicholson, "Introduction," in Alexander von Humboldt, *Personal Narrative of a Journey to the Equinoctial Regions of the New Continent* (London: Penguin, 1995), xxxviii.

5. Humboldt, *Personal Narrative*, 129–30; idem, *Views of Nature: Or Contemplations on the Sublime Phenomena of Creation*, trans. E. C. Otté and Henry G. Bohn (London: Henry G. Bohn, 1850), 2; Humboldt, *Personal Narrative*, 225.

6. Andreas Daum, "Alexander von Humboldt, die Natur als 'Kosmos' und die Suche nach Einheit: Zur Geschichte von Wissen und seiner Wirkung als Raumgeschichte," *Berichte zur Wissenschaftsgeschichte* 23 (2000): 247. I owe the conception of Humboldt's work in terms of space developed here to this article.

7. Susan Faye Cannon, *Science in Culture: The Early Victorian Period* (New York: Dawson and Science History Publications, 1978), 73–110.

8. Daum, "Alexander von Humboldt," 247, 250, 254.

9. Jean Pierre Poirier, *Lavoisier: Chemist, Biologist, Economist* (Philadelphia: University of Pennsylvania Press, 1996), 94–96, 390–95, 401–5.

10. Lissa Roberts, "The Death of the Sensuous Chemist: The 'New' Chemistry and the Transformation of Sensuous Technology," *Studies in History and Philosophy of Science* 26, 4 (1995): 503–29, quotation on 512.

11. Jan Golinski, "The Chemical Revolution and the Politics of Language," *The Eighteenth Century* 33, 3 (1992): 238–51; Roberts, "Death of the Sensuous Chemist."

12. Golinski, "Chemical Revolution," 245.

13. These, at least, are their modern names. See William H. Brock, *Justus von Liebig: The Chemical Gatekeeper* (Cambridge: Cambridge University Press, 1997), 215–49.

14. Frederic L. Holmes, "The Complementarity of Teaching and Research in Liebig's Laboratory," *Osiris* 5, 2d ser. (1989): 121–64.

15. Brock, *Liebig*, 63.

16. Personal communication, Dr. Dietmar Linder, Liebig-Museum, Universität Gießen, June 29, 2006.

17. A. W. von Hofmann in 1875, quoted by J. B. Morrell, "The Chemist Breeders: The Research Schools of Liebig and Thomas Thomson," *Ambix* 19 (Mar. 1972): 36.

18. R. Steven Turner, "Justus Liebig versus Prussian Chemistry: Reflections on Early Institute-Building in Germany," *Historical Studies in the Physical and Biological Sciences* 13, 1 (1982): 131, 136, 137–38.

19. Brock, *Liebig* 48–51; Alan J. Rocke, *Nationalizing Science: Adolphe Wurtz and the Battle for French Chemistry* (Cambridge, Mass.: MIT Press, 2001), 36–41, 51, 65, 84.

20. See Randall Collins, *The Sociology of Philosophies: A Global Theory of Intellectual Change* (Cambridge, Mass.: Harvard University Press, 1998), 524, 533–35.

21. Bruno Latour, "Give Me a Laboratory and I Will Raise the World," in *The Science Studies Reader,* ed. Mario Biagioli (New York and London: Routledge, 1999), 258–75. Illustrative quotations from this article directly paraphrased in this paragraph occur on pp. 261, 262, 263, 264, 268, 271, and 272. This article is a distillation of Latour's book-length study *The Pasteurization of France* (Cambridge, Mass.: Harvard University Press, 1988).

22. Nancy Elizabeth Gallagher, *Medicine and Power in Tunisia, 1780–1900* (Cambridge: Cambridge University Press, 1983), 7–8, 12, 24–41, 83–88, 98.

23. Kim Pelis, *Charles Nicolle: Pasteur's Imperial Missionary* (Rochester, N.Y.: University of Rochester Press, 2006), 39, 66–73, 248 (for quotation); also Anne Marie Moulin, "Patriarchal Science: The Network

of the Overseas Pasteur Institutes," in *Science and Empires: Historical Studies about Scientific Development and European Expansion*, eds. Patrick Petitjean et al. (Dordrecht: Kluwer, 1992), 307–22.

24. Gerald Geison, *The Private Science of Louis Pasteur* (Princeton, N.J.: Princeton University Press, 1995).

25. John Carson, *The Measure of Merit: Talents, Intelligence, and Inequality in the French and American Republics, 1750–1940* (Princeton, N.J.: Princeton University Press, 2007), 131–44; Theta H. Wolf, *Alfred Binet* (Chicago: University of Chicago Press, 1973), 90–91, 153–58, 167–81, 329.

26. Leila Zenderland, *Measuring Minds: Henry Herbert Goddard and the Origins of American Intelligence Testing* (Cambridge: Cambridge University Press, 1998), 66.

27. Ibid., 50–51. The quotation is from Hugo Munsterberg, a German émigré, Wundt student, and Harvard professor.

28. Carson, *Measure of Merit*, 180–82.

29. Zenderland, *Measuring Minds*, 121–22, 131, 138–41.

30. Carson, *Measure of Merit*, 162.

31. Paul D. Chapman, *Schools as Sorters: Lewis M. Terman, Applied Psychology, and the Intelligence Testing Movement, 1890–1930* (New York: New York University Press, 1988).

32. Andrew Dawson, "Origin of Scientific Management: Why Fred Taylor? Why (Not) Philadelphia?" Ms. in preparation. http://www.gre.ac.uk/~da07/6-Research/taylor.doc, accessed July 22, 2006.

33. Thomas P. Hughes, *American Genesis: A Century of Innovation and Technological Enthusiasm* (Chicago: University of Chicago Press, 1989), 250–60.

34. Taylorism even crossed the Atlantic to become a European craze, displacing native alternatives, in the decades after his death; see Anson Rabinbach, *The Human Motor: Energy, Fatigue, and the Origins of Modernity* (New York: Basic Books, 1990), 254, 274–76.

35. Jane Lancaster, *Making Time: Lillian Moller Gilbreth—A Life Beyond "Cheaper by the Dozen"* (Boston: Northeastern University Press, 2006), 111, 119, 126.

36. Peter Liebhold, "Seeking 'The One Best Way': Frank and Lillian Gilbreth's Time-Motion Photographs 1910–1924," *Labor's Heritage* 17, 2 (1995): 61n19.

37. Richard Lindstrom, "'They All Believe They Are Undiscovered Mary Pickfords': Workers, Photography, and Scientific Management," *Technology and Culture* 41, 4 (2000): 725–51, quotation on 739.

38. Lancaster, *Making Time*, 156.

39. For the last three paragraphs, see Richard Gillespie, *Manufacturing Knowledge: A History of the Hawthorne Experiments* (Cambridge: Cambridge University Press, 1991), 133–63.

40. Kathryn Kish Sklar, "*Hull-House Maps and Papers*: Social Science as Women's Work in the 1890s," in *The Social Survey in Historical Perspective, 1880–1940*, eds. Martin Bulmer et al. (Cambridge: Cambridge University Press, 1991), 111–47.

41. Mary Jo Deegan, *Jane Addams and the Men of the Chicago School, 1892–1918* (New Brunswick, N.J.: Transaction, 1988), 35. Also see Rivka Shpak Lissak's critical treatment in *Pluralism & Progressives: Hull House and the New Immigrants, 1890–1919* (Chicago: University of Chicago Press, 1989), esp. 4–7.

42. Shannon Jackson, *Lines of Activity: Performance, Historiography, Hull-House Domesticity* (Ann Arbor: University of Michigan Press, 2001), 75.

43. Ellen Condliffe Lagemann, *The Politics of Knowledge: The Carnegie Corporation, Philanthropy, and Public Policy* (Middletown, Conn.: Wesleyan University Press, 1989), 67–68.

44. On grant-making in natural science, see Robert Kohler, *Partners in Science: Foundations and Natural Scientists, 1900–1945* (Chicago: University of Chicago Press, 1991), 15–40.

45. Martin Bulmer, "The Decline of the Social Survey Movement and the Rise of American Empirical Sociology," in *Social Survey*, ed. Bulmer, 300–304.

46. John H. Stanfield, *Philanthropy and Jim Crow in American Social Science* (Westport, Conn.: Greenwood, 1985), 53–54, 120.

47. Martin Bulmer and Joan Bulmer, "Philanthropy and Social Science in the 1920s: Beardsley Ruml and the Laura Spelman Rockefeller Memorial, 1922–29," *Minerva* 19 (1981): 347–407. In general, see Sarah E. Igo, *The Averaged American: Surveys, Citizens, and the Making of a Mass Public* (Cambridge, Mass.: Harvard University Press, 2007), 25–30.

48. Alexei B. Kojevnikov, *Stalin's Great Science: The Times and Adventures of Soviet Physicists* (London: Imperial College, 2004), 80–85.

49. Donald Fisher, "Rockefeller Philanthropy and the Rise of Social Anthropology," *Anthropology Today* 2, 1 (Feb. 1986): 5–8.

50. James E. Webb, *Space Age Management: The Large-Scale Approach* (New York: McGraw-Hill, 1969), 15–16, 6–7, 29 (with Webb quoting Warren G. Bennis). On Webb, see Walter A. McDougall, . . . *The Heavens and the Earth: A Political History of the Space Age* (New York: Basic Books, 1985), 361–88. On NASA management, see

Stephen B. Johnson, *The Secret of Apollo: Systems Management in American and European Space Programs* (Baltimore: Johns Hopkins University Press, 2002).

51. On Bush's connection to the Hawthorne experiments, see Gillespie, *Manufacturing Knowledge*, 42; also see Daniel Lee Kleinman, *Politics on the Endless Frontier: Postwar Research Policy in the United States* (Durham, N.C.: Duke University Press, 1995), 56–58.

52. Loren R. Graham, "Big Science in the Last Years of the Big Soviet Union," *Osiris*, 2nd ser., 7 (1992): 49–71; Mark R. Beissinger, *Scientific Management, Socialist Discipline, and Soviet Power* (Cambridge, Mass.: Harvard University Press, 1988). For a case study of intra-administrative intrigue within a highly bureaucratized science establishment, see Slava Gerovitch, *From Newspeak to Cyberspeak: A History of Soviet Cybernetics* (Cambridge, Mass.: MIT Press, 2002).

53. Paul Dickson, *Think Tanks* (New York: Atheneum, 1971); William Poundstone, *Prisoner's Dilemma* (New York: Anchor, 1993), 84–96; David Hounshell, "The Cold War, RAND, and the Generation of Knowledge, 1946–1962," *Historical Studies in the Physical Sciences* 27, 2 (1997): 237–67.

54. David Jardini, "Out of the Blue Yonder: The RAND Corporation's Diversification into Social Welfare Research, 1946–1968," Ph.D. dissertation, Carnegie-Mellon University, 1996, 190–232, 304–43; Jennifer S. Light, *From Warfare to Welfare: Defense Intellectuals and Urban Problems in Cold War America* (Baltimore: Johns Hopkins University Press, 2003), 37–45, 108–13.

55. M. Fortun and S. S. Schweber, "Scientists and the Legacy of World War II: The Case of Operations Research (OR)," *Social Studies of Science* 23, 4 (Nov. 1993): 612–13, 620–28. Stephen Johnson, "Three Approaches to Big Technology: Operations Research, Systems Engineering, and Project Management," *Technology and Culture* 38, 4 (Oct. 1997): 891–919; Agatha C. Hughes and Thomas P. Hughes, eds., *Systems, Experts, and Computers: The Systems Approach in Management and Engineering, World War II and After* (Cambridge, Mass.: MIT Press, 2000).

CONCLUSION

1. Walter M. Miller, *A Canticle for Leibowitz* (New York: Harper-Collins, 2006 [1959]), 26.

2. *The Bulletin of Atomic Scientists*, inventor and keeper of the

Doomsday Clock, has included Oppenheimer as a contributor and is still published today.

3. See Katie Hafner and Matthew Lyon, *Where Wizards Stay Up Late: The Origins of the Internet* (New York: Simon & Schuster, 1996), 54–56, 62–63.

4. See, in addition to the discussion of Augustine in Chapter 2, Anthony Grafton and Megan Williams, *Christianity and the Transformation of the Book: Origen, Eusebius, and the Library of Caesarea* (Cambridge, Mass.: Harvard University Press, 2006).

5. Daniel Bell, *The Coming of Post-Industrial Society: A Venture in Social Forecasting* (New York: Basic Books, 1973), 212–50. Peter Drucker was another notable early theorist of "knowledge workers" and the "knowledge society."

6. Clark Kerr, *The Uses of the University*, 4th ed. (Cambridge, Mass.: Harvard University Press, 1995 [1963]), 6, 15.

7. Steven Lubar, "'Do Not Fold, Spindle or Mutilate': A Cultural History of the Punch Card," *Journal of American Culture* 15, 4 (Winter 1992): 43–55; for context, see C. Michael Otten, *University Authority and the Student: The Berkeley Experience* (Berkeley: University of California Press, 1970), 159–88.

8. Nicholas Lemann, *The Big Test: The Secret History of the American Meritocracy* (New York: Farrar, Straus and Giroux, 1999), 125–40, 166–73; see also 5–9, 27–29, 39–56.

9. Louis Menand, "College: The End of the Golden Age," *New York Review of Books* 48, 16 (October 18, 2001): 44–47; John Hardin Best, "The Revolution of Markets and Management: Toward a History of American Higher Education since 1945," *History of Education Quarterly* 28, 2 (Summer 1988): 177–89, esp. 185–86; Roger Geiger, "The College Curriculum and the Marketplace: What Place for Disciplines in the Trend toward Vocationalism?" *Change* 12, 8 (Nov.–Dec. 1980): 16–23, 53–54.

10. Russell Jacoby, *The Last Intellectuals: American Culture in the Age of Academe* (New York: Basic Books, 1987), 140–90. This phenomenon is best approached through the many jeremiads against it: e.g., Allan Bloom, *The Closing of the American Mind* (New York: Simon and Schuster, 1987) and E. D. Hirsch, *Cultural Literacy: What Every American Needs to Know* (Boston: Houghton Mifflin, 1987), and, even more tendentiously, Roger Kimball, *Tenured Radicals: How Politics Has Corrupted Higher Education* (New York: Harper & Row, 1990) and Dinesh D'Souza, *Illiberal Education: The Politics of Race and Sex on Campus* (New York: Free Press, 1991).

11. Ellen Condliffe Lagemann, *An Elusive Science: The Troubling History of Education Research* (Chicago: University of Chicago Press, 2000), esp. 165–83.
12. Daniel Lee Kleinman, *Politics on the Endless Frontier: Postwar Research Policy in the United States* (Durham, N.C.: Duke University Press, 1995).
13. Rebecca S. Lowen, *Creating the Cold War University: The Transformation of Stanford* (Berkeley: Univesity of California Press, 1997); AnnaLee Saxenian, *Regional Advantage: Culture and Competition in Silicon Valley and Route 128* (Cambridge, Mass.: Harvard University Press, 1994), 14–15, 20–25.
14. Margaret Pugh O'Mara, *Cities of Knowledge: Cold War Science and the Search for the Next Silicon Valley* (Princeton, N.J.: Princeton University Press, 2005); Roger Geiger, *Knowledge and Money: Research Universities and the Paradox of the Marketplace* (Stanford, Calif.: Stanford University Press, 2004).
15. As of 2007, Harvard reported 2,497 nonmedical and 10,674 medical faculty members; see http://www.news.harvard.edu/glance/, accessed Aug. 18, 2007. Its medical school complex is located in Boston, several miles from its main Cambridge campus.
16. Sheila Slaughter and Larry L. Leslie, *Academic Capitalism: Politics, Policies, and the Entrepreneurial University* (Baltimore: Johns Hopkins University Press, 1997); Sheila Slaughter and Gary Rhoades, *Academic Capitalism and the New Economy* (Baltimore: Johns Hopkins University Press, 2004).
17. Daniel Lee Kleinman and Steven P. Vallas, "Science, Capitalism, and the Rise of the 'Knowledge Worker': The Changing Structure of Knowledge Production in the United States," *Theory and Society* 30 (2001): 451–92; personal communication, Prof. Itay Neeman, Department of Mathematics, University of California at Los Angeles, Aug. 25, 2007.
18. Christopher D. McKenna, *The World's Newest Profession: Management Consulting in the Twentieth Century* (Cambridge: Cambridge University Press, 2006); Lowell L. Bryan and Claudia I. Joyce, *Mobilizing Minds: Creating Wealth from Talent in the 21st-Century Organization* (New York: McGraw-Hill, 2007).
19. Vannevar Bush, "As We May Think," *Atlantic Monthly* 176, 1 (July 1945): 101–8. See also James M. Nyce and Paul Kahn, eds., *From Memex to Hypertext: Vannevar Bush and the Minds Machine* (Boston: Academic, 1991), 39–66, 113–44.
20. Jennifer S. Light, "When Computers Were Women," *Technology and Culture* 40, 3 (1999): 455–83.

21. Jay Hauben, "Vannevar Bush and J.C.R. Licklider: Libraries of the Future, 1945–1956," http://www.ais.org/~jrh/acn/acn15-2.articles/jhauben.pdf, accessed Sept. 1, 2007.

22. Paul N. Edwards, *The Closed World: Computers and the Politics of Discourse in Cold War America* (Cambridge, Mass.: MIT Press, 1997).

23. Norbert Wiener, *The Human Use of Human Beings: Cybernetics and Society* (Cambridge, Mass.: DaCapo, 1988 [1954]). On the Bush-Wiener connection, see Howard Rheingold, *Tools for Thought: The People and Ideas Behind the Next Computer Revolution* (New York: Simon & Schuster, 1985), 101–3.

24. Licklider's "Man-Computer Symbiosis" is reprinted in *In Memoriam: J.C.R. Licklider, 1915–1990*, ed. Robert W. Taylor (Palo Alto, Calif.: Digital Systems Research Center, 1990).

25. Fred Turner, *From Counterculture to Cyberculture: Stewart Brand, the Whole Earth Network, and the Rise of Digital Utopianism* (Chicago: University of Chicago Press, 2006), 1–28, 54, 71–78, 91, 104–18, 136, 141–53, and plate 10.

26. Alfred D. Chandler Jr. and James W. Cortada, eds., *A Nation Transformed by Information: How Information Has Shaped the United States from Colonial Times to the Present* (Oxford: Oxford University Press, 2000).

27. See Vinton Cerf, "How the Internet Came to Be," in *The Online User's Encyclopedia: Bulletin Boards and Beyond*, ed. Bernard Aboba (Reading, Mass.: Addison-Wesley, 1993), chap. 33. For a more critical perspective, see Rajiv C. Shah and Jay P. Kesan, "The Privatization of the Internet's Backbone Network," *Journal of Broadcasting and Electronic Media* (Mar. 2007): 93–109.

28. http://en.wikipedia.org/wiki/Wikipedia:About, accessed July 25, 2007.

29. http://www.google.com/technology, accessed July 18, 2007.

30. James Surowiecki, *The Wisdom of Crowds: Why the Many Are Smarter than the Few and How Collective Wisdom Shapes Business, Economies, Societies, and Nations* (New York: Doubleday, 2004).

31. See Robert W. Hefner and Muhammad Qasim Zaman, eds., *Schooling Islam: Modern Muslim Education* (Princeton, N.J.: Princeton University Press, 2007).

32. See Timothy B. Weston, *The Power of Position: Beijing University, Intellectuals, and Chinese Political Culture, 1898–1929* (Berkeley: University of California Press, 2004).

33. Joseph S. Alter, *Yoga in Modern India: The Body Between Science and Philosophy* (Princeton, N.J.: Princeton University Press, 2004), 73–108.

34. Richard Florida, *The Flight of the Creative Class: The New Global Competition for Talent* (New York: HarperCollins, 2005), 107–8, citing the work of AnnaLee Saxenian. See Saxenian's "Silicon Valley's New Immigrant High-Growth Entrepreneurs," *Economic Development Quarterly* 16, 1 (2002): 20–31, esp. 24–25 and table 7.
35. Florida, *Flight of the Creative Class*, argues that Europe, New Zealand, and Australia, not so much India and China, are likely to become the first beneficiaries of the globalization of knowledge work.
36. For a polemical treatment of this, see Andrew Keen, *The Cult of the Amateur: How Today's Internet Is Killing Our Culture* (New York: Doubleday, 2007).
37. Lily Kay, *Who Wrote the Book of Life? A History of the Genetic Code* (Stanford, Calif.: Stanford University Press, 2000), 1.
38. Philip Mirowski, *Machine Dreams: Economics Becomes a Cyborg Science* (Cambridge: Cambridge University Press, 2002). See also Thomas Bender and Carl E. Schorske, *American Academic Culture in Transformation: Fifty Years, Four Disciplines* (Princeton, N.J.: Princeton University Press, 1997).

Index

Page numbers in *italics* refer to illustrations.

INDEX

Bologna, University of, *78*, 82, 90, 103, 106
  as center for law studies, 87, 93–99
  origin of, 79
books, 4, 254, 256
  in ancient China, 24–26, 27
  censorship and, 138–40, 164
  Christian ascetics and, 49–55
  codex form of, 45–46, 53
  framing letters and, 137–38
  liturgical, 63, 255
  monastic copying compared with pub-
    lishing of, 141–42
  monastic copying of, 40–42, 52–55
  as museums, 145–47
  papyrus scrolls, 14, 16
  posterity and, 141
  pre-ninth century, 53–54
  Republic of Letters and, 133–42
  Sophists and, 10
  widespread influence of, 141
  see also libraries; writing
Boyle, Robert, 148
Brahe, Tycho, 138
Brahma the Creator, 73, 187
Brahmin caste, 109, 185
Brahmo Samaj, 190
Brand, Stewart, 268
Brandeis, Louis, 236
Breckenridge, Sophonisba, 244
brothels, 80, 188
Buddhism, 73, 75
Bulgaria, 90
Burgundy, 86
Bush, Vannevar, xvii, 248, 251, 253, 260,
  262, 263, 265–67, 269
Byron, George Gordon, Lord, 212, 213
Byzantine Empire, 32, 33, 40, 117, 129

cabinet of curiosities (*Wunderkammer*), *120*,
  143–45, 149, 169
Caesar, Julius, 30–31, 67, 122, 129–30, 133,
  156
calculus, 171
calendars:
  A.D. dating system for, 41, 71
  alternative, 71
  Roman Julian, 66
calendar year, 67
California, University of, 258–59
caliphates, 109
calligraphy, 25

Callimachus, 20, 21, 136, 145
calorimeter, 216
Calvinism, 124, 193
Cambridge University, 80, 89, 166
Canon (Ibn Sina), 99, 115
canons, textual, 28, 44–45, 88, 170, 187,
  229, 256, 261, 271
Canticle for Leibowitz, A (Miller), 251–52
capitalism, 163, 165, 235, 264
Caribbean islanders, 136
caritas, 84
Carnegie, Andrew, 244
Carnegie Corporation, 244
cartography, 21, 134–35, 156
Cassian, John, 51, 56
Cassiodorus, Flavius Magnus Aurelius,
  52–53, 55, 57, 64
Cathars, 90
cathedrals, as astronomical observatories, 68
cathedral schools, 83, 87
causes, Aristotle's typology of, 12
Cavendish, Margaret, 125, 154
censorship, 138–40, 164
Chambers, Ephraim, 164
Charlemagne, 56
Charles IV, Holy Roman Emperor, 105
Chartres, 87
Cheaper by the Dozen (Gilbreth and Carey),
  237
chemistry, 110, 208, 214–23, 230
Chicago, Ill., 238–46
Chicago, University of, 242–43, 244, 245
children, as oblates, 65, 72
Child Study movement, 233
China, xxi, 23–30, 73, 109, 114, 146–47, 271
  academies in, 155–59
  civil service examination system in, 28,
    156, 157, 270
  first imperial libraries of, 27–28
  Hellenistic libraries compared with
    libraries of, 6
  past orientation of, 29
  Qin dynasty book burning in, 24–26, 27
  scholarly political activism in, 270
  unification of, 24
  "Warring States" period in, 22, 23–24
  West compared with, xv
  writing as unifier of greater cultural
    region of, 25–27
China Illustrata (Kircher), 146–47
Chinese language, 25–26

INDEX

INDEX

Jews, 48, 100
  in Alexandria, 18–19, 33, 34
  Islamic rule and, 102, 110, 117
  as moneylenders, 97
  in Republic of Letters, 125
Jobs, Steve, 263
John, Gospel of, 43
Johns Hopkins University, 201
Johnson, Charles S., 245
John the Baptist, 176
Joliot, Frédéric, 207
Judaism, 43, 46, 67, 73, 111
  see also Bible, Hebrew
Judas, Gospel of, 44
Judgment Day, 70
Justinian Code, 95
Justin Martyr, 44

"Kali apparatus," 221–22
kaliyuga, 73
kamasastra, 186
Kamasutra, 186
Kant, Immanuel, 194
Kepler, Johannes, 138
Kerr, Clark, 258–59
kindergartens, 198
Kinsey Reports, 247
Kircher, Athanasius, 146–47
knowledge:
  classification schemes for, 20–21
  commercialization of, 253, 262–65
  as commodity, 163
  democratization of, 253, 257–62
  informal vs. formal, xv
  information identified with, 269, 272
  institution-based approach to history of,
    xvii–xxii, 253–57; *see also* disciplines;
    laboratory, laboratory science;
    libraries; monasteries; Republic of
    Letters; universities
  Internet as repository for entirety of,
    xi
  Library at Alexandria as repository for
    entirety of, 4
  new, 147–49
  organization of, xix–xx
  politics and, 123, 155–56
  production of, 159
  pure vs. applied, 92
  10,000–Year Library and, xi–xii, 268
  today, 270–74

  transition periods for, xii–xiii, xvi–xxii,
    253–54
  "Western intellectual tradition" of, xiii–xv
  western solutions to problems of, xv–xvi
  writing vs. speech in organization of,
    4–5; *see also* oral cultures; writing
"knowledge society," xxii, 253, 257–70, 273

laboratory, laboratory science, xiii, xvi, xx,
    205–50, 262
  "big science" and, 245, 248–50
  dominant status of, 251–53, 257, 264,
    270–74
  as seminar, 218–23
  social science and, 227–47
  spaces of, 210–28
  women and, 58, *206*, 207–9
  as workshop, 215–18
  as the world, 210–15
  world as, 223–28
laissez-faire capitalism, 165
Langevin, Hélène, 207–8
Langevin, Michel, 208
Laon, 87
Laplace, Pierre-Simon, 138, 216
Lathrop, Julia, 243
Latin language, 18, 31, 42, 46, 47, 54, 65,
    74, 102, 125, 128, 150, 156, 164, 170,
    178, 180, 193, 202
Latin schools, 169
Latour, Bruno, 224, 227
Laura Spelman Rockefeller Memorial
    (LSRM), 244
Lavoisier, Antoine, 214–18, 221, 223, 228
law, 194
  canon, 97–98
  dharma, 186, 188
  German, 95
  Islamic, 112–13, 115, 226
  precedent and reason in, 98–99
  Roman, 95, 98
  scholastic, 98
  at University of Bologna, 87, 93–99
leap years, 67
lectio divina, 51, 68
lectionaries, 63
Leeuwenhoek, Antonie van, 132
Left Behind book series, 72
Leibniz, G. W., 171
Leipzig, University of, 107, 199, 231
Lenin, V. I., 236

INDEX

INDEX

humanist interest in writers of, 128–29
law in, 95, 98
libraries of, 31
as oral culture, 42, 43, 53
philosophy in, 48
splitting of, 32
Roman Inquisition, 139
Roman numerals, 68
Rome, 33, 39, 49, 108, 146, 152, 192
Rouelle, Gabriel-François, 216
Royal Swedish Academy, 149
Rule of the Master, 56
ruminatio, 61
Russia, 117, 211

saeculum, 64–65
St. Bartholomew's Day massacre, 152
saints' days, 69
saints' lives, collections of, 63, 64
Salerno, University of, 87, 99–105
salons, 166
salvation, 71–72
Salvation Army, 244
Samarkand, 110
Sanskritic tradition, xv, 73–75, 142, 185
Sanskrit language, 184, 187, 188*n*, 192, 251
sastrarthas, 187
sastras, 185–91, 270
sati, 189
Saxony, 168
scholarly journals, 148–49
scholars, xiii, 4
academies and, 148–59
in Alexandria, 15–16, 17–21, 29, 30
in ancient China, 26, 28
aristocracy and, 109
foundations and, 245
gentlemen's leisure time and, xxi
institutional interfaces between society
and, xvi
Islamic, 109–17
and languages of power and commerce,
22–23
legal protections for, 88
letters of recommendation and, 131–32
primary questions answered by, xviii
truth and knowledge as goals of, 159
vernacular languages and, 164
see also academies; education; Republic
of Letters; teachers; universities
"Scholars at a Lecture," *162*

Scholastic Aptitude Test (SAT), 235, 260, 261
scholasticism, 88
Schopenhauer, Arthur, 196
science, xii, xiv
academies and, 152–55
computus, 68–69
consensus and, 222–23
as craft, 218, 222
Greek, 33
humanities and, 228
Humboldtian, 210–15, 227–28, 233
Islam and, xxi, 82, 99–100, 226
Pasteurian, 223–28
religion and, xxi
social, 209, 228–47, 257
women in, xiii, 154
see also laboratory, laboratory science
Science (Bush), 262
science fiction, 125, 154
scientia, 101, 103, 104
"scientific management," 236–40, 249
scientific method, 139, 148, 149, 153, 155
scientific philanthropy, 240–47, 257
scientific revolution, 122
scriptures, xvi, 41, 43, 46–47, 51, 54, 57,
255
orthodox corruption of, 45
Vedic, 74
see also Bible
Second Coming, 69–72
secular humanists, *see* humanism
secularism, xiv
seminars, 166–83, 184, 191, 199, 200, 208,
256
Semitic languages, 111
Seneca, 106, 129
Septuagint, 18–19, 34, 43, 46
Serampore, 189
settlement houses, 241–43
Seven Years' War, 132
sexual behavior studies, 247
sexuality, in ancient Greece, 7–8
Shi'a Islam, 109, 112
Shockley, William, 263
shuyuan, 155–59
Sic et Non (Abelard), 85, 88
Sicily, 101
sign language, 62
Silicon Valley, 263, 268, 271
Simeon Stylites, 50
Simon, Théodore, 232

INDEX

sin, 58, 62
slaves, in ancient Greece, 14, 45
smallpox, 224
Smith, Adam, 163, 170, 180, 191, 202, 229
socialism, 235
social science, 109, 228–47, 257
sociétés de pensée, 158n
sociology, 245
Socrates, xix, 5, 10–11, 106, 137, 156, 180
Socratic method, 10
solar system, 216
    Copernican (heliocentric), 16, 111, 137–39, 142
    Ptolemaic (geocentric), 16, 111, 142
solar year, 67
soldiering, 239–40
Song of Songs, 86
Sophists, 9–10, 11
Sorbonne, 89, 166, 231
South Asia, 116, 117, 185
    see also India
Soviet Union, 236, 246, 253
Space Age Management (Webb), 247
space program, 247–50
Spain, 32, 101, 102, 110
speech:
    in monasteries, 62
    Roman rhetoric, 42, 43
    see also oral cultures
spring equinox, 67
Squillace, 52
Stanford-Binet test, 234–35
Stanford University, 263, 271
Stoics, 48, 125
studium generale, 80n
studium particulare, 80n
Sufis, 115–16
Summa Theologica (Thomas Aquinas), 92
Sunni Islam, 109, 112
Supreme Court, U.S., 236
sutras, 186
Syria, 50

Talmud, 46–47
tax collectors, 128, 215
Taylor, Frederick Winslow, 236, 249
Taylorism, xvii, 236–40
Taylor Society, 236
teachers, travel by, 82, 92
Ten Commandments, 58

10,000-Year Library, xi–xii, 268
Terman, Frank, 263
Terman, Lewis M., 234–35, 263
Tertullian, 47
textual scholarship, 9–10, 11, 17–18
Thebes, 4
Theologia (Abelard), 87
theologians, xiv
theology, xv, 82, 106–7, 108, 115, 194
    Abelard's coining of term, 85
    Bernard's attack on, 86
    "primordial," 153
    at University of Paris, 87, 88–93
Theon, 33–34
"therbligs," 237
think tanks, 249
Thomas Aquinas, Saint, 92, 98
Thucydides, 30
time:
    as creation of God, 64–65
    guardianship of, 252
    liturgical year, 65–69
    millennarianism and, 69–75
    monasteries and, 39, 41, 56–72, 130
    in Sanskritic tradition, 73–75
time-and-motion studies, 237
Toledo, 82
Toledo, Eleonora, di, 154
Torah, 43, 45, 46
Training School for Feeble-Minded Boys and Girls, 232–33
translation:
    of the Bible, 18–19, 43, 46, 170
    of classic Greek and Roman works, 104, 151
    by Islamic scholars, 110–11
    in languages of India, 189
    of other ancient works into Greek, 18–19
    into vernacular languages, 151
Trinity, 84, 85
trivium, 42, 47, 105, 129, 146
Trojans, 9
Trotula ("Lady of Salerno"), 100
truth, 159, 223, 237
Tunis, 225–27
Turkey, 110
Tuskegee Institute, 245
"two cultures," 228
typhus, 226–27
tyrants, 8